Palestine

Dedicated to the memory of

Mark Jacobsen, PhD
Professor of Military History
Command and Staff College
Marine Corps University
1950–2013

Mark's love of British military history and his astonishing knowledge and understanding of the field of military history in general enhanced the professional education of a generation of Marine Corps field grade officers.

Palestine

*The Ottoman Campaigns
of 1914–1918*

Edward J. Erickson

Pen & Sword
MILITARY

First published in Great Britain in 2016
and reprinted in 2022 by
PEN AND SWORD MILITARY
an imprint of
Pen and Sword Books Ltd
47 Church Street
Barnsley
South Yorkshire S70 2AS

ISBN 978-1-39901-977-4

Printed and bound in England by
CPI Group (UK) Ltd, Croydon, CR0 4YY

Typeset in Times by CHIC GRAPHICS

Pen & Sword Books Ltd incorporates the imprints of
Archaeology, Atlas, Aviation, Battleground, Discovery,
Family History, History, Maritime, Military, Naval, Politics,
Railways, Select, Social History, Transport, True Crime,
Claymore Press, Frontline Books, Leo Cooper, Praetorian Press,
Remember When, Seaforth Publishing and Wharncliffe.

For a complete list of Pen and Sword titles please contact
Pen and Sword Books Limited
47 Church Street, Barnsley, South Yorkshire, S70 2AS, England
E-mail: enquiries@pen-and-sword.co.uk
Website: www.pen-and-sword.co.uk

Contents

Acknowledgements

I must first acknowledge the great intellectual and academic debt that I owe to those who have gone before me. In particular, the authors of the British and Turkish official histories of the Palestine Campaigns in the First World War, including British authors A. F. Becke, Cyril Falls and George MacMunn, as well as Turkish authors Cemal Akbay, Fahri Belen, Şükrü Erkal, Dengiz Kâmuran, Merhum Kâmil Onalp, Yahya Okçu and Hilmi Üstünsoy. All of these men have long passed but their work survives and provides the platform on which my work rests. I would also be remiss if I failed to acknowledge my debt to the late Professor Stanford J. Shaw for his personal encouragement and whose monumental study of the Ottomans in the First World War was prematurely ended with his untimely death. I find it easy to stand on the shoulders of giants.

Among the living I am indebted to the scholarly works of İsmet Görgülü for his efforts in assembling Ottoman and Turkish orders of battle, Hilmar Kaiser for his refreshing and original work on Cemal Pasha and the Armenians, and Ole Nikolajsen for his superb study of Ottoman aviation in the First World War. I am fortunate to count among my personal friends Professors Yigal Sheffy and Matthew Hughes, whose work on intelligence, gas warfare in the Middle East and Allenby's campaigns have been very helpful in filling in parts of this story. My American friends, who are Ottoman historians, include Professors Justin McCarthy and Sean McMeekin, whose work on the Armenian rebellion and its ties to the Entente were incredibly helpful in framing the Ottoman Empire's strategic posture in 1915. Two Turkish friends and colleagues whose brilliant work regarding the Ottoman Special Organization was especially insightful are Dr Polat Safı and Dr Ahmet Tetik. I also owe a very personal and special thanks to two of my dear Turkish friends, who were instrumental in answering my queries about these events. They are Professor Mesut Uyar, whose understanding of the Ottoman Army during this period is unrivalled in the world today, and Dr Yücel Güçlü of the Turkish Ministry of Foreign Affairs, whose knowledge of the Armenian threat to the Fourth Army is unmatched anywhere.

The maps in this book are used with the permission of the Askeri Tarıhıve Stratejik Etut Başkanlığı (ATASE) (Strategic Studies Institute, Turkish General Staff) in Ankara, Turkey. I gratefully thank the commander and his staff, especially Mr Serdar Demirtaş, for this permission.

This book could not have been produced without the encouragement and assistance of my friend and acquisitions editor at Pen and Sword, Mr Rupert Harding. Moreover, all readers (myself included), will also note the superb attention to detail of my friend and copy editor, Ms Alison Miles.

In Quantico, Virginia, this book could not have been written without the efforts of Colonel Steve Grass, USMC and Dr Doug McKenna, respectively the Director and the Academic Dean of the Marine Corps Command and Staff College, whose approval of (and constant support throughout) of a six-month sabbatical leave from my teaching responsibilities enabled me to complete this book on time. Lastly, and most importantly, I owe a tremendous thanks to my wife, Ms Jennifer Collins, for her unstinting and tireless encouragement of my writing.

List of Plates

Commanders
1. Zeki Bey and his staff, 1914
2. Cemal Pasha at his field headquarters
3. Enver Pasha and Cemal Pasha leaving Fourth Army HQ
4. 'Little Cemal' Pasha in Jerusalem
5. Fahrettin Pasha inspecting troops in Medina, 1917
6. Fahrettin Pasha inspecting a fortified position.
7. Friedrich Kress von Kressenstein
8. Erich von Falkenhayn inspecting Ottoman soldiers
9. Sureya Bay, Ottoman Camel Corps commander
10. Colonel Esat with 3rd Cavalry Division staff
11. Otto Liman von Sanders
12. Mustafa Kemal Atatürk

The Ottoman Army in Palestine
13. VIII Army Corps encampment
14. An infantry column departing for the Suez Front, late 1914
15. An infantry column, early in the war
16. A hastily prepared infantry defensive position
17. Entrenched infantry
18. A machine-gun section
19. Field artillery with a range finder
20. Mountain artillery
21. 6th Cavalry Regiment
22. Infantry and cavalry awaiting attack at Beersheba
23. Von Kress inspecting Ottoman assault troops

Aviation and Logistics
24. German aircraft at Huj
25. German Albatross DV fighters at Huj
26. German Captain Felmy in his aircraft at Huj
27. A labour battalion road building and laying pipe
28. A railway dump, Jerusalem, 1917
29. Kuseimih Watering Point
30. El Arish Watering Station

List of Maps

Map Symbol Key

Infantry

Artillery

Engineer

Cavalry

Medical

Logistics Trains

Communications

Artillery Piece: Gun

Artillery Piece: Howitzer

Search Light

Observation Outpost

Machine Gun

Headquarters Locations

List of Maps

Chapter 1

Introduction

Palestine, The Ottoman Campaigns of 1914–1918 is intended to be a companion volume to *Gallipoli, The Ottoman Campaign*, which Pen and Sword Publishing graciously published for me in 2010. Like its predecessor, *Palestine, The Ottoman Campaigns of 1914–1918* is written to present the Ottoman and Turkish side of a four-year series of campaigns in Palestine during the First World War. The existing historiography of these campaigns in English is written from a very Anglo-centric point of view; it includes the magnificent British official histories, a large corpus of secondary works about these events, and a vast array of participant memoirs. Like its predecessor, this book is intended to be a corrective to the Anglo-centric historiography. Moreover, *Palestine, The Ottoman Campaigns of 1914–1918* is not designed to be a comprehensive history that tells the entire story from both sides or from all perspectives in a balanced narrative. Rather, this is the account of the campaigns and battles as the Turks understand them and this book tells the Ottoman story.

The Syria-Palestine-Hejaz Theatre of Operations

While the Ottoman province known as Palestine occupies the central position in the British view of the battles and campaigns fought there in the First World War, for the Ottomans the operational theatre was much larger. In fact, the Ottoman theatre included three entire Ottoman provinces – Syria, Palestine and the Hejaz. (See map 1.1.) After mobilization in September 1914 the geographic area of operations of the pre-war Ottoman Second Army Inspectorate transferred to its wartime successor, the Ottoman Fourth Army. The three Ottoman provinces in the Fourth Army's area included the modern countries of Israel, Jordan, Lebanon and Syria. Moreover, it also included the western coast of Saudi Arabia as far south as Mecca and Medina, Egypt's Sinai Peninsula and Gaza, and a large part of what is now south-eastern Turkey. It is wrong

Map 1.1: The Ottoman theatre of operations

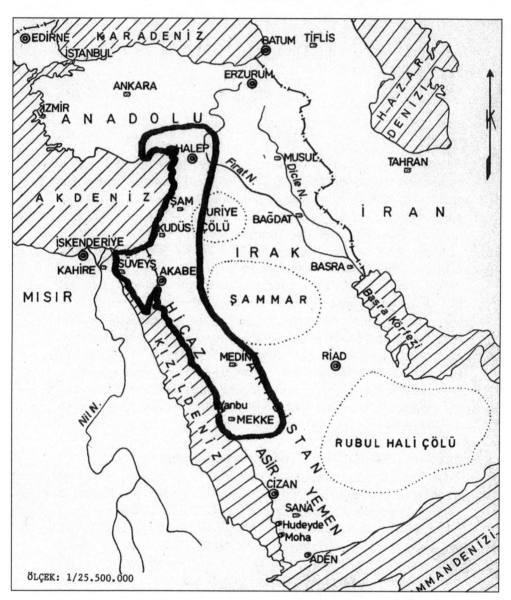

ÖLÇEK: 1/25.500.000

today to equate the British effort in Palestine with the much larger in scope Ottoman military effort in the region. A more accurate description of the Ottoman Army's operational area would be to call it the Syria-Palestine-Hejaz theatre. This is the story of that larger theatre and that larger effort.

In terms of military geography, the area comprised rugged mountains, coastal littorals, semi-arid agricultural land and the sandy deserts of Arabia. The operational area's inhabitants included Ottoman Turks, a large variety of Arabs (both tribal and city dwellers), Maronite Christians, Zionist Jews, Armenians, Kurds and Bedouins. A large portion of the population was illiterate and many did not speak Ottoman Turkish. The area had, for the most part, a very primitive transportation infrastructure that included a single-track railway leading to Medina. Its climate was dangerously hot in the summer, the southern parts were net importers of food, there was almost no industrial infrastructure and the entire area would be characterized as water deficient today. The operational area also included numerous religious sites, which were significant to Muslims, Christians and Jews. These factors created operational challenges that the Ottoman armies operating in the region had to overcome in order to remain combat effective in the field.

To think that the complexities of the operating environment were simply 'difficult' vastly understates the reality facing the three operational commanders who commanded in this theatre during the First World War – Cemal Pasha, Erich von Falkenhayn and Otto Liman von Sanders. These commanders continuously dealt with a number of competing demands that began with conventional frontal warfare which pitted the poorly equipped Ottoman Army against the wealth and power of the British Empire and its armies, but which included other significant challenges as well. For example, they were also constantly threatened on their western flank by an immense coastal littoral which was vulnerable to amphibious attack by the Royal Navy. Moreover, until January 1916, the rear areas of the northern part of the theatre were threatened by an Armenian rebellion, which, when dealt with, was superseded by an active Arab rebellion in the south. Compounding these operational realities the supporting logistics architecture was notably weak, vulnerable to interdiction and breakdown, and funnelled through two narrow passes containing uncompleted tunnel complexes in the Taurus and Amanus mountains. This theatre was an exceptionally complex operational environment and was characterized by competing demands that forced hard choices on the men commanding there.

The Last Nineteenth-Century War

The conventional First World War campaigns in Palestine were unlike the contemporary First World War campaigns fought on the major fronts in Europe. It may be argued that the war in Palestine was, in fact, the last nineteenth-century war. In fact, the very signatures of the First World War were absent in the Palestine theatre. There were few continuous lines of trenches and the battles in Palestine were never battles of materiel, involving large numbers of crew-served weapons and huge expenditures of munitions. Most of the individual battles fought there were of very short duration, most lasting only one or two days, and battlefield casualties were minimal (in comparison to the European fronts) reflecting a lower intensity of combat. Logistics played a key role, but neither side had enough resources to wage war on a continuous basis and active campaigning in Palestine followed a sine curve-like rhythm based on the availability of supplies. Lastly and importantly, the anonymity of the mass armies in Europe stood in stark contrast to the sharply defined role of individual personalities in Palestine who had a measurable impact on battlefield success or failure.

The most distinct characteristic of the war in Palestine was that it was a war of manoeuvre rather than a war of static and deadlocked trench warfare. While there certainly were periods of trench warfare, both sides engaged in operational and tactical manoeuvre and both sides sought envelopment solutions to the tactical dilemma. This was possible because the densities of men on the ground were low and quite often the armies' flanks were open in the desert. It was possible, therefore, for commanders in Palestine to envision and plan campaigns in a similar way to that of commanders in the nineteenth century. There were of course, periods of static warfare characterized by entrenchments and frontal assaults across no-man's-land, but these trench systems were never constructed to the degree of battlefield width and depth seen in Europe. The defensive systems in Palestine were often only one or two trenches deep, with very little defensive barbed wire, behind and beyond which lay open ground. In turn, operational and tactical breakthroughs and manoeuvre warfare that were impossible in Europe, were possible in Palestine.

The art of command also seems easier to identify and understand in Palestine, at least in comparison with the Western Front. This is the result of the fact that the campaigns in Palestine were discrete in time and space and the battles themselves of such short duration. In comparison with the Western Front it is far easier here to study the opposing plans and to understand the impact of individual commanders on the success or failure battlefield operations. Additionally, the campaigns in Palestine were never as dependent on technology and massive fire support which makes it easier to separate the decisions and actions of commanders from the steamroller tactics employed elsewhere in the First World War.

Ottoman Army Leadership in the Syria-Palestine-Hejaz Theatre
Remarkably, the Ottoman Army in Palestine was still in being and fighting when the Mudros Armistice, which was signed on 30 October 1918, ended the First World War in the Middle East. It had survived Edmund Allenby's magnificent breakthrough and envelopment at Megiddo, as well as Allenby's pursuit from Galilee to Aleppo, and it was preparing its final defence of the Anatolian heartland. How was it possible for such an under equipped and poorly resourced army composed mostly of illiterate and unindustrialized conscripted men to remain in the field in such disastrous circumstances? To understand this the reader must understand the nature of the Ottoman Army itself and especially its leadership.

This book shows both the weaknesses and the strengths of the Ottoman Army during the First World War. However, since the Ottoman Army in Palestine remained combat effective until the very end of the war, arguably, its institutional strengths overcame most of whatever weaknesses it had. In fact, the weaknesses of the army were primarily logistical rather than weaknesses in command, doctrines or training. As at Gallipoli, this was often misunderstood by its British opponent. As a result, in their planning processes, the British focused on the apparent weaknesses of the Ottoman Army rather than focusing on how to overcome their enemy's demonstrated strengths. It is significant to note that the British Army was not able to defeat the defences of the Ottoman Army in Palestine until the late autumn of 1917. Even then it still took the British Army, with vastly superior resources, another year to push the Ottoman Army entirely out of Palestine and Syria.

The primary strength of the Ottoman Army in Palestine lay in its commanders at the tactical level rather than at the operational level. The three operational commanders, Cemal, von Falkenhayn and Liman von Sanders, were all highly trained and experienced general staff officers but all three were defeated and all three made mistakes in over estimating the operational capabilities of the Ottoman armies in Palestine. Cemal demonstrated a finely honed ability to balance competing requirements, including expanding the divisional base while losing his mainstay trained formations (to the Gallipoli campaign) and simultaneously managing a counter-insurgency campaign. These activities were essentially reactive and it must be noted that he was unable to envision and effectively plan offensive campaigns. Cemal's successor, Erich von Falkenhayn, presided over the loss of the Gaza–Beersheba line and the loss of Jerusalem. He proved realistic in deflecting minister of war Enver Pasha's overly ambitious offensive plans and played a crucial role in hammering out a sound defensive strategy for the Ottoman fronts in the Middle East in 1917. However, as an operational commander, von Falkenhayn proved unable to convert ideas into successful battlefield operations and he repeatedly failed to concentrate his forces at decisive points. Liman von Sanders understood the Ottoman Army's strengths and weaknesses and the finesse with which he handled the successful Jordan River defensive operations in the spring of 1918 showcased his ability to rely on and trust the judgements of his subordinate Ottoman commanders. Later in the autumn it is doubtful that any action on his part might have reversed the catastrophic defeat at Megiddo, but consideration should be given to the fact that Liman von Sanders handled the retreat under pressure to Aleppo with great skill.

It was at the tactical level in Palestine where it may be argued that Ottoman and German commanders provided brilliant leadership. At corps and field army levels Ottoman commanders proved very capable as a group and performed exceptionally well. İsmet's leadership of the III Corps withdrawal from encirclement at Beersheba was a brilliant display of tactical decision-making. His command of III Corps in the withdrawal from Galilee and the retreat to Aleppo also showed considerable tactical skill and acumen. Likewise, Mustafa Fevzi demonstrated masterful tactical skills in task-organizing his army into the counter-attack forces which stopped Allenby from taking Amman in the spring of 1918. 'Little Cemal', who led the VIII Corps and fought in Palestine for almost the entire duration of the war, proved admirably resilient and capable. In the Hejaz Fahrettin Pasha restored a deteriorating operational situation and turned in a remarkable performance by holding out in Medina for months after the armistice.

At divisional level there were a number of Ottoman commanders whose performance may be characterized as brilliant. Time and time again Colonel Esat of the 3rd Cavalry Division salvaged a bad tactical situation with his superb handling of mixed infantry and cavalry forces. Under his exceptional leadership, the 3rd Cavalry Division became something of a 'fire brigade' and was routinely committed to repair breaches in the line. Likewise, Lieutenant Colonel Asım's leadership in command of the 48th Infantry Division in the spring 1918 counter-attacks against Allenby's trans-Jordan raids was brilliant. Asım's ability to create ad hoc but remarkably effective combined arms teams and vigorously lead them against the British is worthy of study today. Colonel Refet's retreat from Romani and his subsequent defence of Gaza were also notably excellent performances under difficult circumstances.

But without doubt, the finest demonstration of battlefield leadership and tactical skill came at field army level from Mustafa Kemal (later Mustafa Kemal Atatürk), whose masterful retreat from Galilee to Aleppo is a model of its kind. A defeated army being pursued by a more mobile and confident enemy is considered by military professionals as one of the most difficult situations for a commander to deal with. Kemal's handling of the withdrawal of his Seventh Army behind the Jordan River after Megiddo saved the Yildirim Army Group from certain destruction. Subsequently in the retreat under pressure to Damascus and then to Aleppo, Kemal's ability to position rear guards and blocking forces in a 'just-in-time' manner prevented the pursuing British cavalry forces from trapping the army group on numerous occasions. Throughout the retreat his dynamic leadership held his army together and ensured its survival when the other two Ottoman armies in Palestine were destroyed. Mustafa Kemal's inspired performance under these severe and arduous conditions can only be described as brilliant.

It would be wrong to ignore the contributions of a number of capable German commanders in explaining why the Ottoman Army in Palestine remained in the field until 1918. Certainly Kress von Kressenstein's restless and relentless activity and propensity for offensive operations were instrumental in keeping the British off balance during the first two years of the war. Other officers at corps and division levels also played an important part in the defence of Palestine, including Major Tiller, Colonel Hergote and Colonel von Oppen. That these officers were able to lead Ottoman soldiers effectively was a triumph of interoperability and an example of exceptionally effective military cooperation.

Palestine, The Ottoman Campaigns of 1914–1918

The research methodology utilized in this book employs a close examination of the official histories of Turkey and Great Britain as the vehicle by which these events are analysed. This study relies on the following overlapping official histories (the publishing details may be found in the bibliography).

British Official Histories Taken from Official Documents
1) MacMunn, George and Cyril Falls. *Military Operations Egypt and Palestine, From the Outbreak of War with Germany to June 1917.*
2) Falls, Cyril and A. F. Becke. *Military Operations Egypt and Palestine, From June 1917 to the End of the War.*

Turkish Official Histories Taken from Official Documents
1) Akbay, Cemal. *The Ottoman Empire's Military Mobilisation and Entry into the War.*
2) Okçu, Yahya and Hilmi Üstünsoy. *The Sinai-Palestine Front, From the Beginning of the War to the Second Gaza Battles.*
3) Onalp, Merhum Kâmil, Hilmi Üstünsoy, Kâmuran Dengiz and Şükrü Erkal. *The Sinai-Palestine Front, Operations from the Second Gaza Battle to the Mudros Armistice, 21 April 1917–30 October 1918.*
4) Erkal, Şükrü. *The Hejaz, Asir and Yemen Fronts and Libya Operations.*
5) Belen, Fahri. *The Turkish Fronts in the First World War, Years 1914–1915*, 5 vols.
6) Koral, Necmi, Remzi Önal, Rauf Atakan, Nusret Baycan and Selâhattin Kızılırmak. *The Ottoman State in the First World War,*

Administration and Logistics.
7) Göymen, İhsan. *Turkish Air Operations.*
8) Karamatu, Selâhattin. *Turkish Armed Forces History, 1908–1920.*

Where possible reports and plans from the Turkish and British archives supplement these books. Additionally, after the war, many of the Ottoman and German participants wrote memoirs about their experiences, including Cemal Pasha, Hüseyin Hüsnü, Ali Fuat Erden, Ali Fuat Cebesoy, Kress von Kressenstein and Liman von Sanders. Through comparison and contrast of these sources the author's intent is to provide the reader with a fresh narrative about these battles and campaigns that is absent from the English language historiography.

Conclusion
For the most part the Palestine campaigns of the First World War were campaigns of operational and tactical manoeuvre. In this regard they showcase leadership and battlefield mobility. The Ottoman and German commanders in Palestine displayed great skill in creating organizations that could manoeuvre rapidly and decisively. At the tactical levels they

demonstrated that they knew how to employ effectively the forces under their command in a highly fluid operational and tactical environment. This capability eroded in the final months of the war when logistical support failed to keep up with tactical demands. Likewise, the British Army in Palestine evolved an exceptionally well-developed manoeuvre capability under Edmund Allenby and his final campaigns in 1918 became models of the operational art.

It should also be noted that both the Ottoman and British armies in Palestine made continuous deliberate and conscious efforts to understand and employ the latest tactical innovations from the Western Front. For the Ottomans this manifested itself in the importation of modern fighting methods from the Germans including the reorganization of infantry battalions and the creation of assault troops (*stosstruppen*). For the British this is seen in the evolution of superb state-of-the-art combined arms tactics in 1918. These innovations were somewhat self-balancing until the final campaigns of 1918. However, in the final campaigns of the war neither great commanders nor tactical innovations could save the out-numbered and out-matched Ottoman Army in Palestine from defeat.

Chapter 2

1914

Planning and Concentration

Introduction

As a result of its alignment with Great Britain and France against Russia throughout most of the nineteenth century, the Ottoman Empire enjoyed friendly relations with those two countries. However, as Europe cascaded toward war in 1914, the Ottomans found themselves increasingly alienated from the British and leaned evermore towards the Germans. Exacerbating this was the fact that many of the Young Turks (member of the westernizing and modernizing Committee of Union and Progress) were Ottoman general staff officers, who had strong intellectual ties with the German Army and personal relationships with its officer corps. Moreover, the Ottoman Empire stood outside the architecture of the system of alliances that tied the Great Powers into two opposing power blocks. As such, other than keeping an eye on the Balkan states and their traditional Russian enemy, the Ottomans had no notions of going to war in the summer of 1914. Furthermore, any idea that the empire might find itself at war with Britain or France was inconceivable for Ottoman military planners.

The strategic consequence of this dilemma was that the Ottoman Empire found itself going to war with adversaries for which situation it had no defined objectives or war plans. Surprised by the unfolding events of the summer of 1914 and bound in turn by a secret treaty with Germany, the planners of the Ottoman general staff were confronted by strategic uncertainty. The Ottoman Army's concentration plan moved the army's divisions to the Bulgarian and Russian frontiers and left minimal forces to confront the British in the Sinai and Mesopotamia. The result was an early defeat on the Euphrates–Tigris and the loss of Basra and the ad hoc cobbling together of an inadequately resourced and poorly conceived offensive against the Suez Canal.

The Ottoman Army

The year 1914 was a period of recovery and reconstitution as the Ottoman Army returned to its peacetime garrisons and reorganized after the First and Second Balkan Wars of 1912–13. These wars had destroyed about a third of the pre-war Ottoman infantry divisions as well as forfeiting the productive and populous Balkan provinces. The new minister of war, Enver Pasha, with the renewed assistance of a German military reform mission, led by Major General Otto Liman von Sanders, struggled to rebuild the capability and capacity of the Ottoman Army.[1] The reconstructed Ottoman Army comprised thirty-six infantry divisions organized into four army inspectorates and one independent army corps. Commanding generals under the inspectorate system, which was based on the German model, were responsible for the organization and training of active and reserve units within their areas. The Ottoman VII Corps, with four infantry divisions, was headquartered in San'a and was operational, conducting counter-insurgency operations in Yemen and Arabia. Under wartime conditions the army inspectorates mobilized as numbered field army headquarters (i.e. when mobilized the First Army Inspectorate became the Ottoman First Army).

In the west the First Army Inspectorate, headquartered in Constantinople, comprised the fifteen infantry divisions of the Ottoman I, II, III, IV and V Corps. These were the most well-equipped and well-trained divisions in the army. The Third Army Inspectorate in the east at Erzincan commanded nine infantry divisions of the IX, X and XI Corps as well as the army's four reserve cavalry divisions. The smaller Fourth Army Inspectorate in Mesopotamia comprised the XII and XIII Corps with four badly under-strength infantry divisions. Relative to this study, the Second Army Inspectorate garrisoned the Levantine coast, Syria and Palestine. The headquarters of the Second Army Inspectorate was located in Damascus and commanded by Major General Zeki Pasha.[2]

The Second Army Inspectorate supervised the VI Corps with headquarters in Aleppo, which commanded the 16th Infantry Division in Adana, the 24th Infantry Division in Gaziantepe and the 26th Infantry Division in Aleppo.[3] The inspectorate also supervised the VIII Corps, headquartered in Damascus, with its subordinate 23rd Infantry Division in Homs, the 25th Infantry Division in Damascus and the 27th Infantry Division in Jerusalem. Additionally, the inspectorate supported the independent 22nd Infantry Division at Medina, although this division fell under the VII Corps operationally for the protection of the Hejaz railway. All of the Second Army and Fourth Army Inspectorate subordinate units were, in comparison to those in the First and Third Army Inspectorates greatly under strength and poorly equipped. For example, the infantry regiments assigned to the infantry divisions in both the Mesopotamian and Syrian/Palestinian inspectorates were maintained at two-battalion strength instead of the three-battalion standard in the rest of the army. Artillery, cavalry, engineer and service support units were similarly drawn down in strength.

Ottoman War Plans and Movements

In early April 1914, the newly arrived German Colonel Fritz Bronsart von Schellendorf completed the staff work on the Primary Campaign Plan for the Ottoman Army. The plan reflected a strategic situation based on a renewal and expansion of the war in the Balkans. The Ottoman general staff believed that the empire would simultaneously oppose both a renewed Balkan coalition of Bulgaria and Greece in the west, and Russia in the east. The mobilization plans subsequently developed supported this appreciation. The Primary Campaign Plan specified that three basic tasks were to be initially accomplished by the military: the army had to secure key terrain along the frontiers, while bringing a majority of forces to decisive points, and ensuring at the same time that enough time was available to complete mobilization and concentration. The plan specifically forbade units being committed piecemeal to combat as had occurred in 1912.[4]

Under this plan the Ottomans would field an army of observation on the Greek and Bulgarian frontiers and, although this army was prepared to fight, it would not act provocatively, nor would it engage in offensive operations. In the east against Russia, the Ottomans would attempt to gain the tactical initiative by conducting limited attacks should favourable operational conditions exist in Caucasia. After completion of mobilization, the static inspectorates transitioned to mobile field army headquarters. The plan established an integrated defence of Constantinople incorporating the Çatalca lines covered by the Fortress City of Adrianople and the army of observation. To achieve the force structure required under this scheme, the general staff planned to move the Second Army and the Fourth Army to the straits region from Syria and Mesopotamia respectively. In their places, the army would establish area commands which would take over the remaining truncated inspectorate functions of conscription and depot training. Importantly, since the war plans did not envision conflict with Britain and France,

Mesopotamia and Syria/Palestine were not considered to be under imminent threat.

Although the Ottoman Empire was not immediately a belligerent in the First World War, the events of late July and early August 1914 were sufficient to cause the government to mobilize. On 1 August 1914, most of the major European powers and several minor powers were mobilizing their forces. The empire followed suit by issuing partial mobilization instructions to selected units. On Friday afternoon, 2 August 1914, the Ottoman general staff ordered general mobilization effective from 9.00 am that day. For planning purposes, the following day, 3 August, became the first 'numbered' day in the mobilization schedule. In theory, the army could be mobilized in about twenty-two days; however, the Ottoman general staff expected that delays and mismanagement would extend the mobilization window to about forty to forty-five days.[5] In addition to the missing regiments, battalions, and companies in Ottoman infantry divisions, the peacetime army had significant shortfalls in cavalry, communications, field bakery and combat engineer detachments. Ottoman infantry divisions had no munitions reserves or depots. At corps level, severe shortages existed in animal depots, bakery detachments, telegraph detachments and field hospitals. Only one corps had its allotted howitzer battalion, only one corps had a full strength telegraph battalion and only one corps had its assigned cavalry regiment.[6] Crippling shortages of all kinds characterized the logistical capability of the Ottoman Army to carry out mobilization. In Palestine, the VIII Corps needed thirty-six days to mobilize instead of the twenty-six days that the plan specified.[7]

After the events of July 1914, the empire found itself bound to Germany in a secret treaty signed on 2 August, and a second secret treaty with Bulgaria quickly followed. Although these treaties were not formal alliances, they served to align the Ottoman Empire with the Central Powers against the Entente Powers. In effect, by eliminating Bulgaria as an enemy, these treaties negated the strategic priorities with which Bronsart von Schellendorf formulated the Primary Campaign Plan earlier that spring and potentially added the Entente Powers as opponents.[8] Unfortunately for the Ottoman war planners, the movements required in the war plan had already begun with the Second Army headquarters and VI Corps headquarters moving to the Constantinople region. On 6 August, Enver Pasha relieved Zeki Pasha (who remained in Damascus) and assigned command of the Second Army to Ahmet Cemal Pasha, who would join the staff as it arrived in Constantinople.[9]

Cemal Pasha (sometimes referred to as Büyük Cemal or 'Big Cemal' to distinguish him from Küçük Cemal or 'Little Cemal', a similarly named corps commander in Palestine), a Young Turk and member of the inner circle of the ruling Committee of Union and Progress, held the portfolio of the minister of the navy but wanted to serve in a more active role. Cemal was an experienced military officer and he was well qualified for field army command. He was a graduate of the Ottoman War College (*Erkan-ı Harbiye Mektebi*) and a trained general staff officer. Cemal graduated from the college on 28 January 1896 (his class graduated early due to the diplomatic crisis with Greece that ended in war).[10] During the First Balkan War, Cemal served as an infantry division commander.

The VIII Corps remained behind in Syria and Palestine under the supervision of the newly activated Syrian Area Command, which was established on 13 August under Zeki Pasha's command.[11] Six days later, Zeki Pasha received an instruction from the general staff to begin planning an Egyptian campaign. The high command envisioned a campaign using the infantry divisions of the VIII Corps in combination with jandarma battalions and local Arab tribal levies. Several officers arrived in Syria shortly thereafter – Major Mümtaz, Lieutenant Colonel Eşref (later Eşref Kuşçubaşı), Captain İnsan and Jandarma Lieutenant Saip, who went to the Gaza–Beersheba line to organize irregular Arab tribal cavalry.[12] Mümtaz and Eşref were agents of the clandestine *Teşkilat-ı Mahsusa*, or Special Organization (hereafter SO), and it is unclear whether Zeki Pasha was aware of their role or subsequent activities.

As the strategic imperatives changed, Bronsart von Schellendorf began to adapt the Primary Campaign Plan on 20 August 1914. The possibility of a direct attack on Constantinople receded with the signing of the treaty with Bulgaria. Ottoman forces would continue to concentrate in Thrace, but with an eye towards conducting possible operations with the Bulgarians against either the Romanians or the Serbs. Although Russia maintained strong forces on the Caucasian Front, the Ottomans thought that they would not be inclined to attack, since Russia was already heavily engaged against Germany and Austria-Hungary. As a result, the idea of a large-scale Ottoman offensive using the Ottoman Third Army in Caucasia began to be seen as a viable option, in spite of the deplorable logistical and communications difficulties involved. Since eventual hostilities against Great Britain were likely, the Ottomans also began to consider the possibility of an offensive against Egypt and the Suez Canal. With the continuing security of a friendly

Bulgaria and with the increasing likelihood of a neutral Greece, staff work and estimates continued supporting these twin offensives.

Planning the Egyptian Campaign

On 6 September 1914, the Ottoman general staff reactivated a new Fourth Army in Damascus and assigned the VIII Corps and the XII Corps, which were moving north west from Mesopotamia, to join the new army headquarters. Additional artillery units, including 150mm howitzers, were sent to the new army as well. At Gaza, Major Mümtaz attempted to round up 20,000 camels for military operations. Zeki Pasha issued planning guidance for an offensive campaign into Egypt on 7 September, which soon became known as the Egyptian campaign project. In this way the pre-war Primary Campaign Plan was formally and significantly altered as contingency planning took over. In addition to the Fourth Army's proposed Egyptian offensive, the general staff ordered the Third Army in Caucasia to plan for offensive operations towards Ardahan and Batum. Furthermore, Enver decided that a wing of the Third Army would manoeuvre from a base formed by the Erzurum fortress and crush Russian forces in the area of Sarıkamış.

To support the Primary Campaign Plan, the Ottoman general staff had a Concentration Plan distinct from the mobilization plan. The purpose of the Concentration Plan was to task organize the command and control of the Ottoman Army and to position it to execute the Primary Campaign Plan.[13] In the planning endeavours of the more sophisticated armies of the major powers, these plans tended to merge into one nearly simultaneous effort. However, in the poorly developed Ottoman Empire, these plans were three distinct procedures separated in time, scope and intent. The Concentration Plan shifted major forces to European Ottoman Thrace for the protection of the Ottoman Straits, to Caucasia for the Third Army's winter offensive and to Palestine for the attack on the Suez Canal. The IV Corps deployed north from Smyrna and was reassigned to the Second Army. The XIII Corps from Mesopotamia was assigned to the Third Army, while its sister XII Corps went to Syria. As economy of force measures to support these deployments, both Mesopotamia and the Smyrna region were stripped of regular corps and divisions and were converted into area commands. However, the re-activation of Fourth Army in Damascus for an unanticipated offensive into Egypt threw the plan into disarray.

The Concentration Plan itself seemed to be fairly simple in transferring the centrally positioned corps, located in the interior of

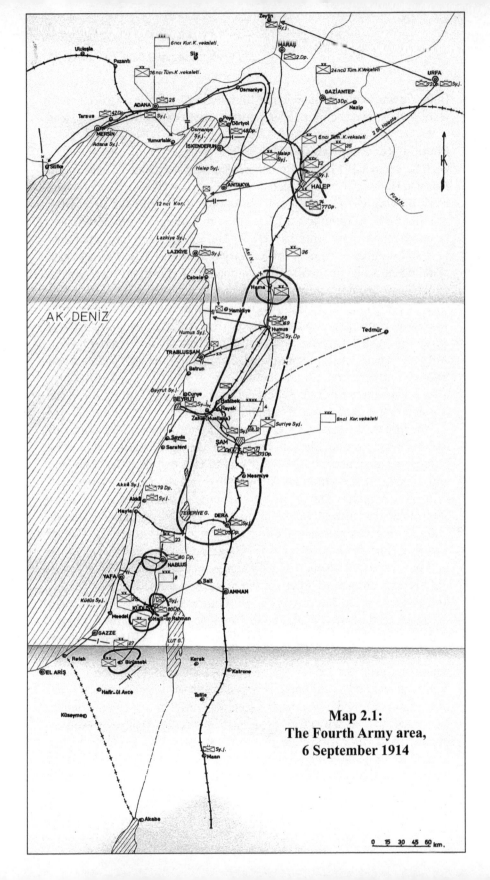

Map 2.1:
The Fourth Army area,
6 September 1914

AK DENIZ

0   15   30   45   60 km.

Anatolia, in Syria and in upper Mesopotamia, to concentration positions on the frontiers. However, as in the Balkan Wars, once again movements were delayed and the plan proved much slower to execute than expected. These slow movements presaged future problems with the empire's inadequate infrastructure and weak transportation system.

An important component in Ottoman strategic and operational planning early in the war was the idea of organizing and instigating Islamic rebellions in Allied territories, including British India, the Sudan, French North Africa, Russian Caucasia and trans-Caucasia, Persia and Egypt.[14] To oversee this endeavour the Young Turks had created the unique SO organization in 1913, the leadership of which was composed of hard-line nationalists with military experience.[15] In Egypt there were a number of anti-British nationalists, who are known today to have been SO agents, among whom were Abdülaziz Shawish and Muhammad Farid.[16] These agents were important because one of the SO's major strategic efforts involved instigating a rebellion in Egypt to overthrow the British occupation in conjunction with the Fourth Army's planned invasion. The SO charged one of its most experienced and dedicated agents, Lieutenant Colonel Eşref, to orchestrate the rebellion in conjunction with conventional operations. According to Eşref's memoirs, 'Egyptians who had fled to Constantinople from the British occupation of their country now returned as Ottoman agents and worked to prepare the local populations for revolt as soon as the Ottoman Army . . . advanced to attack the Suez Canal'.[17] In the early autumn of 1914, 600 agents and agitators led by Abdülaziz Shawish and Süleyman el-Baruni began to organize and lead strikes and demonstrations in Egypt, which were suppressed in turn by the British. Abdülaziz Shawish narrowly escaped capture and fled but was replaced by Muhammad Farid, Dr Nasır and Dr Tabit Maheab.[18] The SO also began a serious propaganda effort involving the publication of revolutionary Islamic monthly and daily journals to inflame the population against the allies.

Although not yet at war with Great Britain, Ottoman intelligence officers believed that the British garrison in Egypt was about 20,000 men but they read in British newspapers that 40–50,000 Indian soldiers were deploying into Egypt as well. Taking this into account, the Fourth Army staff developed planning assumptions about the campaign, the principal of which was that the operation must involve at least three infantry divisions.[19] The staff envisioned a two-phase operation, initially moving to the Suez Canal from the Ottoman–Egyptian frontier and then secondarily crossing the canal into Egypt to take Cairo. Three routes were considered viable, from Gaza by El Arish to Al Qantara, from Beersheba to Ismailia, and from Aqaba to Suez. Plans were made to move the 25th Infantry Division to Maan by train while the 23rd Infantry Division would march by road from Nablus to Maan as well. Early on in planning, the poor state of logistics was known to be a serious problem because the advanced positions along the frontier were not serviced by rail lines of communications nor was the local infrastructure robust or self sufficient. This was especially true for medical and veterinary services.[20] To offset these problems the general staff began to send supplies to the Fourth Army including conserves, munitions, additional draft animals, wagons and locomotives. The general staff also sent word that it had dispatched a well-trained German general staff officer to assist in planning.

On 27 September 1914, Lieutenant Colonel Friedrich Freiherr Kress von Kressenstein (hereafter von Kress) and seven German officers and officials arrived in Damascus.[21] Captain Ekrem Bey accompanied von Kress, a 44-year-old Bavarian who did not speak Ottoman Turkish, as his translator. Zeki immediately assigned von Kress duties as the VIII Corps chief of staff and von Kress began to push the planning aggressively forward. He ordered Major Mümtaz, who was now styled commander of the Bedouin Arabs, to scout the three routes to the canal for distances and suitability for artillery movement. Von Kress had more questions at this point than answers and he was very aware of the difficulty of the operation and also of the strength of the British garrison, including the Royal Navy's ships which could be positioned in the canal itself. In early October, the XII Corps headquarters, commanded by Major General Fahrettin Pasha, arrived in Aleppo and his major subordinate units, the 35th and 36th Infantry Divisions, concentrated in Aleppo and Hama respectively.[22] This reinforcement relieved Zeki Pasha from worrying about the protection of the Levant coast and enabled the Fourth Army to begin moving forces to the Palestine–Sinai frontier.

As Ottoman units moved southward in the middle of October 1914, von Kress persuaded Zeki Pasha to change the campaign project to a more deliberate design. Von Kress envisioned an expeditionary force arranged in three echelons, which would advance over the three routes scouted by Major Mümtaz. The determination to use a sequentially ordered echelon arrangement was a function of the army's capability and capacity to deliver water forward over the Sinai desert.[23] The 25th Infantry Division, commanded by Colonel Hilmi, advancing in the centre, formed the heart of the first echelon. Battalions from other divisions provided a right-flank column along the coast and a left-flank column from Aqaba. Staff Major Rıfat from the 27th Infantry Division commanded the right-flank column, with his 1st Battalion, 80th Infantry Regiment which would be accompanied by Major Mümtaz and his Bedouin Arab irregulars. The left-flank column would be led by Lieutenant Colonel Musa Kâzım and composed of the 1st Battalion, 69th Infantry Regiment. The second echelon would comprise the remainder of the 27th Infantry Division, while the 23rd Infantry Division followed as the third echelon.

Von Kress and his Ottoman staff were very aware of the great difficulty involving operations in waterless terrain with no real roads or towns. To mitigate this, the planners brought together men with experience in living in the desert and formed them into the 'Desert Staff' (*çöl kadrosu*).[24] The Desert Staff was then distributed among the three elements of the first echelon, which had to make their way across the barren terrain. The two trailing echelons had less need for such advice as they would be traversing already scouted terrain. Logistically the staff calculated that 30,000 camels were needed to support the operation, however, the army had nowhere near that number available. In order to procure camels from the local population, the general staff provided 150,000 gold liras to the VIII Corps with which to purchase enough camels necessary for the operation.[25]

Convinced that the Ottomans would enter the war sooner or later against them, the British and the Russians used the time generated by the slow Ottoman concentration to prepare measures against them. Both Allied countries prepared to take the offensive immediately upon commencement of hostilities and both countries proved more capable than the Ottomans in their ability to position and to direct forces for immediate use. On 31 October 1914, several days prior to the official start of hostilities, Russian army units began cross-border operations and British operations began the following day in the Persian Gulf with the landing of troops near Fao and in the Mediterranean with a Royal Navy bombardment of Gaza. A major Russian attack on the Third Army's defensive lines began on 5 November and, on 7 November, major British forces landed at Basra. By 19 November, the Ottomans had lost Basra in Mesopotamia and the Russians began larger operations aimed against Saray and Van.

In the Syria and Palestine theatre, Royal Navy gunboats and cruisers began immediate bombardments of coastal cities, including Aqaba where a landing party briefly came ashore. The outbreak of war spurred the efforts of the VIII Corps to complete its preparations for the offensive. On 2 November von Kress issued secret orders to Major Mümtaz to push his irregulars out to Al Arish, Bir Hasanah and An Nakhl.[26] Staff Major Rıfat and Mümtaz were ordered to occupy Al Arish and prepare to move forward. The next day von Kress issued an instruction organizing these advanced forces as the Khan Yunis Detachment under the command of Staff Major Rıfat, who was ordered to establish forward logistical nodes at the town of Khan Yunis as well. A second ad hoc command, the Maan Detachment, was established under the commander of the 69th Infantry Regiment. Infantry companies, artillery batteries and engineers were also assigned to these detachments. An additional irregular force of Circassian volunteers under the command of Lieutenant Colonel Eşref of the SO also made its way to the frontier.

Ahmet Cemal Pasha Takes Command
By mid-November there was gathering concern in Constantinople that the Egyptian campaign was under-resourced in combat capability and in the ability of the commanders in theatre. Consequently, Enver had discussions with Cemal, who was then commanding the Ottoman Second Army, suggesting that Cemal take command of the Fourth Army in order to assure adequate oversight of the endeavour. Although Cemal was concurrently the minister of the navy, he was a trained general staff officer with considerable experience in the army and, more importantly, Enver had confidence in him. On 18 November 1914, Enver ordered Cemal to take command of the Fourth Army and also attached German Colonel Werner von Frankenberg und Proschlitz as his chief of staff. Enver also assigned some of the most promising young officers in the army to the expedition including Staff Lieutenant Colonel Ali Fuat (later General Ali Fuat Erdem) and Staff Major Refet (later General Refet Bele).[27]

On the same day, Enver ordered the general staff to divert the 10th Infantry Division, which was then en route to the Bandirma area, from the First Army to the Fourth Army.[28] This division, from the pre-war Smyrna garrison, was in better condition than the Fourth Army's divisions from Syria. Enver also ordered a heavy artillery battery and several ammunition columns south from the IV Corps as well, which added significant combat capability to the planned campaign. Enver alerted the 8th Infantry Division, from the pre-war III Corps Tekirdağ garrison, for movement to Syria at the same time. This III Corps division was one of the best infantry divisions in the Ottoman Army and was very well trained and equipped. However, the 8th Infantry Division did not begin its movement south until mid-December.[29] Consequently, it would arrive too late to participate in the canal offensive.

While preparing for departure, Cemal ordered increased munitions and supplies to Palestine and sent orders to the Fourth Army to construct 500 portable water containers. He also requested and received permission to deploy two aircraft, which were very scarce at that time, to Palestine. At the operational level, additional major forces were also dedicated to the Palestine theatre when Enver Pasha recognized that IV Corps units might be better employed there. Cemal and his staff officers departed Constantinople by train on 21 November and, on the same day, a volunteer group of Mevlevis also left Konya for Palestine.[30]

Cemal proved to be a very active commander while travelling. On 21 November he cabled the XII Corps commander asking for reports about the condition of infantry and artillery units, the status of individual training, the availability of medical, veterinary and engineer units, and finally asking 'what are your thoughts about the situation?'.[31] He requested updates from the VIII Corps commander regarding the locations of all of his units, the status of logistics and the activities of the volunteer groups. He received some of this information at train stops en route. Cemal arrived in Adana on 26 November where he stayed for two days examining the coastal defence arrangements. He sent a lengthy report to Enver about the condition of the defences in the Adana–Osmaniye region.[32] In the report he expressed apprehension about the ability of the VI Corps to defend the region against an Allied amphibious attack and he was very concerned about the timely arrival of the 10th Infantry Division. Cemal also commented on the low morale of the soldiers he had encountered. On 1 December, he reached the XII Corps headquarters where he remarked on the ragged clothing of the soldiers and deficiencies in discipline and training for which he blamed Lieutenant Colonel Ali, the chief of the general staff's Soldier's Directorate. He also noted the severe shortage of draft animals and Cemal was so troubled by the condition of the officers and men in the 104th Infantry Regiment that he forced its commander, Lieutenant Colonel Mahmut, to retire.[33]

On 6 December 1914, Cemal arrived in Damascus, where he immediately demanded full briefings from the Fourth Army staff and VIII Corps commanders. Cemal had evidently had been thinking deeply about his command while travelling because he immediately ordered a reorganization of the Fourth Army which separated responsibility for the defences in the rear from the offensive elements aimed at the Suez Canal. As finally configured, Cemal divided his army area into four zones numbered I–IV from north to south. Integral to this scheme was persuading Enver to release control of the rump VI Corps headquarters and units remaining near Adana. Accordingly, in Zone I the 16th Infantry Division garrisoned Adana and the coast, in Zone II the VI Corps staff took over defensive responsibility from Alexandretta to Tripoli, in Zone III the XII Corps commander (Fahrettin Pasha) took over and operated from the Fourth Army headquarters in Damascus, and the IV Zone from Jaffa to Gaza passed to the 27th Infantry Division in Jerusalem.[34] This command arrangement was improvisational but reflected the capability of the Ottoman Army to task organize effectively commanders and units on an ad hoc basis to accomplish terrain-based missions.[35] This left the VIII Corps commander, Brigadier General 'Little' Cemal (later Cemal Mersinli), and his staff to focus exclusively on offensive operations.

On 8 December Cemal undertook to purchase additional camels from the Ottoman Army's Medina Detachment and two days later he wrote to Sherif Hussein and Colonel Vehip, commander of the 22nd Infantry (Hejaz) Division, asking for support.[36] In this letter Cemal explained the campaign as a battle for Islam. Subsequent letters to the Sherif outlined the gathering strength of the Fourth Army's Bedouin volunteers and asked him to provide similar volunteer groups from his Arab tribes. This correspondence was reinforced by the Jihad which Sultan Mehmet V, as caliph of the Islamic world, had declared against the allies on 12 November 1914.[37] Cemal also intimated that the brief British landing at Aqaba was a harbinger of things to come, and an exchange of ciphered cables between Cemal and Vehip followed. By 24 December these communications had solidified into actual commitments for the Egyptian campaign with the Sherif contributing several hundred Arab tribesmen under the command of his son, Ali, and Vehip promising to provide several infantry regiments to the left flank at Maan.[38] Cemal's active engagement in the command posture of his army, and with the Ottoman commanders and Arabs in the Hejaz, was a significant gain for the Fourth Army which protected the army's rear as well as its left flank.

As a result of the recruiting efforts of the SO, the number of volunteer groups increased as 1915 approached. The SO was assisted in these efforts by an Arabic nationalist member of parliament named Abdurrahman Pasha, who was supplied with 100,000 gold liras to purchase camels as well as to recruit men.[39] Eşref's irregular Circassian group grew to 270 men, and a 200-man company of irregular Kurdish cavalry recruited by Abdurrahman Pasha and commanded by Lieutenant Hilmi Musallimi arrived, as did a detachment of 200 Libyan volunteers. The Şekip Arslan (a Lebanese nationalist) Detachment of 150 Druze volunteers from Lebanon and the Nurettin Volunteer Detachment of some 270 Muslim Bulgarian refugees also arrived. Altogether the total of irregular volunteer groups totalled about 1,200 men.[40] The SO leaders hoped by bringing these non-Turkic Muslim volunteer groups into Egypt in concert with the invading Ottoman Army that their example would inflame and enthuse the Egyptian population to active rebellion.

Cemal was extremely concerned about the inadequate logistics posture of his army and assigned Lieutenant Colonel Behçet of the general staff as the commander of a Desert Lines of Communications Inspectorate.[41] Behçet was responsible for developing and pushing the logistics infrastructure forward in order to support the offensive with water, food, munitions and other supplies. He initially established two main supply bases at Al Arish and Kalatünnahil, and Maan would be added later when Vehip's infantry division joined the expedition. From the main bases von Kress and the VIII Corps staff also established a network of six smaller supply points to distribute supplies forward. The logistics goal for the campaign was to establish a fourteen-day supply of the vast array of consumables and commodities required by an army at war. Campaigning in the desert placed water and weight at a premium because everything had to be brought forward by animals or men. The Fourth Army developed what it called the Desert Ration which provided sufficient nutrition for a man for one day but did not weigh more than 1kg.[42] The Desert Ration was composed mostly of biscuits, dates and olives and each man carried a gourd of water. The daily water allotment for each man was 4kg (or just under 2 litres). Each horse was allotted 5kg of barley and 18kg of water (about 8 litres) while camels were allotted 3kg of barley and 5kg of water (just over 2 litres).[43] The privileges of rank allowed officers an additional 15kg of personal baggage and imams and officials were allowed to bring the books and utensils of their profession. In order to conserve water marches were planned to be conducted at night allowing the men and animals to rest during daylight hours. The stage was now set for Cemal to move into an offensive posture in 1915.

British Planning and Concentration
Great Britain had occupied Egypt in 1882 and, as empire commerce through the Suez Canal grew in strategic importance, undertook its

defence seriously. In 1906, Lord Esher estimated that the Ottomans could set up a logistic infrastructure in the Sinai to support 100,000 men.[44] Another study in 1909 opined that although a raid on the canal might be attempted, a serious invasion of Egypt 'could not be undertaken without much previous preparation and without the construction of a railway'.[45] While these threats placed imperial communications between Britain and the East in peril, 'a popular revolt in Egypt was considered the most dangerous'.[46] Additionally, a number of topographic surveys focusing on routes and water points were conducted by the British as well. These led to staff appreciations in 1911, which advanced the idea that the Ottomans could place 10 infantry divisions with 100,000 men within 45 days along the Sinai border, of which 10–20,000 men could cross the peninsula in 10–15 days.[47]

On 8 September 1914, Lieutenant General Sir John Maxwell arrived to command British forces in Egypt and was charged with the defence of the Suez Canal.[48] By October, his forces grew as the 42nd East Lancaster Division (Territorial) and the Lucknow Brigade (Indian Army) arrived to reinforce the Egyptian Camel Corps. Major General A. Wilson arrived on 16 November and assumed duties as GOC Canal Defences. On 20 November men of the Camel Corps clashed with Mümtaz's Bedouins at Bir en Nuss, 30km east of Al Qantara. In December enough Indian Army brigades had arrived to organize the 10th and 11th Indian Army Infantry Divisions in Egypt.[49] Moreover, the 1st Australian Infantry Division, a light horse brigade, and the New Zealand Infantry Brigade also arrived in Egypt in December. General Wilson organized the canal defences around the trained regulars of the two Indian infantry divisions, the Imperial Service Cavalry Brigade and the artillery brigades of the East Lancashire Division. The remaining East Lancashire infantry brigades with the Australians and New Zealanders remained in training camps but could be quickly moved by rail from Cairo to the canal as a reserve. In all, as 1915 approached, the British had some 60,000 combat troops in Egypt, albeit in various stages of training.

Conclusion
In the summer and autumn of 1914, the Ottoman Empire and its army were unprepared to wage a multi-front war against the Entente Powers. The Palestine and Syrian theatres were particularly unprepared and ill-equipped to go to war with Great Britain. Yet, when Cemal Pasha arrived, he immediately began to contemplate and plan for offensive operations against Egypt.

In retrospect, the complexity of the Palestine theatre is immediately apparent when considering that Cemal planned a tactically complicated and logistically difficult combat operation at the same time that he had to deal with restive Arab tribes, an active naval threat and coastal defence, and an inadequate theatre-wide logistics infrastructure. Moreover, his strategic lines of communications reached back to Constantinople leaving his army at the distant end of a very long pipeline which could not provide supplies, men and resources for his army in real time. His army also had to manage the climactically intense Palestinian and Sinai Peninsula summers, where the temperatures could reach 50 °C. All of these concerns created difficulties in 1914 and each continued in some form and became magnified as the years passed. And, as British strength grew in the region and able commanders were sent to fight Cemal's army, additional operational problems arose.

Notes

1. See Edward J. Erickson, *Ottoman Army Effectiveness in World War I, A Comparative Study* (Abingdon: Routledge, 2007), pp. 7–15 for details of these reform efforts.
2. Yahya Okçu and Hilmi Üstünsoy, *Birinci Dünya Harbinde Türk Harbi IVnü Cilt, 1nci Kısım, Sina-Filistin Cephesi, Harbin Başlangıcından İkinci Gazze Muharebeleri Sonuna Kadar (First World War, Turkish War, Sinai-Palestine Front, From the Beginning of the War to the Second Gaza Battles)* (Ankara: Genelkurmay Basımevi, 1979).
3. Fahri Belen, *Birinci Cihan Harbinde Türk Harbi 1914 Yılı Hareketleri (The Turkish Front in the First World War, Operations in 1914)* (Ankara: Genelkurmay Basımevi, 1964), p. 40.
4. Cemal Akbay, *Birinci Dünya Harbinde Türk Harbi, 1nci Cilt, Osmanli Imparatorlugu'nun Siyası ve Askeri Hazırlıkları ve Harbe Girisi (Ottoman Empire Military Mobilisation and Entry into the War)* (Ankara: Genelkurmay Basımevi, 1991), p. 157.
5. Ibid., p. 167.
6. Ibid., p. 171.
7. Ibid., pp. 175–6.
8. See Edward J. Erickson, *Ordered To Die, A History of the Ottoman Army in the First World War* (Westport, CT: Greenwood Press, 2000) and AKSAKAL.
9. Okçu and Üstünsoy, *Sina-Filistin Cephesi, Harbin Başlangıcından İkinci Gazze Muharebeleri Sonuna Kadar*, p. 105.
10. Email correspondence with Professor Mesut Uyar, 7 January 2015. I am indebted to Professor Uyar for this information about Cemal Pasha's background.
11. Okçu and Üstünsoy, *Sina-Filistin Cephesi, Harbin Başlangıcından İkinci Gazze Muharebeleri Sonuna Kadar*, pp. 108–9.
12. Ibid., p. 108.
13. Akbay, *Birinci Dünya Harbinde Türk Harbi*, pp. 176–8.
14. See Edward J. Erickson, *Ottomans and Armenians, A Study in*

Counterinsurgency (New York: Palgrave Macmillan, 2013), pp. 111–18 for a brief overview of the origins and missions of the *Teşkilat-ı Mahsusa*.

15. Stanford J. Shaw, *The Ottoman Empire in World War I, Volume 1* (Ankara: Turkish Historical Society, 2008), pp. 352–69.

16. Ibid., p. 369.

17. Stanford J. Shaw, *The Ottoman Empire in World War I, Volume 2, Triumph and Tragedy November 1914–July 1916* (Ankara: Turkish Historical Society, 2008), p. 1167.

18. Ibid., p. 1171.

19. Okçu and Üstünsoy, *Sina-Filistin Cephesi, Harbin Başlangıcından İkinci Gazze Muharebeleri Sonuna Kadar*, pp. 118–19.

20. Necmi Koral, Remzi Önal, Rauf Atakan, Nusret Baycan and Selâhattin Kızılırmak, *Türk Silahli Kuvvetleri Tarihi Osmanli Devri Birinci Dünya Harbi Idari Faaliyetler ve Lojistik, Xncu Cilt* (*Turkish Armed Forces History, Ottoman State in the First World War, Administration and Logistics*) (Ankara: Genelkurmay Basımevi, 1985), p. 145.

21. Okçu and Üstünsoy, *Sina-Filistin Cephesi, Harbin Başlangıcından İkinci Gazze Muharebeleri Sonuna Kadar*, p. 122.

22. İsmet Görgülü, *On Yillik Harbin Kadrosu 1912–1913, Balkan–Birinci Dünya ve Istiklal Harbi* (Ankara: Türk Tarih Kurum Basimevi, 1993), p. 138.

23. Okçu and Üstünsoy, *Sina-Filistin Cephesi, Harbin Başlangıcından İkinci Gazze Muharebeleri Sonuna Kadar*, pp. 125–6.

24. Ibid., p. 126.

25. Ibid.

26. Ibid., p. 128.

27. Ibid., p. 134.

28. Ibid., p. 133.

29. Muhratem Saral, Alpaslan Orhon and Şükrü Erkal, *Birinci Dünya Harbinde Türk Harbi Vncü Cilt, Çanakkale Cephesi Harekati Inci Kitap (Haziran 1914–Nisan 1915)* (*First World War, Turkish War, Gallipoli Front Operations, June 1914–April 1915*) (Ankara: Genelkurmay Basımevi, 1993), pp. 85–6.

30. Okçu and Üstünsoy, *Sina-Filistin Cephesi, Harbin Başlangıcından İkinci Gazze Muharebeleri Sonuna Kadar*, p. 135.

31. Ibid., p. 136.

32. Cemal to Enver, Cipher message, 26 November 1914, reproduced in Okçu and Üstünsoy, *Sina-Filistin Cephesi, Harbin Başlangıcından İkinci Gazze Muharebeleri Sonuna Kadar*, pp. 139–41.

33. Ibid., p. 145.

34. Ibid., Kroki (Sketch) 6 and pp. 145–6.

35. See Erickson, *Ottoman Army Effectiveness in World War I* for a comprehensive summary of the capabilities and capacities of the Ottoman Army in the First World War.

36. Cemal to Hussein, 10 December 1914 reproduced in Okçu and Üstünsoy, *Sina-Filistin Cephesi, Harbin Başlangıcından İkinci Gazze Muharebeleri Sonuna Kadar*, p. 150.

37. Shaw, *The Ottoman Empire in World War I, Volume 2*, pp. 751–8.

38. Okçu and Üstünsoy, *Sina-Filistin Cephesi, Harbin Başlangıcından İkinci Gazze Muharebeleri Sonuna Kadar*, pp. 152–7.

39. Shaw, *The Ottoman Empire in World War I, Volume 2*, p. 1628.

40. Okçu and Üstünsoy, *Sina-Filistin Cephesi, Harbin Başlangıcından İkinci Gazze Muharebeleri Sonuna Kadar*, p. 174.

41. Djemal Pasha (Cemal Pasha), *Memories of a Turkish Statesman 1913–1919* (New York: George H. Doran Company, 1922), p. 148.
42. Ibid., p. 149.
43. Belen, *Birinci Cihan Harbinde Türk Harbi 1914 Yılı Hareketleri*, p. 61.
44. Yigal Sheffy, *British Military Intelligence in the Palestine Campaign 1914–1918* (London: Frank Cass, 1998), p. 3.
45. The Morley Sub-Committee Report, 1 March 1909, cited in Sheffy, *British Military Intelligence in the Palestine Campaign*, p. 9.
46. Ibid., p. 10.
47. Ibid., p. 16.
48. George MacMunn and Cyril Falls, *History of the Great War, based on Official Documents: Military Operations Egypt and Palestine, From the Outbreak of War with Germany to June 1917* (London: HMSO, 1928), p. 15.
49. Ibid., p. 20.

Chapter 3

1915
The First Suez Offensive

Introduction

The Ottoman Fourth Army began 1915 with an ambitious plan to cross the Suez Canal with several infantry divisions. The invasion was closely coordinated with the subversive activities of the SO, which was encouraging unrest in Egypt. Crossing the canal, in turn, would spark a rebellion by the Egyptian people. However, by the time the operation was underway and reached the Suez Canal, the British had positioned 100,000 men to repel Cemal's men. The comic opera operation collapsed rapidly and the rebellion was stillborn. Casualties on both sides were very light and Cemal's forces returned to their frontier positions. While a complete failure, the aborted campaign did demonstrate Ottoman capability and capacity for large-scale trans-Sinai operations and encouraged Cemal to think about a second attempt later in the year.

After 25 April 1915, the demands of the Gallipoli Campaign gutted the Fourth Army's strength when Enver withdrew three infantry divisions for service at Gallipoli as well as a number of battalions for service in Mesopotamia. In return, the Fourth Army activated three new under-strength infantry divisions made up mostly of jandarma and depot battalions. To maintain pressure on the British in Egypt during this period, von Kress conducted a series of raids on the Suez Canal. In the midst of this drawdown, Cemal and the Fourth Army dealt with the relocation of a large number of Ottoman Armenians and conducted counter-insurgency operations against rebels and those who refused relocation. Despite these operational demands, by the end of 1915, the Fourth Army had been reduced to a coastal defence and internal security force, which had very little offensive capability or capacity.

Planning and the Approach March to the Suez Canal

The geography of the Sinai Peninsula was not conducive to either sustained operations or to the movement of large forces across its breadth. There were only two semi-improved roads leading from Palestine, one along the northern coast and the second along the ancient Route of the Patriarchs in the arid and desolate middle of the peninsula. The second route led to Ismailia on the canal. The terrain was waterless and afforded no fodder for the draft animals, which meant that everything that the army needed for survival had to be brought forward. Water, in particular, consumed in large quantities by both men and animals, posed a particular problem. For this reason the Fourth Army maintained its original plan to move its forces forward in tactical echelons.

The mature Ottoman tactical plan for the attack on the Suez Canal envisioned a daring *coup de main* crossing of the canal between Tussum and Serapeum by a single infantry division from the first echelon. This attack in the mid-point of the Suez Canal would be coordinated with two reinforced regiments from the first echelon conducting supporting diversionary attacks on both flanks. After forcing a passage over the canal itself another infantry division from the second echelon would cross the canal at Tussum and seize Ismailia. Early planning ideas included adding a newly available infantry division to reinforce the bridgehead on the west bank of the canal, but this proved impossible when Cemal decided to strengthen his coastal defences with the division instead. However, planners did include in the second echelon an infantry regiment to reinforce the right and a small infantry division to reinforce the left. The Ottomans hoped that by cutting the mid-point of the canal that they could reduce the effects of the gunfire of Royal Navy warships, which would inevitably assist any British counter-attack. Furthermore, they hoped that such an audacious manoeuvre would incite the Muslim populations of Egypt to rise in revolt against the British.[1]

The VIII Corps staff spent the first half of January 1915 moving its first echelon forces into assembly areas along the frontier from which to begin the approach march west. Occasionally, enemy aircraft were observed flying over the gathering Ottoman host. As these units moved forward the second echelon moved into the vacant camps. In this way the 10th and 22nd Infantry Divisions made their way into assembly areas near Jerusalem and Aqaba respectively.

The Centre Column, accompanied by VIII Corps commander Little Cemal, was the first echelon's main effort and it began to move forward on the night of 14/15 January. It was composed of the 25th Infantry Division, commanded by Staff Colonel Ali Fuat with Staff Major Mustafa İzzet as his chief of staff, and numbered about 13,000 men and 7,500 animals. The division comprised its organic 73rd, 74th and 75th Infantry Regiments and was reinforced by the 68th Infantry Regiment from the 23rd Infantry Division.[2] Unfortunately, these regiments were still organized with their pre-war authorization of two battalions each instead of the normal army standard of three-battalion regiments, altogether giving the division eight infantry battalions instead of the nine-battalion army standard for an Ottoman infantry division. Likewise, the 25th Artillery Regiment comprised two artillery battalions, although the artillery was reinforced by one 150mm howitzer battery (four howitzers). Accompanying the under-strength division were five bridging companies with pontoon platoons and a regiment of irregular Arab cavalry.[3] The Centre Column's mission was to make the assault crossing of the Suez Canal.

The Right Column of the first echelon, under the command of Major Rıfat, comprised the reinforced 1/80th Infantry Regiment (from the 27th Infantry Division) and an artillery battery. It was accompanied by Major Mümtaz and his irregular Bedouin cavalry. The Right Column's mission was to conduct diversionary attacks near Al Qantara to confuse the British as to the exact location of the attack and also to block maritime movement on the canal itself.

The Left Column of the first echelon comprised the 1/69th Infantry Regiment, under the command of newly promoted Lieutenant Colonel Musa Kâzım, and an artillery battery. Accompanying Musa's command were the Circassian, Druze, Kurdish and Bulgarian irregulars led by Eşref, who had been given additional SO instructions.[4] The Left Column's mission was to conduct a diversionary attack on the canal at Suez with the same objectives as its Right Column sister. Eşref, however, was instructed by his SO headquarters in Constantinople to break across the canal and lead his irregulars to Zagazig, some 50km inside Egypt west of Ismailia, to raise the rebellion there.[5]

Movement forward began on 14 January 1915, and for the first week, movement was conducted in daylight. (See map 3.1.) The Ottomans advanced with three columns abreast with the main effort in the centre. Large water tanks and storage depots were moved forward in an unprecedented and sophisticated logistical operation, and artesian wells were also drilled. By 22 January the advancing columns had reached a north–south line in the vicinity of Habra (about mid-way in the

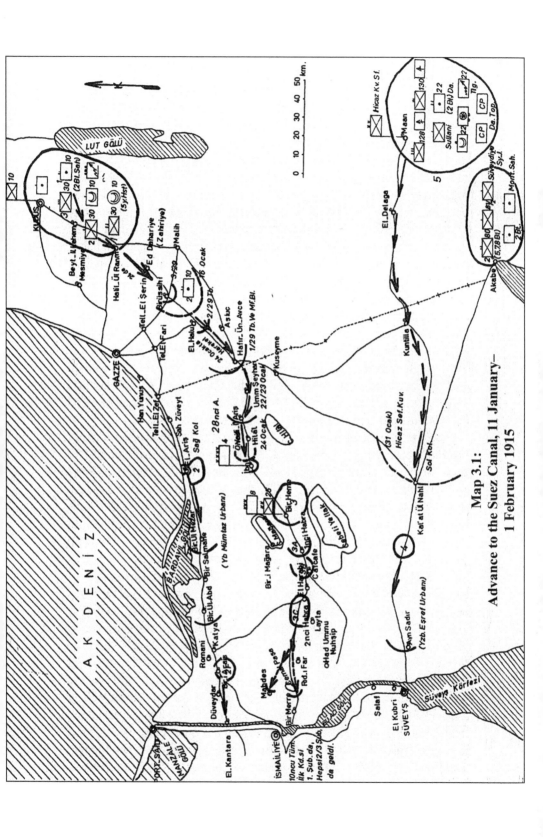

Map 3.1:
Advance to the Suez Canal, 11 January–
1 February 1915

peninsula). Because of the danger of discovery by French reconnaissance seaplanes, the Ottomans decided to conduct the final approach march under the cover of darkness. In a series of rapid night marches conducted over the next seven days, the 25th Infantry Division (the main centre column) reached its planned assembly area, 10km east of Ismailia, on 31 January 1915. There the force rested while the supporting engineers and trains brought forward pontoons, boats and bateaux, which had been requisitioned in Gaza and laboriously transported across the desert from Beersheba. Cemal's Fourth Army headquarters reached Hilal on 24 January and three days later established itself near Al Harabi. The Right and the Left Columns also reached their flanking assembly areas in the north halfway between Katia and Al Quantara and in the south near Bir Mab'uk. On 31 January, the second echelon 10th Infantry Division reached Al Harabi. Of note, on 28 January, the 25th Infantry Division's 1st and 2nd Battalions, 68th Infantry Regiment were detached and sent south toward Suez and north of Lake Timsah respectively. The 2/68th Infantry Regiment was reinforced with artillery and irregulars, designated as the Muhaddes Detachment and assigned to attack the canal and Ismailia bridge. This further reduced the main assault crossing force to six infantry battalions.

The Ottoman offensive was no secret and British intelligence easily tracked the massing of the Fourth Army largely because Cemal had attempted to generate public support from the Arab inhabitants of Syria and Palestine. On 11 January 1915, the British command released a statement to the Egyptian press that an attack on the canal was imminent.[6] Major General Wilson organized the canal defences into three sectors held by Indian Army soldiers. Wilson's Sector I ran from the port of Suez north to Geneffe at the southern point of the Great Bitter Lake, Sector II ran north from there to an old army camp just north of Ismailia, and Sector III ran north from there to Port Said. Sector I was held by the 30th Infantry Brigade and Sector III by the reinforced 29th Infantry Brigade. Wilson's most heavily defended sector was Sector II, where Cemal's main blow would fall. Moreover, this sector had the shortest frontage and was held by the 22nd (less one battalion) and 28th Infantry Brigades. The defences were trenches constructed on the west bank and held by small detachments until 26 January when Wilson ordered the trenches to be manned in full force.[7] In general reserve the British maintained the 31st and 32nd Infantry Brigades and the Imperial Service Cavalry Brigade. Even the Advanced Ordnance Base at Zagazig contained an entire infantry battalion (about a thousand Indian infantrymen). Not counting the 3 infantry divisions of Territorials, Australians and New Zealanders training in camps near Cairo, Maxwell disposed over 40,000 men in the defence of the Suez Canal, the central mass of which were stationed in the critical sector between the Great Bitter Lake and Lake Timsah. Additionally, the Royal Navy and French Navy stationed two battleships and a half-dozen cruisers in the canal itself to provide naval gunfire support.

Based on the appreciations of the Fourth Army intelligence division, Cemal was very aware that the British had at least 35,000 men on the canal and another 150,000 in Egypt, but he hoped to surprise the enemy and achieve local superiority at the point of crossing.[8] Cemal's tactical objective was to cross the Suez Canal and seize Ismailia, thereby triggering a country-wide rebellion in Egypt (which was the operational objective of the campaign) which no amount of enemy soldiers could then contain. Final orders for the attack were issued on 1 February and, unknown to Cemal, his main effort in the centre pitted seventeen infantry battalions and an irregular cavalry regiment against nineteen Indian infantry battalions and a cavalry brigade.[9]

In order to command and control the main effort, the Fourth Army headquarters and VIII Corps headquarters were moved forward to a small hill 6km south east of Ismailia. The VIII Corps attack orders specified that on the night of 2/3 February the attack force would move forward to assembly areas 3–4km from the canal and organize itself for the crossing, which would be made by four infantry battalions (from north to south, 2nd Battalion, 75th Infantry Regiment, 1st and 2nd Battalions, 74th Infantry Regiment and 1st Battalion, 73rd Infantry Regiment). The crossing itself would be made by two infantry companies and the machine-gun platoon from each of the four battalions in the first wave, to be followed by the remaining four infantry companies in a second wave. Twenty-four pontoons would carry the men of the first wave.[10] Two companies of a fifth battalion (2nd Battalion, 73rd Infantry Regiment) were immediately available as a reserve. The 2nd Battalion, 25th Artillery Regiment and bridging and pontoon platoons would go forward as well. Of the remaining divisional strength, 1st Battalion, 75th Infantry Regiment would move into blocking position facing Ismailia on the north flank and the 5th Company of the 2/73rd Infantry Regiment would move to the canal to secure the left flank. A heavy artillery battery was positioned to fire on enemy warships that were expected to offer resistance from Lake Timsah. The orders also specified that the Left Column would conduct a demonstration at Suez at the same time and that the irregular cavalry units should be prepared to move forward rapidly.[11]

The Assault on the Suez Canal

At 6.00 pm on 2 February 1915, the twenty-four assault infantry platoons began to move forward. It was a dark night and smoking was prohibited, as was unnecessary noise. Each company advanced with officers leading two platoons of the first wave forward with a third platoon following and comprising the second wave. Every third pontoon carried engineers and there were rafts available as well. It is unclear today whether the seven machine guns available in the first wave were dedicated to covering fire from the east bank or whether these guns were intended to make the crossing. The VIII Corps commander, Little Cemal, located himself on Çifte Hill (3km from the canal) and he intended to cross the canal when a bridgehead was established. At 10.00 pm the regiments of the second echelon 10th Infantry Division began to move forward. At 2.00 am, 3 February, the assault platoons advanced to within 600m of the canal where they began to assemble with their associated engineer pontoons. But, within the hour, the assault platoons stumbled across enemy sentry posts, which contained Indian soldiers alerted by barking dogs, and enemy rifle fire began at about 4.00 am.[12] Under fire and with dawn approaching, the men in the assault platoons began to run forward dragging their pontoons and equipment.

As the Ottomans pushed their pontoons into the canal the cloud cover broke revealing an almost full moon which illuminated the crossing to Indian riflemen, machine-gunners and an Egyptian artillery battery.[13] The soldiers who were making the assault were completely untrained in water crossing operations and panicked. Some of the men jumped out of the pontoons and fled inland while others dropped their pontoons even before entering the water. The carefully prepared attack plan disintegrated. By 4.20 am the canal was alive with British fire and, according to the British official history, only three pontoons made it to the west bank. Maps in the modern Turkish official history show a platoon from the 3rd Company, 1/74th Infantry Regiment and a platoon from the 4th Company, 2/74th Infantry Regiment as well as a platoon from the 1/73rd Infantry Regiment reached the west bank.[14] Every Ottoman officer and soldier who made the crossing was subsequently killed or captured.

At 5.30 am, Cemal sent an aide-de-camp over to the VIII Corps headquarters to receive the first reports, which noted heavy enemy firing but not much else. Cemal immediately ordered the 28th Infantry Regiment from the second echelon forward to reinforce the VIII Corps. At this time firing was heavy and Ottoman riflemen and machine-gunners, firing from the east bank, were raking the Indian positions causing 'casualties among the defenders to mount up'.[15] On the division's northern flank, the 1/75th Infantry Regiment pushed onward towards the canal bridge at Ismailia and became engaged in a firefight with British outposts. This attack failed as well and a British counter-attack at midday took several hundred prisoners. The VIII Corps headquarters sent the 1st and 2nd Battalions of the 28th Infantry Regiment to reinforce this effort.

The Ottomans pulled back from the east bank of the canal and could hear the destruction of their small bridgeheads on the west bank. The Fourth Army's artillery engaged several British warships throughout the day with some success but the main effort was effectively stalled. At 2.00 pm, Cemal convened a council of war with Fourth Army chief of staff Colonel von Frankenberg and chief of operations Lieutenant Colonel Ali Fuat as well as with VIII Corps commander Little Cemal and his chief of staff von Kress to discuss the situation.[16] The meeting was held at Cemal's command post just 800m from the firing line. The VIII Corps officers were willing to attempt another crossing but Cemal pointed out that there were only three undamaged pontoons remaining. Cemal concluded that retreat, in order to preserve the force from an immediate enemy counter-attack, was the only logical decision. All present agreed with the exception of a despairing von Kress, who, according to Cemal, was emotionally committed to the campaign.[17] At 3.10 pm, 3 February, Cemal issued orders ending the battle.[18] He ordered the fresh 10th Infantry Division to establish a defensive position on the higher ground about 5km east of the canal with its remaining battalions. The surviving officers and men of the 25th Infantry Division were to withdraw behind the defences and reconstitute (Cemal noted that they had been without water or food for 23 hours). He ordered the units on the northern flank to maintain contact until dark and then withdraw and he tasked the men of the withdrawing 25th Infantry Division to assist in pulling all of the heavy artillery and field artillery back as well. While the disengagement was conducted successfully, the bulk of the boats and pontoons were abandoned, ending any hopes that the Ottomans might have had of renewing the offensive. Cemal himself was one of the last men to pull back.

To the north of the 25th Infantry Division the Muhaddes Detachment split into two columns and conducted a feint with several companies of the 68th Infantry Regiment to the canal at Al Ferdan on 3 February, while the 2/68th Infantry Regiment swept south and established a position 5km east of Ismailia. From there irregular cavalry conducted a raid to the banks of the Suez Canal opposite the Ismailia train station. These forces withdrew on 4 February.

The Right Column arrived in its assembly area north of Katia at 2.00 pm on 31 January 1915. It began its advance on 2 February toward Al Qantara where, at 9.00 pm, two infantry companies and two infantry companies of the 80th Infantry Regiment under Major Mahmut and Staff Major Rıfat respectively occupied attack positions on the high ground overlooking the British trenches east of the canal.[19] They conducted a coordinated attack at 3.00 am on 3 February. Mahmut was handily repulsed while Rıfat's forces closed to the defences and remained there. Both forces withdrew to the column's assembly area on the night of 3/4 February. The force withdrew on 5 February except for Major Mümtaz and 400 of his 1,300 irregular Bedouin cavalry, who remained behind and left at 7.30 am on a diversionary raid north to the Nile River from the vicinity of Port Said.

The Left Column reached its assembly area 10km east of the town of Salute, which lay across the canal from Suez city on the night of 25/26 January. The force left in the morning and pushed to the outskirts of the town of Salute. It launched two minor attacks at 4.00 am and 1.00 pm on 27 January that were repulsed by the British.[20] The powerful second echelon of the Left Column, composed of Staff Colonel Vehip's 22nd Infantry Division, with three infantry regiments and artillery, reached Kalatünnahil on 31 January and joined the first echelon forces two days later. This created an extremely powerful Ottoman force opposite Suez, although when the Centre Column's assault crossing failed further operations were pointless. The Left Column remained in place in its assembly area when it finally withdrew on 6 February.

Altogether, the British captured about 300 Ottoman soldiers. Ottoman casualties were relatively light, with 14 officers and 178 soldiers dead, 15 officers and 360 soldiers wounded and 15 officers and 711 soldiers missing or captured, for a total loss of 1,293 men.[21] British losses for all ranks and nationalities were 32 killed and 130 wounded.[22] After the action, the British thought that they had simply countered a reconnaissance-in-force rather than a major Ottoman offensive aimed at severing the vital Suez Canal upon which Imperial communications depended. Cemal Pasha decided to retreat back to an advanced line to be established near El Arish–Magdaba and which would be held by three infantry battalions and two batteries of field artillery. From there, he hoped to be able to harass and interdict British shipping on the Suez Canal with mobile columns.

Planning a Second Egyptian Campaign

On the morning of 4 February, the 23,106 men and 12,007 animals of the VIII Corps began to withdraw. A fortnight before, in the Centre Column, 25,000 men and 13,873 animals had departed the concentration area near Beersheeba.[23] Water and food were not an issue because the depots at Birinci Habra and Al Ibn were well stocked. Undeterred by his failure, Cemal began immediately to plan for a second offensive. In order to begin preparations for a second canal expedition, Cemal decided to split his army into two components as it withdrew. The larger part would pull back into Palestine and Syria and begin training and preparations for renewing the offensive. A smaller part would be detached and designated as the Desert Force Command (DFC), which would guard the frontier as well as push occasional reconnaissance raids forward to the canal. On 5 February 1915, Cemal activated the DFC and assigned the Desert Lines of Communications Inspectorate as its logistical element.[24] He assigned von Kress as its commander, Lieutenant Colonel Behçet as commander of the logistics inspectorate and Major Şakir as the DFC chief of staff.

During the retreat Cemal analysed why he had failed and he began to consider what it might take in the future to conduct a successful campaign. He tasked Major Ali Fuat to summarize these thoughts in a formal report.[25] Cemal believed that future expeditions needed heavy artillery, two zeppelins, a dozen aircraft, more engineers and water specialists. Cemal came to see the first expedition as a reconnaissance-in-force which provided him with a personal understanding of the conduct of a future campaign against the Suez Canal. He was extremely disappointed with the inability of the SO to raise rebellion in Egypt and he thought that better coordination with the Egyptian SO agents as well as with the Senussi tribes in Libya would prove extremely valuable.[26] Cemal also thought that three army corps, each with a strength of two infantry divisions, an engineer battalion, a quick-firing artillery battalion, a heavy artillery battalion and a half-battalion of howitzers would be needed.[27] In a second campaign, one corps would advance to Al Qantara, a second corps would advance to Ismailia and the third would remain in reserve. Supporting these forces, the 22nd Infantry Division would separately threaten Suez, while the two forward corps simultaneously attacked Al Qantara and Ismailia. Cemal sent this revised plan to Enver in a report and began work on its implementation.

Most of the Fourth Army was back behind the frontier by 15 February. As the army withdrew, it left detachments behind which came under von Kress' command to become the DFC. Lieutenant Colonel Musa Kâzım, with the 1st Battalion, 61st Infantry Regiment, Nurettin's volunteers and the Bedouin irregulars, with artillery and machine guns, became the Left Wing Detachment at Nahil. Von Kress and his Desert Force headquarters, with the 1/73rd Infantry Regiment from the 10th Infantry Division, the Libyan volunteers, with artillery, engineers, and machine guns, occupied Ibn as the Centre Detachment.[28] German Lieutenant Colonel Laufer and the two battalions of the 81st Infantry Regiment, with artillery and machine guns, occupied El Arish and became designated as the Right Wing Column. The Camel Cavalry Regiment under Lieutenant Colonel Sadık remained behind with von Kress at Ibn. Cemal also assigned the headquarters and remaining elements of Lieutenant Colonel Ali Fuat's 25th Infantry Division to the DFC with most of the division in cantonments at Gaza.

After organizing the DFC, Cemal turned his attention to the main elements of the Fourth Army and on 17 February reorganized his forces.[29] The 27th Infantry Division, which had been conducting rear area security as the Provisional Jerusalem Division, was reactivated and assigned to the VIII Corps. Cemal organized a provisional army corps under Brigadier General Fahrettin, which ultimately became the XIV Corps and assigned the 8th and 10th Infantry Divisions to it.[30] The provisional corps headquarters was in Jerusalem with most of the 8th Infantry Division. The 22nd Infantry Division, still under Cemal's command, remained in and around Maan. Cemal re-established his own Fourth Army headquarters in Jerusalem.

During the advance from Gaza to the canal and during the retreat, Cemal was beyond the last telegraph post. Consequently, information reached him only after considerable delays and he was often out of touch with the strategic situation elsewhere in the empire. As such he was unaware of the gathering storm of the empire's competing strategic priorities which would turn his theatre into an operational backwater. Previously, on 14 December 1914, Enver sent the 35th Infantry Division back to Mesopotamia to assist in halting the deteriorating situation there and now, after the disastrous Sarıkamış offensive, Enver sent the 36th Infantry Division to the Ottoman Third Army on 22 March 1915.[31]

These deployments gutted the Fourth Army's defences along the Levant coast and left the XII Corps with only a handful of depot battalions. Because of concerns about the loyalty of the Arab tribes in the Hejaz, the 22nd Infantry Division withdrew back to Medina leaving only the 130th Infantry Regiment at Maan on 8 March 1915. The Royal Navy's climactic assault on the Dardanelles on 18 March resulted in a 150mm howitzer battery being sent to the straits region.

However, the worst was yet to come. Three days after the Gallipoli landings on 25 April 1915, Enver ordered the crack 8th Infantry Division, the 10th Infantry Division and the newly activated XIV Corps headquarters to deploy to the Gallipoli Peninsula.[32] On 2 June, Enver ordered the 25th Infantry Division to Gallipoli as well. Cemal attempted to retain the 25th Infantry Division but was overruled by Enver. The successful British offensive up the Tigris River in Mesopotamia also took its toll on Cemal's army. The Ottoman general staff ordered 3,000 newly conscripted and partly trained men to Mesopotamia and then, on 30 May, ordered a mountain howitzer battalion to Mosul. Between 5 and 9 June 1915, the 33rd Cavalry Regiment, the 130th Infantry Regiment, the 2nd Battalion, 129th Infantry Regiment, two machine-gun companies and another mountain artillery battery were ordered to Mesopotamia.[33] The 2nd Battalion, 131st Infantry Regiment, the 2nd Camel Cavalry Regiment, more artillery and 4,000 more conscripts were sent to Mosul in July and August. Finally, by the end of the summer, most of the remainder of the Fourth Army's machine guns and quick-firing artillery had been sent to Gallipoli as well.

This situation obviously ruined any thoughts that Cemal had for another offensive against Egypt and forced him to reorganize his army. Moreover, Italy entered the war against the Central Powers on 23 May 1915 renewing Ottoman fears that Entente forces would conduct amphibious operations somewhere along the littorals of the north-east Mediterranean coast. Thus, in the first six months of 1915, the operational posture of the Ottoman Fourth Army changed from an offensive to defensive alignment.

Maintaining the Initiative – the Von Kress Raids

Although it was clear that an operational offensive could not be conducted in the near term, Cemal was keenly aware of the strategic need to maintain operational and tactical pressure on British forces in Egypt. This was especially important after the amphibious landings on the Gallipoli Peninsula since most of Britain's available theatre reserves were stationed along the Suez Canal.[34] In order to accomplish this Cemal ordered von Kress and his DFC to conduct a series of raids designed to demonstrate Ottoman capability on a continuing basis. The prospect of action excited the aggressive von Kress and he began planning immediately. Cemal gave von Kress additional assets in the form of a small aviation detachment which gave him access to aerial reconnaissance of British activities. Von Kress organized a raiding force and titled it the Kalatünnahil Detachment (the town of Kalatünnahil is given as Nekhl in British histories) and gave command to Lieutenant Colonel Musa Kâzım.

Von Kress launched the first raid on the canal on 15 March 1915 from Ibn, some 50km south of El Arish. Musa Kâzım was taken sick and von Kress took direct command of the operation. As configured, he established two echelons, the combat echelon, which was built around the 3rd Battalion, 30th Infantry Regiment, the 27th Machine Gun Company, the 4th Mountain Battery from the 27th Artillery Regiment, the 1st Battery, 22nd Mountain Artillery Battalion and a fifty-man detachment from the Camel Regiment (under Lieutenant Colonel Sadık), as well as engineer, medical, transport and water portage units.[35] Von Kress established a support echelon, composed of the 2nd Battalion, 129th Infantry Regiment under Major Kemal, with two attached infantry companies, a machine-gun platoon and the mixed camel supply column. The force was deliberately light and tailored for speed. Three days later von Kress passed through Kalatünnahil and then turned west toward the canal. On 19/20 March, he reached an assembly area 14km from Giyum.

On 21 March, the detachment moved the infantry battalions to positions directly on the canal with the four 75mm guns of the artillery battery overlooking the eastern shore.[36] Firing was exchanged the next day when the gunners sent a few shrapnel shells westward. Von Kress sent fifty men of the camel cavalry on a diversionary raid north toward Şaluf on the night of 22/23 March as he prepared to withdraw his force. The camel cavalry ran into an Indian Army patrol and lost several men in a firefight before pulling back.[37] The raid failed to impress the British but did serve to demonstrate a continuing Ottoman capability to interdict the Suez Canal.

Von Kress launched another raid on 23 April 1915 against the mid-point of the canal. German Major Fischer and a reserve Hungarian captain named Gondos led this raid.[38] After a 125km march the force reached positions near Kilometre 69, south of Al Qantara. As the Ottomans approached the canal they encountered a strong British camel cavalry patrol and engaged in a brief firefight. That night the Ottomans launched a minor attack on Branch Mark Post and then withdrew. Just to the north another small Ottoman detachment led by German Major Hunger, composed of the 3rd Battalion, 28th Infantry Regiment and the regimental machine-gun company, reached positions near the canal on 28 April. From there, Hunger launched small raids to the canal before withdrawing on 5 May.[39] According to the British official history, this ended enemy activity 'of any importance' along the Suez Canal until the autumn.[40] However, von Kress continued to press the British by launching several additional raids between 17 June and 23 July 1915. These raids were led by First Lieutenant Sırrı and were composed of fast-moving camel cavalry. The purpose of these raids was to plant German mines in the Little Bitter Lake under the supervision of a German officer named Kaltenbah and a mine specialist named Schuh.[41] According to the Turkish official history, mines were successfully planted in the canal on 28 June after which the detachment sabotaged the railway near Al Qantara.[42] Another raid from El Arish by irregular cavalry planted dynamite on the Port Said–Al Qantara railway, cutting the tracks on 12 August 1915.

These raids did not impress Maxwell and failed to prevent him from sending major elements from his forces in Egypt to reinforce the ongoing Gallipoli campaign. The raids did serve, however, to maintain Cemal's interest in Ottoman capability and capacity. Cemal came to the conclusion that, while a crossing of the Suez Canal was impossible, a major movement to the eastern shore was well within the Fourth Army's capability.[43] Such an effort would block British maritime traffic in the canal. Combined with the enthusiastic and aggressive von Kress's offensive ideas, and encouraged by Enver, Cemal began to formulate a plan for a second Suez Canal campaign with this in mind during the autumn of 1915.

The Reorganization of the Fourth Army

To meet the needs of a multi-front war against the Entente the Ottoman Army began expanding its base of infantry divisions beginning in December 1914.[44] In the Fourth Army area, the general staff activated four new infantry divisions in 1915, one of which would be sent immediately to Mesopotamia. The first new division was the 41st Infantry Division in Adana, which was built around a nucleus of the Aleppo Jandarma Division as its cadre on 27 March 1915. Its three infantry regiments (the 131st–133rd), and an under-strength artillery regiment (the 41st) of three independent batteries were activated using untrained, newly conscripted men taken directly from the area depot battalions and by recalling older reservists. As a mobile reconnaissance element the irregular Humus Volunteer Cavalry Company was assigned to the division as well as an engineer and medical company. The division would not be ready for combat for months but, even so, two battalions were sent to Mesopotamia that summer.[45]

In May 1915, von Kress decided to release most of the volunteer units from government service.[46] It is unclear why he did this but, with the abandonment of offensive operations aimed at raising rebellion in Egypt, these forces became irrelevant. Another reason might have been the difficulty of supplying a large number of men forward of the Gaza lines.[47]

The general staff activated the 44th Infantry Division in Osmaniye on 15 June and the 43rd Infantry Division activated in Syria on 26 June 1915.[48] The 44th Infantry Division was truncated with only two new infantry regiments (the 139th, composed of three depot battalions, and the 140th, which was made up of two jandarma battalions), rather than the army standard of three regiments, and an artillery regiment (the 44th) of three batteries of obsolete cannon. The new 43rd Infantry Division also had two new infantry regiments (the 137th and the 138th, which were both composed of two jandarma battalions) and a similar artillery regiment (the 23rd) but the general staff also assigned the division the active army's 67th Infantry Regiment raising it to the triangular regimental army standard. The newly activated regiments using mobile (*seyyar*) jandarma battalions, which were trained and disciplined, were better off than the 139th, which was composed of untrained conscripts and older reservists. In any case, like the 41st Infantry Division, neither of these two divisions would be operationally capable for months. Almost all of the men in the three new infantry divisions were locally conscripted or reservist Arabs, whose motivation and patriotism Cemal continued to have concerns about.[49] On the plus side of the ledger, the three infantry regiments of the 27th Infantry Division were all augmented with a mobile jandarma battalion, as was the 130th Infantry Regiment. Of Cemal's five infantry divisions, only the 27th Infantry Division was at war strength (nine infantry battalions and three artillery battalions, augmented by three jandarma battalions).[50]

Cemal began the Fourth Army's reorganization on 15 June 1915 and it was completed on 15 July. Little Cemal's VIII Corps, headquartered in Jerusalem, comprised the 23rd and 27th Infantry Divisions, three independent batteries of artillery, two companies of engineers, the surviving elements of the bridge train, medical and bakery companies. Fahrettin's XII Corps, headquartered in Damascus, comprised the newly activated 41st, 43rd and 44th Infantry Divisions with no additional corps units other than medical and bakery companies. Cemal's headquarters transferred to Damascus, which had better lines of communications, and retained command of four 120mm howitzer batteries, an aviation detachment, a company of Nurettin's irregular volunteers, the headquarters cavalry company and communications units.[51] After 15 July 1915, the main effort of the Fourth Army turned to training the newly activated divisions in an attempt to bring their combat effectiveness up to the standard of the active army.

In spite of these difficulties, the Fourth Army still carried the mission of coastal defence and internal security, which Cemal was forced to attend to as well. On 14 July, Cemal organized the army into four operational areas of responsibility. In the north he assigned the 44th Infantry Division the First Area (the *1st Bölge*, which may be translated as zone, district or a defined area) around Adana, its coast line and hinterlands. The Second Area, centred on Aleppo but stretching from the coast north to Karamanmaraş and Gaziantepe, was assigned to the 41st Infantry Division and the Third Area, essentially modern-day Lebanon, was assigned to the 43rd Infantry Division. The southernmost Fourth Area, most of modern-day Israel, was assigned to the 27th Infantry Division in Jerusalem.[52]

Unrest in the Fourth Army Rear Areas
In addition to the ongoing imperatives of a conventional war, the Ottoman Fourth Army experienced a significant threat from the restive peoples who inhabited its rear areas. According to Cemal's memoirs, the most important military events in late 1915 were the Armenian uprisings in Zeytun and Urfa.[53] While the Armenian incidents were, militarily, the most compelling problem for the Fourth Army, there were other disaffected Ottoman minorities in its operational area which included Syrian Arabs, Lebanese Christians, Kurds, Zionists and the tribal Arabs of the Arabian Peninsula. This is not to say the entirety of these minorities were engaged in subversive or revolutionary activities, or even that a majority of them supported such goals, nevertheless, it is true that small secret revolutionary committees existed within the Armenian, Syrian Arab, Lebanon Christian and Zionist communities.[54] The separatist ambitions of the Kurds and tribal Arabs were, on the other

hand, long standing and well known.[55] The separatist activities of these varied groups were tracked by Ottoman intelligence services and by the field army staffs. The Ottoman Third and Fourth Armies were particularly affected by this situation and were continually developing tactical intelligence that would enable the armies to deal with potential problems.

Much of the problem dealt with the fragile logistics architecture that sustained the Fourth Army. When the Fourth Army formed on 6 September 1914, it activated the Fourth Army Lines of Communications Inspectorate (*4ncü Ordu Menzil Müfettişliği*, or 4 LoCI) on 12 November 1914, with the headquarters in Damascus.[56] The activation of 4 LoCI, commanded by Major Kâzım, occurred after the declaration of war, and there was no opportunity to stockpile munitions or supplies. The Fourth Army was responsible for the security and maintenance of the railway line that led from the Pozantı Gap to the Euphrates River and south through Palestine to Medina. The railway posed particular problems because it was constructed by European entrepreneurs rather than by military planners. There were two uncompleted gaps in rugged mountains at Pozantı (54km) and Osmaniye (36km), different gauge tracks (e.g. 100cm wide from Remleh to Jerusalem but 105cm wide from there to Damascus), and the entire line was in an extremely poor state of repair.[57] Compounding the difficulties, all supplies for the Mesopotamian theatre were shipped through the 4 LoCI area and competed for the inadequate transportation resources. The most vulnerable point in the 4 LoCI lines of communication was near the seacoast town of Dörtyol. Sometimes called the 'Berlin to Baghdad Railway' because of German investments, the railway split near Dörtyol with the pilgrimage route leading south to Medina and an uncompleted spur leading east for about 48km.[58] Of particular concern were the tracks and bridges near Dörtyol that lay close by the Mediterranean Sea, making them tempting targets for Allied naval interdiction.

Throughout the spring of 1915, the British and French raided the Levant coast, damaging infrastructure and landing spies and agents into the Fourth Army's rear area. Of these, the activities of Captain Frank Larkin and HMS *Doris*, as well as those of the French and Russian navies, are the most well documented and alerted the Ottomans to the profound operational weaknesses in their Levantine coastal defence posture, especially around Dörtyol, and soon intelligence reports began to arrive in Constantinople.[59] On 12 February 1915, three Armenians were caught contacting a British ship off Dörtyol.[60] The same report identified a man named Agop hiding in the reeds on shore, who was caught with signalling equipment, and who testified that the three Armenians were conveying information about Ottoman army positions. This information was forwarded to the headquarters of the Fourth Army in Damascus on 5 March; however, the army staff was already aware of the situation and had previously, on 26 February, begun to reinforce the region with a detachment of troops from the 8th Infantry Division.[61] In this alert, the problems in Dörtyol and Aleppo took priority in the first paragraph. Cables from the Ministry of War and interior minister Talat Pasha to Fourth Army commander Cemal in March and April identified Dörtyol again, as well as Alexandretta and Adana, as locations from which Armenians needed to be relocated away from for security reasons.[62] German consular reports titled 'The unrest in Dörtyol' outlined more problems in the village and noted that inhabitants were friendly toward the British landing parties.[63] Moreover, the German reports identified several Armenians, who came ashore from British ships, to recruit and organize a revolution. Raids uncovered large quantities of explosives cached in Armenian homes.[64]

The sensitivity of the Ottomans to threats to their railway lines of communications, as the dangerous spring of 1915 arrived, is illustrated by further message traffic from Constantinople. In a ciphered message to the Fourth Army Talat Pasha specifically requested that relocated Armenians from the towns and villages of the Alexandretta and Bilan districts, within which lay Dörtyol, be managed in a particular manner. Talat proposed guidelines for the resettlement of displaced Armenians in temporary villages, but directed that the relocated Armenians from these areas 'be definitely resettled at least twenty-five kilometers away from the Baghdad railway lines running to the frontier as well as away from other railway lines'.[65]

The relocations of the Ottoman Armenians from eastern Anatolia began in earnest after what the Ottoman government characterized as the Van rebellion began in mid-April 1915.[66] Regardless of cause, in late April 1915, Armenian revolutionaries, the Russian Army and Armenian volunteer regiments (*druzhiny*) were in firm possession of the strategic city of Van and were advancing toward Bitlis. In response to this battlefield reverse, the Ottoman government began a deliberate relocation campaign of the Ottoman Armenian inhabitants of six eastern provinces on 31 May 1915. Localized relocations in the Third Army and Fourth Army areas had occurred earlier and this directive widened the relocations to include significant parts of Aleppo and Adana.[67] In any event, Cemal's Fourth Army was now tasked to accomplish the following:

> The conduct of such rebel elements rendered it necessary to remove them from the areas of military operations and to evacuate the villages serving as bases of operations and shelters for the rebels. To achieve this, a different course of action has begun to be implemented. Within that framework, the Armenians living in the provinces of Van, Bitlis, Erzurum, with the exclusion of the centers of Adana, Sişs, and Mersin; the sanjaks of Adana, Mersin, Cebel-i Bereket and Kozan; the sanjak of Maras with the exclusion of the center of Maras; the towns and villages of Inkenderun, Bilan, Cisr-i Sugur and Antakya of the province of Aleppo; with the exclusion of the central district of Aleppo have begun to be rapidly transferred to the southern provinces.[68]

Cemal Pasha is known to have resisted the idea of blanket removal of Ottoman Armenians but nevertheless the Fourth Army carried out the military application of the directive.[69] There were numerous incidents along the 4 LoCI lines of communications including small attacks and incidents in the Armenian-manned labour battalions which kept the roads repaired and operational.[70]

The British staffs in Cairo were especially energized with the idea of conducting an amphibious landing near Dörtyol and Alexandretta, in conjunction with a large Armenian uprising in the Zeytun region, for the purposes of cutting the Ottoman railway lines. One of the personalities behind this was Lieutenant Colonel Sir Mark Sykes, an expert on the Ottomans and the Near East, who was sent from London to Egypt to study and coordinate the idea with Armenian expatriates. On 14 July 1915, Sykes met with Sourene Bartevian, editor of the Armenian newspaper *Houssaper* and a prominent *Dashnak* (member of the Armenian Revolutionary Federation), who tried to persuade Sykes of the viability of an autonomous Armenia.[71] Letters between Sykes and Major General Charles E. Callwell, author of the already well-known *Small Wars*, then a senior staff officer at the War Office and Sykes's superior, indicated that the Armenians hoped to be in possession of Muş very soon.[72] Sykes also reported to Callwell that the Armenians were prepared to provide 5,000–6,000 men for a landing, if the British would supply weapons and ships. What is interesting about this particular exchange of correspondence is the fact that, subsequently, Sykes helped orchestrate the Arab Revolt in 1916, as well as co-author the infamous Sykes-Picot Agreement that divided the pre-war Ottoman Middle East into independent states and European protectorates. On 22 July 1915, a delegation from the Armenian National Defence Committee approached Sir John Maxwell, British commander in chief in Egypt, to reinforce the offer of coordinated Armenian rebellions, and to offer positive internal military assistance to the British. Boghos Nubar, a notable member of the delegation, claimed that the British could 'rely on 25,000 Armenian insurgents in Cilicia and 15,000 from nearby provinces' to support an Allied landing in the Alexandretta area, which would cut the 4 LoCI's communications to the Sinai front.[73] The details of the plan were transmitted to the Foreign Office by Sir Henry McMahon, British high commissioner in Egypt, who was at the same time engaged in a famous exchange of letters with the Arabs also encouraging them to revolt as well.[74] Belatedly, McMahon followed up in the autumn with messages to the Foreign Office pointing out that an 'unexpected descent' on Alexandretta would cut off the Ottoman armies in Arabia, Mesopotamia, Palestine and Syria.[75]

Although the British never landed at Alexandretta, it should be noted that these particular personalities were heavily involved in Britain's subsequent, and successful, effort to start an Arab revolt against the Ottomans. It is fair to say that the British were instigating very actively both Armenian and Arab rebellions in mid-1915. German consular reports from Constantinople and Damascus reveal that the Ottoman Ministry of War was aware of these schemes.[76] Baron Max von Oppenheim also sent reports to Berlin from Damascus noting that an accumulation of evidence had aroused the fear of the Ottoman authorities that a landing was expected near Alexandretta.[77]

The Armenian relocations went as planned in some areas but in many locations the Ottomans met fierce resistance. The only forces available to the Fourth Army were the barely trained and under-strength regiments of the newly activated 41st, 43rd and 44th Infantry Divisions. The governor of Adana reported on 29 July 1915 that Armenians on the Ayvajik plateau near Maraş were resisting relocation, and that Armenians from Zeytun and Hadjin were gathering there as well.[78] Cemal ordered the 132nd Infantry Regiment to destroy them and reinforced the regiment with a mountain artillery platoon and a regular infantry battalion.

From 17 July to 4 August, the Diyarbekir Stationary Jandarma Regiment and the Midyat Mobile Jandarma Battalion reported the suppression of 500 rebels, who had taken shelter in Ziyor village and who had been under siege since 17 July.[79]

On 29 July 1915, the 1st Battalion, 133rd Infantry Regiment was sent to Antep (Gaziantepe) to fight insurgents.[80] At the same time, the 132nd Infantry Regiment was ordered to suppress 500 Armenian guerrillas near Zeytun. The fight to subdue Zeytun was costly and was only resolved by a direct assault on the town.[81] On 30 July 1915, the 3rd Battalion, 131st Infantry Regiment was sent to Antakya (Antioch), where it went into action against 500–600 insurgents. Contemporary Ottoman observers also noted that the only way to root out the rebels was at the point of a bayonet.[82]

The most well-known battles occurred south west of Antioch on the Musa Dağ mountain and were immortalized in Franz Werfel's novel *The Forty Days of Musa Dagh*.[83] The Armenians on Musa Dağ numbered about 5,500, of whom several thousand were men equipped with a variety of rifles.[84] By mid-July, the Armenians were hard at work fortifying their villages and the entire population was put to work in this endeavour. On 7 August 1915, the 41st Infantry Division began its counter-insurgency operations against Musa Dağ. In the first encounter the Armenians routed the overconfident Ottomans, who had launched a poorly coordinated frontal attack. The 1st Battalion and 2/131st Infantry Regiment (870 infantrymen) renewed the assault and began an encirclement supported by artillery. After a brief bombardment, the Ottomans assaulted and carried the village with a bayonet attack. The 41st Infantry Division began further operations on 13 August 1915. After several more days of search-and-destroy operations the division reported that 'no Armenians remained in nearby Antakya' on 20 August 1915.[85] The 41st Infantry Division finished clearing the mountain on 31 August.

Operations continued against insurgent Armenians in September 1915. Moreover, French agents had come ashore from French naval vessels, including the French battleship *Victor Hugo*, and the 41st Infantry Division staff was very concerned about the possibility of the Armenian insurgents supporting a French amphibious landing in the Gulf of Iskenderun.[86] However, the anticipated landing never occurred, although French naval operations continued including the evacuation of some of the survivors of Musa Dağ by the French cruisers *Guichen* and *Jeanne d'Arc*. After November 1915, the 41st Infantry Division resumed coastal and internal security duties in the Iskenderun vicinity.

Rebellions broke out in Urfa, a centre of known Armenian revolutionary committee activity throughout 1915. On 9 August 1915,

Armenians rose up in the nearby village of Germüş. The uprising quickly spread and within ten days had become what the Ottomans called a 'large insurrection' and because the town was strongly fortified, the governor asked for 'the dispatch of a military force with artillery'.[87] The Fourth Army was forced to send in reinforcements to assist the 41st Infantry Division. The 3/130th Infantry Regiment was dispatched from the 23rd Infantry Division in Syria, arriving in Urfa on 30 September 1915.[88] Accompanying the Ottoman troops was a German captain named Eberhard Count Wolffskeel von Reichenberg, who recorded his observations in a diary. He noted that 'the entire defence is very well prepared and led. The band is well provided with weapons and ammunition.'[89] A bitter struggle ensued with the Ottomans finally overcoming resistance on 23 October.

In September 1915, the Fourth Army began to relocate the Armenians of Mersin and Tarsus. Toward the end of these relocations, resistance broke out and a second battalion from the 23rd Infantry Division deployed on 28 October to fight Armenian guerrillas around the city of Tarsus. These operations concluded the Fourth Army's military counter-insurgency efforts.

Cemal was also extremely worried about Entente-inspired Arab insurgencies in Syria and minority Christian uprisings in Lebanon.[90] This was a result of the information gathered by the SO's counter-espionage cells operating in the Fourth Army area, which had been tracking the activities of Syrian and Christian notables.[91] Moreover, the counter-espionage cells also collected evidence that implicated a number of Ottoman Army officers of Arab ethnicity, who were in contact with French agents. The British were also very active in this period dropping dozens of agents along the Levant coast, a number of whom were apprehended by Ottoman authorities.[92] British intelligence services in Cairo were also in communication with a Zionist volunteer group called Nili, which was coordinated by Avshalom Feinberg and Aaron Aaronsohn.[93] The Zionists were too small in number to instigate rebellion actively but they became an important source of information for British intelligence.

At first, Cemal attempted conciliatory declarations to counteract the Entente's efforts to instigate rebellion but these failed in the face of resentment and rising nationalism. Armed with intelligence provided by the counter-espionage cells, Cemal began operations against the Syrian Arabs in the early summer of 1915. This became an operational imperative when Cemal's best combat infantry divisions were withdrawn for the Gallipoli campaign.[94] The conspiracy involved a number of Syrian notables including the *El Mufit* newspaper publisher Abdülgani, tribal leader Nuri Şaalan and several Bedouin sheiks.[95] The ring leader of the Syrian Arabs was Abdul Kerim el Halil, who was caught with a number of his accomplices and put on trial in June and July 1915. Military courts martial found them guilty and condemned them to death.[96] The speedy executions served to spread panic among the rebels and before they were executed in August, Cemal's intelligence services extracted enough information to destroy the conspiracy. For reasons similar to the Armenian relocations, the Fourth Army deported hundreds of Syrian Arab and Druze families to various places in Anatolia in the autumn of 1915.[97] Cemal also took punitive action against the Lebanese Christians, who were also implicated, by abrogating the *Reglement Organique*, under which Lebanon had enjoyed autonomy since 1861. This harsh measure enabled the Fourth Army to establish direct martial law in Beirut and the Lebanese hinterlands.[98]

As the winter of 1915 approached the Fourth Army had effectively ended, for the time being, the internal threats to its rear area. Whether the Armenian, Syrian Arab or Lebanese Christian peoples would have rebelled in numbers sufficient to cripple the Fourth Army is problematic at best. It is clear, however, that Entente efforts to instigate rebellion among these peoples failed in the face of effective Fourth Army operations enabled by SO counter-espionage activities and conventional Ottoman Army intelligence services.

Conclusion – Final Operations in 1915

On 26 November 1915, Cemal and von Kress began actively planning the second Suez Canal campaign. This was enabled by the arrival of the 3rd Infantry Division, under the command of Staff Colonel İbrahim Refet.[99] This division had been withdrawn from the Gallipoli Front on 8 October and Refet's and his headquarters arrived in Beersheba at the end of December 1915. The 3rd Infantry Division was tactically very experienced and a highly regarded fighting organization. Refet's division comprised the 31st, 32nd and 39th Infantry Regiments and a heavily reinforced composite artillery regiment. This division formed the backbone of the First Expeditionary Force, which Cemal activated on 26 December 1915.[100] Von Kress took command of the new organization and was assigned Staff Major Kadri as his chief of staff. Additional forces from the Gallipoli campaign, which was ending, were also allocated to the First Expeditionary Force and would arrive in the late winter of 1916.

Overall, the operations of the Ottoman Fourth Army in 1915 may be characterized as operationally and tactically complicated. Cemal attempted a major offensive, which was under-resourced, against the Suez Canal which ended in failure. In his rear area a gathering insurgency by Armenian committees supported by the Entente reared its head and had to be dealt with. Compounding these competing operational demands, the Arab Revolt was about to begin in earnest. At the strategic level, the Ottoman general staff took most of Cemal's pre-war active and trained divisions to support the increasing demands of the unfolding Gallipoli campaign. These departing units were, in turn, replaced by newly activated infantry divisions, which needed to be manned, equipped and trained. Some of these divisions found themselves in action in the autumn against Armenian rebels. Altogether, it was a full plate of decisions and dilemmas that Cemal and his Fourth Army staff were forced to deal with.

Notes

1. Commandant M. Larcher, *La Guerre Turque Dans La Guerre Mondiale* (Paris: Chiron & Berger-Levrault, 1926), p. 251.
2. Okçu and Üstünsoy, *Sina-Filistin Cephesi, Harbin Başlangıcından İkinci Gazze Muharebeleri Sonuna Kadar*, Kuruluş (Order of Battle Diagram) 4.
3. Belen, *Birinci Cihan Harbinde Türk Harbi 1914 Yılı Hareketleri*, Kuruluş (Diagram) 3.
4. Shaw, *The Ottoman Empire in World War I, Volume 2*, pp. 1637–8.
5. Ibid., p. 1638.
6. MacMunn and Falls, *Military Operations Egypt and Palestine, From the Outbreak of War with Germany to June 1917*, p. 29. In an earlier work the author of the current volume incorrectly noted that the Ottomans had achieved some measure of surprise, a statement that is clearly in error.
7. Ibid., pp. 329–33.
8. Djemal Pasha, *Memories of a Turkish Statesman 1913–1919*, pp. 155–6.
9. Belen, *Birinci Cihan Harbinde Türk Harbi 1914 Yılı Hareketleri*, p. 72.
10. Ibid., p. 73.
11. Okçu and Üstünsoy, *Sina-Filistin Cephesi, Harbin Başlangıcından İkinci Gazze Muharebeleri Sonuna Kadar*, pp. 203–4.
12. Ibid., p. 212.
13. MacMunn and Falls, *Military Operations Egypt and Palestine, From the Outbreak of War with Germany to June 1917*, pp. 39–40.
14. Okçu and Üstünsoy, *Sina-Filistin Cephesi, Harbin Başlangıcından İkinci Gazze Muharebeleri Sonuna Kadar*, Kroki (Sketch) 10.
15. MacMunn and Falls, *Military Operations Egypt and Palestine, From the Outbreak of War with Germany to June 1917*, p. 41.
16. Okçu and Üstünsoy, *Sina-Filistin Cephesi, Harbin Başlangıcından İkinci Gazze Muharebeleri Sonuna Kadar*, pp. 216–17.
17. Djemal Pasha, *Memories of a Turkish Statesman 1913–1919*, pp. 156–8.

18. Fourth Army Orders, 1510 hours, 3 February 1915, reproduced in Okçu and Üstünsoy, *Sina-Filistin Cephesi, Harbin Başlangıcından İkinci Gazze Muharebeleri Sonuna Kadar*, p. 217.

19. Ibid., Kroki (Sketch) 13.

20. Ibid., Kroki (Sketch) 14a.

21. Belen, *Birinci Cihan Harbinde Türk Harbi 1914 Yılı Hareketleri*, p. 78.

22. MacMunn and Falls, *Military Operations Egypt and Palestine, From the Outbreak of War with Germany to June 1917*, p. 50.

23. Okçu and Üstünsoy, *Sina-Filistin Cephesi, Harbin Başlangıcından İkinci Gazze Muharebeleri Sonuna Kadar*, p. 219.

24. Ibid., pp. 263–4 and Djemal Pasha, *Memories of a Turkish Statesman 1913–1919*, pp. 163–4.

25. Djemal Pasha, *Memories of a Turkish Statesman 1913–1919*, p. 159.

26. Okçu and Üstünsoy, *Sina-Filistin Cephesi, Harbin Başlangıcından İkinci Gazze Muharebeleri Sonuna Kadar*, pp. 260–1.

27. Ibid., p. 262.

28. Ibid., pp. 266–7.

29. Ibid., pp. 268–70 and Djemal Pasha, *Memories of a Turkish Statesman 1913–1919*, pp. 164–5.

30. Fahrettin is also known as Fahreddin, Fakhri and Fakhreddin. All are the same officer (1868–1948), who took the name Ömer Fahrettin Türkkan in 1934 and was known as the 'Lion of Medina' for his stalwart defence, which lasted until January 1919. He was detained by the British on Malta until 1921 when he was released and joined Mustafa Kemal's nationalist forces.

31. Belen, *Birinci Cihan Harbinde Türk Harbi 1914 Yılı Hareketleri*, p. 84.

32. Okçu and Üstünsoy, *Sina-Filistin Cephesi, Harbin Başlangıcından İkinci Gazze Muharebeleri Sonuna Kadar*, pp. 272–3.

33. Ibid.

34. Ibid., p. 301.

35. Ibid., p. 303.

36. Ibid., pp. 304–5.

37. MacMunn and Falls, *Military Operations Egypt and Palestine, From the Outbreak of War with Germany to June 1917*, p. 61.

38. Okçu and Üstünsoy, *Sina-Filistin Cephesi, Harbin Başlangıcından İkinci Gazze Muharebeleri Sonuna Kadar*, pp. 306–7.

39. Ibid., pp. 308–11.

40. MacMunn and Falls, *Military Operations Egypt and Palestine, From the Outbreak of War with Germany to June 1917*, p. 64.

41. Okçu and Üstünsoy, *Sina-Filistin Cephesi, Harbin Başlangıcından İkinci Gazze Muharebeleri Sonuna Kadar*, pp. 312–15.

42. Ibid., p. 316.

43. Djemal Pasha, *Memories of a Turkish Statesman 1913–1919*, p. 168.

44. See Erickson, *Ottoman Army Effectiveness in World War I*, pp. 21–8, 68–74 for an overview of how the Ottoman Army expanded its number of infantry divisions in the war.

45. Okçu and Üstünsoy, *Sina-Filistin Cephesi, Harbin Başlangıcından İkinci Gazze Muharebeleri Sonuna Kadar*, p. 282.

46. Fahri Belen, *Birinci Cihan Harbinde Türk Harbi 1915 Yılı Hareketleri* (*The Turkish Front in the First World War, Operations in 1915*) (Ankara: Genelkurmay Basımevi, 1964), p. 84.

47. Shaw, *The Ottoman Empire in World War I, Volume 2*, p. 1742. Shaw noted the low morale on the front caused by little food and no pay.
48. Fahri Belen, *Birinci Cihan Harbinde Türk Harbi 1918 Yılı Hareketleri* (*The Turkish Front in the First World War, Operations in 1918*) (Ankara: Genelkurmay Basımevi, 1967), chart after p. 250, 'Divisions Organized in the War'. The 45th Infantry Division, organized in Aleppo on 22 August 1915, deployed to Mesopotamia.
49. Djemal Pasha, *Memories of a Turkish Statesman 1913–1919*, p. 167.
50. Okçu and Üstünsoy, *Sina-Filistin Cephesi, Harbin Başlangıcından İkinci Gazze Muharebeleri Sonuna Kadar*, Kuruluş (Order of Battle Diagram) 7.
51. Ibid., pp. 2805.
52. Ibid., Kroki (Sketch) 18.
53. Djemal Pasha, *Memories of a Turkish Statesman 1913–1919*, p. 167.
54. This literature on this subject is vast and outside the scope of this work. Of particular interest are Erickson, *Ottomans and Armenians, A Study in Counterinsurgency*, Shaw, *The Ottoman Empire in World War I, Volume 2* and Sheffy, *British Military Intelligence in the Palestine Campaign*.
55. See also James Barr, *Setting the Desert on Fire, T.E. Lawrence and Britain's Secret War in Arabia 1916–1918* (New York: W. W. Norton and Company, 2009), Şükrü Erkal, *Birinci Dünya Harbinde Türk Harbi VIncı, Hicaz, Asir, Yemen Cepheleri ve Libya Harekâtı 1914–1918* (*First World War, Turkish War, Hicaz, Asir and Yemen Front and Libya Operations*) (Ankara: Genelkurmay Basımevi, 1978), David Murphy, *The Arab Revolt, 1916–18* (Oxford: Osprey Publishing Ltd, 2008) and Elizer Tauber, *The Arab Movements in World War I* (London: Frank Cass, 1993).
56. Fourth Army Orders, Damascus, 12 November 1914, reproduced in Okçu and Üstünsoy, *Sina-Filistin Cephesi, Harbin Başlangıcından İkinci Gazze Muharebeleri Sonuna Kadar*, pp. 765–7.
57. Ibid., pp. 675–6.
58. Ibid., pp. 698–704.
59. Instructions from the minister of the interior to the governor of Adana, 16 February 1915, BOA DH, File 50/141 reproduced in Arş.Ş.Mud.lüğü (T. C. Başbakanlık Devlet Archives staff), *Osmanli Belgelerinde Ermenile (1915–1920)* (Ankara: Osmanlı Arşivi Daıre, 1995), p. 20.
60. Report from governor of Adana to Ministry of Internal Affairs, National Police Directorate, ATASE, Archive 13, Record 63, File 1-3.
61. Report from Ministry of Internal Affairs to Fourth Army, 4 March 1915, and Headquarters Fourth Army Cipher Number 2247, 28 February 1915. ATASE BDH, File 13, Folder 63, index 2 (1–3).
62. Orders from Ministry of the Interior, General Secretariat of Security to the governor of Adana, 2 March 1915. BOA DH (Başbakanlık Osmanlı Arşivi–Dahiliye Nezareti Arşivi), File 50/141 reproduced in Hikmet Ozdemir and Yusuf Sarinay (eds), *Turk-Ermeni Ihtilafi Belegeler* (Ankara: Egemenlik, n.d.)., document 3. Also ciphered telegram from Talat, minister of the interior to Fourth Army commander Cemal Pasha, 11 April 1915. BOA DH, File 52/93, reproduced in Ozdemir and Sarinay (eds), *Turk-Ermeni Ihtilafi Belegeler*.
63. Report N. 226 from Vice Consul Alexandretta (Hoffman) to Ambassador Wangenheim, Constantinople, 7 March 1915. AP-AA (Politisches Archiv des Auswartigen Amts) (German Foreign Ministry), Embassy Constantinople/Vol. 168, translated and reprinted at http:// www.armenocide.de. Also Report No. 2234

from Consul Adana (Brüge) to Ambassador Wangenheim Constantinople, 13 March 1915. AP-AA, Embassy Constantinople/Vol. 168, translated and reprinted at http://www.armenocide.de.

64. Ali Fuat Erden, *Birinci Dünya Harbinde Suriye Hatiraları* (Istanbul: Arma Yayınları, 2003), p. 26. At the time of the incident Ali Fuat was a staff officer in the Ottoman Fourth Army.

65. Message from the Directorate of Security, Ministry of the Interior to the Fourth Army Command, 23 May 1915. BOA DH, File 53/94, reproduced in Ozdemir and Sarinay (eds), *Turk-Ermeni Ihtilafi Belegeler*.

66. For the Ottoman view of the Van Rebellion, see, Erickson, *Ottomans and Armenians, A Study in Counterinsurgency*, pp. 165–9.

67. The movement and disposition of the relocated Ottoman Armenian civilians is outside the scope of this book. For varied commentary see Yücel Güçlü, *Armenians and the Allies in Cilicia 1914–1923* (Salt Lake City, UT: University of Utah Press, 2012), Raymond H. Kévorkian, *The Armenian Genocide, A Complete History* (London: I.B. Tauris, 2011) and Guenter Lewy, *The Armenian Massacres in Ottoman Turkey, A Disputed Genocide* (Salt Lake City, UT: The University of Utah Press, 2005).

68. Sublime Porte to Ministry of War, 842, 31 May 1915, ATASE, Archive 401, Record 1580, File 1-36 and Department of Critical Affairs Document No. 63 to ministries, 31 May 1915, BOA, 3267598, Siyasi, 53, reproduced in Ozdemir and Sarinay (eds), *Turk-Ermeni Ihtilafi Belegeler*, document 17b.

69. See Hilmar Kaiser, 'Regional Resistance to Central Government Policies: Ahmed Djemal Pasha, the Governors of Aleppo, and Armenian Deportees in the Spring and Summer of 1915', *Journal of Genocide Research*, Vol. 12, No. 3 (2010), 173–218.

70. Ciphered message, Ministry of the Interior to governor, Sivas province, 20 July 1915, BOA, DH, Ş fr., No. 54-A/50, reproduced in Ozdemir and Sarinay (eds), *Turk-Ermeni Ihtilafi Belegeler*, document 58 and Aleppo to Maj Gen Veli, 28 August 1915, ATASE, Archive 15, Record 63, File 8, *Arşiv Belgeleriye Ermeni Faaliyetleri 1914–1918, Cilt I*, p. 232.

71. Salahi Sonyel, *The Great War and the Tragedy of Anatolia* (Ankara: Turk Tarih Kurumu, 2001), pp. 128–9.

72. Major General C. E. Callwell, War Office to Foreign Office, 6 August 1915, enclosing letters from Sykes to Callwell, 14 July 1915, NA, FO 371/2940/108253.

73. Announcement by ANDC to Maxwell, C in C, Egypt, 24 July 1915, Vatche Ghazarian, *Boghos Nubar's Papers and the Armenian Question 1915–1918* (Waltham, MA: Mayreni Publishing, 1997), document 119, p. 203.

74. McMahon to Grey, 17 July 1915, NA, FO 371/2485/1067960.

75. McMahon to Foreign Office, 24 September 1915, NA, FO 371/2480/138051.

76. Notes of the Naval Attache, Constantinople, 6 August 1915, PA-AA/BoKon/170, Dok. 131. A53a/1915/4647, translated and reprinted at http://www.armenocide.de.

77. Oppenheim to Bethmann-Hollweg, 29 August 1915, PA-AA/R14087, 1915-A-27584, translated and reprinted at http://www.armenocide.de.

78. Governor of Adana to Ministry of the Interior Police Directorate, 29 July 1915, ATASE Archive 311, Record 1264, File 9, reproduced in İnanç Atılgan and Garabet Moumdjian, *Archival Documents of the Viennese Armenian-Turkish Platform* (Klagenfurt: Wieser Verlag, 2010), pp. 370–1.

79. Suleyman Faik, acting corps commander to Headquarters, 3rd Army, 4 August 1915, ATASE Archive 2835, Record 127, File 4-11, reproduced in Atılgan and Moumdjian, *Archival Documents of the Viennese Armenian-Turkish Platform*, pp. 388–9.

80. M. Atamer, *41nci Piyade Tumen Tarıhcesi (41st Infantry Division History)*, ATASE, Archive Folder 26–344 (unpublished staff study), p. 5.

81. Erden, *Birinci Dünya Harbinde Suriye Hatiraları* , pp. 144–5.

82. Ibid., p. 146 (see note 65).

83. Franz Werfel, *The Forty Days of Musa Dagh*, trans. Geoffrey Dunlop (New York: Viking Press, 1934).

84. Ibid., p. 166.

85. Atamer, *41nci Piyade Tumen Tarıhcesi*, p. 8.

86. Ibid., p. 9.

87. District governor of Urfa to Ministry of the Interior, 29 September 1915, ATASE Archive 2287, Record 11, File 4-13, reproduced in Atılgan and Moumdjian, *Archival Documents of the Viennese Armenian-Turkish Platform*, pp. 598–9.

88. Mete Şefik, *23ncu Piyade Tumen Tarıhcesi* (Ankara: Genelkurmay Basımevi, n.d.), ATASE, record 26–412, p. 24.

89. Hilmar Kaiser (ed.), *Eberhard Count Wolffskeel von Reichenberg, Zeitoun, Mousa Dagh, Ourfa: Letters on the Armenian Genocide, Second Edition* (London: Gomidas Institute, 2004), p. 21.

90. Djemal Pasha, *Memories of a Turkish Statesman 1913–1919*, p. 206.

91. Shaw, *The Ottoman Empire in World War I, Volume 2*, p. 1696.

92. Sheffy, *British Military Intelligence in the Palestine Campaign*, pp. 78–81.

93. Ibid., pp. 82–3.

94. Okçu and Üstünsoy, *Sina-Filistin Cephesi, Harbin Başlangıcından İkinci Gazze Muharebeleri Sonuna Kadar*, p. 336.

95. Ibid., pp. 336–7.

96. Djemal Pasha, *Memories of a Turkish Statesman 1913–1919*, pp. 212–13.

97. Shaw, *The Ottoman Empire in World War I, Volume 2*, p. 1704. Shaw asserted that these deportations apparently happened without Cemal's knowledge or orders.

98. Ibid., pp. 1696–7.

99. Okçu and Üstünsoy, *Sina-Filistin Cephesi, Harbin Başlangıcından İkinci Gazze Muharebeleri Sonuna Kadar*, p. 338. Refet Bele, first in the Ottoman War Academy class of 1912, went on to a distinguished career and retired as a major general in 1926.

100. Ibid., p. 339.

Chapter 4

1916
The Second Suez Offensive

Introduction

January 1916 saw the ending of the Gallipoli campaign, which released substantial British and Ottoman forces for active service elsewhere. The British and Imperial divisions went initially to Egypt, but ten infantry divisions were sent to France by mid-summer, leaving four infantry divisions under the command of Sir Archibald Murray in Egypt. The Ottoman divisions were scattered throughout central Europe, Caucasia and Mesopotamia, with only a single infantry division reaching Palestine. Additionally, small German and Austro-Hungarian specialized formations, including heavy artillery, aircraft and machine-gun detachments were dispatched to the Fourth Army as well. Nevertheless, Cemal and von Kress were determined to regain the initiative by launching offensive operations against the Suez Canal. Competing for the Fourth Army's scarce resources, Sharif Hussein ibn Ali raised the standard of revolt in western Arabia, which Cemal was forced to deal with in the summer.

In spite of these dilemmas, Cemal and von Kress organized a large raid against Katia, which was successful. They followed this with a subsequent offensive campaign against Romani, which was spectacularly unsuccessful. At the tactical level, the Ottoman Army in Palestine performed very well throughout 1916, but overly ambitious plans at the operational level destroyed any gains it made over the year.

General Situation in January 1916

The ending of the Gallipoli campaign brought the Mediterranean Expeditionary Force (MEF) back to Egypt. The MEF was a massive army of fourteen infantry divisions and created what the War Office designated as the Imperial Strategic Reserve.[1] All of these divisions were battered, understrength and in need of rest and reconstitution. Nevertheless, all of them took their place along the Suez Canal for its defence. Murray established a large number of training centres that offered specialized instruction to the officers and men of the reconstituting divisions. This training base remained in Egypt throughout the rest of the war. By June 1916, ten of the divisions were deployed to France but the 42nd, 52nd, 53rd and 54th Infantry Divisions remained in Murray's Egyptian Expeditionary Force (EEF), the headquarters of which was located in Ismailia. The EEF also had the Australian and New Zealand Mounted Division and a brigade of Imperial Camel Cavalry on its rolls. With such a large force, Murray determined that standing on the defensive along the canal was inefficient. He wrote an appreciation stating that it was preferable to push out into the Sinai and establish an active defence, fixed on four places – El Arish, El Hassana, Nekhl and El Kossaima. Murray noted that, 'Strategically . . . the base of the defensive zone of Egypt . . . were the 45 miles between El Arish and El Kossaima'.[2] In accordance with Murray's appreciation, the EEF began to push out men, water pipelines and railways east into the Sinai.

Likewise, after the ending of the Gallipoli campaign, the Ottoman general staff enjoyed a surplus of forces, which could be deployed after a period of refitting and rest. Many of the Ottoman divisions were sent to the crumbling Caucasian Front over the spring and summer of 1916, as well to Galicia, Romania and Greece. This left only a small number of forces available to reinforce the Fourth Army. The German and Ottoman general staffs were very aware of the massive British force in Egypt and regarded it as an ever-present amphibious threat to landing in the Fourth Army's rear area near Alexandretta.[3] Cemal pressed for a large number of reinforcing divisions with which to take the offensive a second time. However, Enver decided to send him only a single infantry division, as well as a number of unique subordinate units, providing the Fourth Army with a very small offensive capability beyond its five infantry under-strength divisions (which were already committed to coastal defence and internal security).

The Arab Revolt[4]

Cemal's Fourth Army area also included most of the Arabian Peninsula, which was inhabited by a number of Arab Bedouin tribes. The term Arab Revolt in the context of the war in the Middle East in the First World War has come to mean the rebellion of the Hashemite leader, Sharif Hussein ibn Ali, and his struggle against Ottoman rule in the Hejaz. In the context of modern military history, the term has become synonymous with the irregular guerrilla operations of the Arab armies of Hussein's sons Abdullah ibn Hussein, Ali ibn Hussein and Feisal ibn Hussein. Geographically, the revolt encompassed the western coastal littoral of the Arabian Peninsula from Mecca northward to Amman. From the Ottoman strategic and operational perspective, the centre of gravity of the campaign to control the Hejaz was the town of Medina, which also had significance as a religious and cultural objective as well. However, in the larger strategic sense, Medina (and the Hejaz itself) had almost no military value except that its retention directly affected the prestige of the Ottoman caliphate. Although today, one might think that the possession of Mecca might serve Ottoman interests more that Medina, it was always the retention of Medina that occupied the attentions of the Ottoman military in the First World War.

It is fair to say that Sharif Hussein ibn Ali brilliantly played both sides of the street until he decided to support the British. As early as April 1914, he sent his son to Cairo for secret negotiations with General Sir H. H. Kitchener and, throughout 1915, he was in contact with the Damascus-based Syrian rebels. The Sharif was also in direct contact with Sir Henry McMahon, the British High Commissioner in Egypt, exchanging letters that have come to be known as the Hussein-McMahon letters. The letters committed the British to military support and Arab independence in exchange for Hussein raising rebellion against the Ottoman Empire. Cemal was aware of Hussein's contacts with the Entente but did not know the full details of his duplicity until after the war. In an attempt to keep the Hashemites loyal, Cemal brought Hussein's son, Feisal, to Damascus and Constantinople, where he delivered assurances of loyalty.[5] In February 1916, Enver Pasha came to Damascus to inspect the Fourth Army and review plans for the invasion of Egypt. He continued on to Medina, where he feted Hussein with gifts.[6]

Alarmed by the Arab conspiracy in Damascus, Cemal demanded further assurances from Feisal in April 1916. By this time, Fourth Army chief of staff, Ali Fuat, was certain that Hussein was committed to rebellion and told Cemal so.[7] On 22 May 1916, Cemal discussed his suspicions with XII Corps commander, Fahrettin, and a week later dispatched Fahrettin to Medina. This was not a moment too soon when on 10 June 1916, Hussein fired a single rifle shot from his window in Mecca initiating the Arab Revolt.

The Fourth Army's garrison in the Medina–Mecca area was known as the Hejaz General Force. The headquarters of the Hejaz General Force, commanded by Major General Galip (late known as Galip Paşinler), was the town of Taif in the cooler hill country east of Mecca.[8] The principal component of the force was the 22nd Infantry Division, under the command of Colonel Ahmet. Arab forces under Emir Abdullah isolated the town of Mecca and, on 12 June, began to surround Taif.

At the time the town was isolated, its garrison composed of the 1st and 3rd Battalions, 129th Infantry Regiment and the 22nd Artillery Battalion, as well as gendarmes, signals troops and engineers. Colonel Ahmet had about 3,000 Ottoman soldiers, but they were short of artillery shells and rifle ammunition. Galip was initially confident that he could successfully hold the town. The defence of the town was partitioned into three sectors with the 3/129th Infantry Regiment commanded by Captain İsmail Hakkı, holding the northern perimeter and two companies from the 1st Battalion holding the south-east and south-west sectors respectively, with the remaining two companies of the battalion held in reserve near the town's central citadel. The garrison made a number of offensive sorties, on 18/19, 19/20 and 27 June to disrupt the occupation of hills overlooking the town by Abdullah's encircling forces.

By mid-July it was evident to Galip that he was in serious trouble and he sent messages to Mecca for a relief column to launch toward Taif. The Mecca garrison was itself weak and composed of the 3rd Battalion, 128th Infantry and the 2nd Battalion, 130th Infantry Regiments, with an irregular cavalry detachment and a few howitzers. Moreover, Mecca was intermittently under siege and its commander lacked the strength to defend the town simultaneously with assisting Galip. Other potential Ottoman reinforcements were penned in Jeddah and unavailable as well. By mid-July Galip's men were running low on artillery shells and the Sharif brought in howitzers, supplied by the British, to shell the town. The situation for the Ottoman defenders grew increasingly desperate in August when extremely hot weather set in. Colonel Ahmet's divisional orders on 25 August 1916 notified his men that the defence of the town now rested on his riflemen due to the shortage of artillery shells.[10] Unable to break out, starving and ridden with sickness, Galip surrendered the Hejaz General Force on 22 September.[11] Ottoman records listed 138 officers and men killed, 238 wounded, 62 deserted and 16 missing and state that the Arab losses were known to be significantly greater.[12] When combined with surrenders at Mecca and Jeddah, the Ottoman Army lost over six battalions of infantry in this period as well as the headquarters and artillery of the 22nd Infantry Division.

As a result of the deteriorating situation in the Hejaz, Enver and Cemal decided to reinforce Fahrettin, who had arrived earlier in Medina. The Ottoman high command reorganized its forces in the Hejaz by activating the Hejaz Expeditionary Force under the command of Fahrettin Pasha on 30 June 1916.[13] With Galip surrounded in Taif, Fahrettin took command of the defence of Medina and, after Galip's surrender and the loss of Mecca and Jeddah, became the single overall Ottoman commander in the Hejaz in the autumn of 1916. Fahrettin Pasha was an extremely able and aggressive officer and decided to secure Medina by conducting punishing attacks on Ali's Southern Arab Army, which threatened the town from the south.

On 30 June 1916, Enver ordered the 55th Infantry Regiment from the 14th Infantry Division to the Hejaz.[14] This regiment then formed part of the new 58th Infantry Division organizing in Medina between 25 and 28 June 1916 to replace the 22nd Infantry Division, which was trapped in Taif.[15] The now-orphaned 42nd and 130th Infantry Regiments were also assigned to the new division along with machine-gun companies and artillery batteries. The Ottoman high command dispatched additional reinforcements from Anatolia, including the 1st Battalion, 138th Regiment, the 1st Battalion, 79th Infantry Regiment and two artillery batteries from the 6th Artillery Regiment to the Arabian theatre.[16] Later that summer, Cemal dispatched additional reinforcements in the form of the 161st and the 162nd Infantry Regiments from Aleppo to Medina as well.

The First Expeditionary Force
Beginning in January 1916, reinforcing forces from Gallipoli began to reach the Fourth Army. The headquarters of the 3rd Infantry Division, under the command of Staff Colonel Refet, reached Beersheba, where von Kress had established the headquarters of the First Expeditionary Force. İbrahim Refet was a general staff officer, who had finished first in the War College class of 1912, with experiences on army staffs and in command of infantry divisions.[17] By the beginning of February, Refet's 32nd and 39th Infantry Regiments, the artillery headquarters and a mountain artillery battalion also reached Beersheba.[18] The incoming 31st Infantry Regiment and the 1st Mountain Howitzer Battalion deployed to Halilürrahman as did the 2nd, 3rd, 4th, 5th and 6th Field Hospital Medical Companies. Unusually for the Ottoman Army in the First World War, these three infantry regiments were composed of four infantry battalions each (the army's regimental standard was three

infantry battalions) making them very powerful combat assets. Also at that location were the Camel Cavalry Regiment, the 1st and 2nd Camel Cavalry Companies, the Fourth Army's chief of engineers and three engineer companies. Other Ottoman Army units included an explosives and mine detachment, a rapid tactical bridge train, telephone, telegraph and wireless detachments, and a labour battalion. The army also sent a 150mm howitzer battery and six German machine-gun companies from Gallipoli to Cemal's Fourth Army.

The first of an increasing number of German and Austro-Hungarian formations and personnel began to arrive. These were important because, over time, they included modern technical combat assets that the Ottoman Army did not possess. Germany sent the Pasha I Column comprising three batteries of 210mm mortars, a battery of 100mm-long guns, four platoons of anti-aircraft guns and the 300th Pasha I Flying Squadron.[19] Austria-Hungary sent two six-gun batteries of 105mm mountain howitzers.

Throughout the war the flow of reinforcements to Palestine was perennially afflicted by the abysmal state of the Ottoman railway system, which itself became the determinant in the kinds and strength of the formations sent to Palestine (as well as to Mesopotamia).[20] The formations sent to Palestine in the winter and spring of 1916 may be characterized as firepower intensive and manpower light. These formations gave the Fourth Army a much-improved tactical capability that included aircraft, long-range howitzers and a large number of machine guns. Moreover, the experienced 3rd Infantry Division was full of hardened and disciplined men, who were combat veterans of the Gallipoli campaign. By late March, Cemal's revived attack force grew to 11,873 men armed with 3,293 rifles, 56 machine guns and 30 artillery pieces.[21]

Von Kress began to push the attack force out along the coast road in March 1916, although smaller independent detachments had come within 40km of the canal in February. At the same time, the British began to push east toward Katia and by early April had laid 26km of railway track from Al Qantara. By the third week in April, British yeomanry cavalry held Katia and the 5th Mounted Brigade was disposed along the new railway. A smaller mixed infantry and yeomanry forces held a flanking position 21km to the south west of Katia. Von Kress learned of the British push forward on 15 April and four days later moved forward picquets of Ottoman and Bedouin cavalry to gain contact with the enemy force. He also deployed two aircraft from the Pasha I Squadron forward to El Arish. Sensing an opportunity and, in spite of severe overall numerical inferiority, the aggressive von Kress decided to attack.

The Affair of Katia

Von Kress organized a small attack force composed of his own headquarters, the 1st and 2nd Battalions, 32nd Infantry Regiment, the 8th Battery, 9th Artillery Regiment, the 8th Battery, 1st Artillery Regiment, the 1st and 2nd Camel Cavalry Companies, a machine-gun company, an engineer detachment, medical and logistics columns, and an aviation detachment.[22] He also committed the Camel Cavalry Regiment to the force. Altogether von Kress marshalled 95 officers, 3,560 men, 4 machine guns and 6 howitzers, which he organized at El Arish on 19 April into 2 columns. Von Kress, with chief of staff Staff Major Kadri, personally commanded the Right (northern) Column, which included both infantry battalions, the 1st Artillery Regiment battery and the machine-gun company. Major Carl Mühlmann, who had joined von Kress after serving in the Gallipoli campaign, commanded the Left Column, with his chief of staff, Major Mehmet. The Left Column comprised the Camel Cavalry Regiment (about 600 men), the 9th Artillery Regiment battery and a single machine gun. Both columns brought medical and logistics detachments.[23]

Conventional combat action renewed itself in this theatre when von Kress pushed forward towards the British outpost at Katia. At 6.00 pm, 22 April 1916, the Right Column reached assault positions 5km east of Katia, where von Kress issued his operations order.[24] (See map 4.1.) He ordered German Major Tiller to take command of the infantry battalions, the artillery and howitzers as the main assault force. He organized a small flanking detachment under the command of Captain Sırrı composed of Sırrı's camel cavalry company and the 1st and 2nd Companies, 32nd Infantry Regiment. Von Kress intended to pin the British in their defensive positions and sweep into their rear using Sırrı's detachment. Von Kress accompanied Tiller and began the approach march reaching an assault position 5km east of Katia at midnight. At the same time, Mühlmann's Left Column continued its advance as well. From here the infantry moved forward to a position 500m from the British advanced outpost at Oghratina (east of Katia) and at 4.30 am Tiller began his attack. By 7.30 am, most of the British were wounded and surrounded and the outpost fell an hour later. Von Kress and Major Kadri established their command post on a sand hill 3km east of Katia to observe the final assault.[25] At about 9.00 am, he unleashed Sırrı's flanking detachment

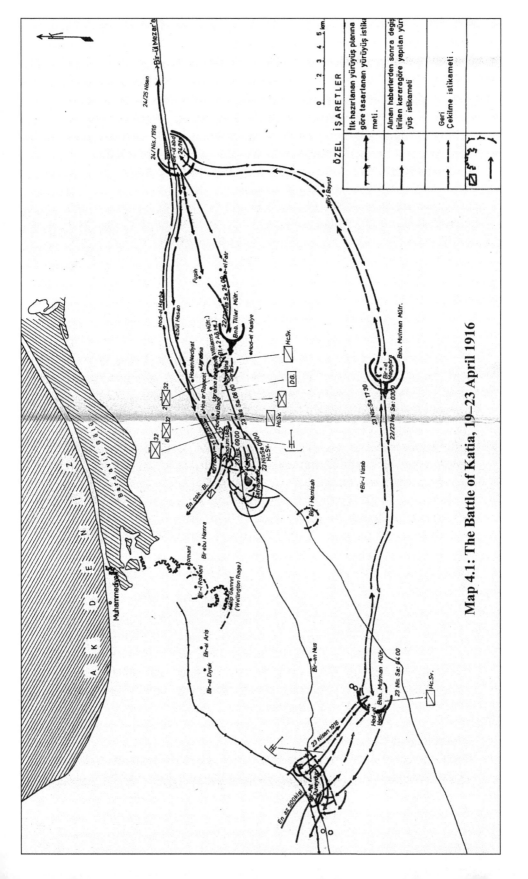

Map 4.1: The Battle of Katia, 19–23 April 1916

around the British left. Tiller's detachment continued towards Katia and his artillery joined in the fight at 9.45 am. British efforts to reinforce Katia with yeomanry cavalry ran into Sırrı's men and then fell back to Romani.[26] Katia was cut off and Tiller's infantrymen overran the position at 3.00 pm, capturing the remnants of several squadrons of British cavalrymen.

To the south Mühlmann's Left Column reached an assault position at Hod el Hasia at 4.00 am, 23 April, 5km south-east of Dueidar. This small oasis was held by a small detachment of Royal Scots Fusiliers. Mühlmann launched his attack an hour later with his small infantry force and 2 hours later split his camel cavalry in two wings to surround the oasis. Resistance was fierce and the Ottomans were unable to break into the position or completely surround the oasis. At about noon, a British relief column arrived forcing Mühlmann to break off the engagement and retreat.[27]

Unable to remain forward in such a tactically exposed position, von Kress ordered a general withdrawal back to El Arish, which was strongly held by several companies from the 81st Infantry Regiment and two batteries of artillery from the 5th Artillery Regiment. Arriving there, von Kress kept his headquarters elements in El Arish but he sent his infantry back to Beersheba, where there was a railhead and they could be supplied more easily. He also sent his artillery to Cemone, which was on the railway to the west of Gaza.

From the British perspective, the Affair at Katia was 'a lamentable occurrence, resulting as it did in the total loss of three and half squadrons of Yeomanry'.[28] Von Kress also reported capturing 98 rifles, 163 swords, 2 machine guns and a large number of animals and supplies. Total Ottoman losses were reported as 154 killed, 174 wounded and 46 missing. While this was a minor engagement, it was hard fought with Ottoman casualties exceeding 10 per cent over the course of 23 April 1916. MacMunn and Falls argued correctly that the affair had 'no effect other than to delay the progress of the railway for a few days'.[29] With that said, British losses were almost double that of the Ottomans and the incident served to illustrate that the Ottoman Army was a combat force that could manoeuvre rapidly and fight effectively using combined arms tactics.

The Battle of Romani
The Ottoman counter-offensives in the Caucasus in the summer of 1916 by the Second Army created difficulties for the Fourth Army.[30] Not only

did the Caucasian offensives prevent badly needed reinforcements from being assigned to the Fourth Army, but the general staff required Cemal to provide 6,000 trained individual replacements for the Second Army. Many of these men came out of his Fourth Army formations (in addition to the depot training battalions within his operational area). The start of the Arab Rebellion also drew forces away from the Syrian–Palestine area when the destruction of the 22nd Infantry Division forced Cemal to send reinforcements to Medina. Reflecting concern at strategic levels in Constantinople, on 15 May 1916, the Ottoman general staff activated the 53rd Infantry Division in Aleppo, however, there were no trained men to man the regiments and the division remained in a cadre status throughout the summer and autumn. In spite of these difficulties, Cemal and Enver agreed on 30 May 1916 to renew the offensive in the Sinai in July.[31]

Von Kress, who was concerned about elaborate British offensive preparations extending forward along the coast agreed with Cemal, and they decided to launch a second expedition against the British defences. Cemal decided that this would be a strictly limited attack that was only intended to keep the British off balance and to spoil their plans. On 28 June, Cemal sent von Kress, who maintained his headquarters in El Arish and had screening forces running south from there to Kalatünnahil, orders to this effect. Cemal noted that there were 200,000 enemy soldiers in Egypt but asserted that the fragile British lines of communications made the enemy forward elements positioned in a fortified salient around the small village of Romani vulnerable. He also pointed out that the British build-up increasingly created a dangerous situation for the First Expeditionary Force. Both Cemal and von Kress thought that failure to act aggressively must result in the retreat of the First Expeditionary Force to Gaza. To support the offensive, Cemal ordered the Desert Logistics Inspectorate to push supplies forward to El Arish.

Von Kress began tactical planning and envisioned a larger version of his victorious encirclement at Katia. The attack force comprised the headquarters of the First Expeditionary Force and the 3rd Infantry Division, the 31st, 32nd and 39th Infantry Regiments, and the 32nd Regiment Machine Gun Company. The 3rd Division also provided its Mountain Howitzer Battalion, Camel Cavalry Company, Engineer Company and Medical Detachment. Von Kress also took the Austro-Hungarian howitzer battalion, the 1st and 2nd Heavy Mortar (210mm) Batteries, the 150mm howitzer battery, the 100mm gun battery and two anti-aircraft guns. The six companies of German machine guns had been reorganized into a Heavy Machine Gun Battalion of eight companies (which also included two light trench mortar detachments) and von Kress took it along as well. He also planned to send the Camel Cavalry Regiment and the Bedouin Volunteer Camel Cavalry Company well to the south to conduct a diversionary operation opposite Ismailia. On the evening of 4 July 1916, von Kress began to bring his regiments from their garrisons in Beersheba to El Arish and by 14 July, his forces were assembled and prepared for action. Because of the larger force involved in the offensive and the extended battle space, von Kress decided to move his forces forward in six administrative echelons.[32] The first two echelons, composed of most of the infantry, mountain artillery, machine guns and engineers, moved west the next day. The third echelon comprised the heavy artillery and the 39th Infantry Regiment. The fourth, fifth and sixth echelons were made up of the logistical and medical trains as well as the 4th Battalions of the three infantry regiments. By 22 July the last echelon had departed from El Arish.

In the meantime, the British noticed increasing Ottoman air activity over Romani and Katia and Murray decided to reinforce the Romani position. By 19 July, Murray had stationed the 53rd Infantry Division and the Australian and New Zealand Mounted Division (less one brigade) in the Romani position, with a total rifle strength of 14,000 men.[33] Water shortages limited the number of artillery that could be deployed at Romani but there were a total of nine artillery batteries (thirty-six guns and howitzers) supporting the defence. In early August, Murray brought the 42nd Infantry Division forward from Al Qantara and stationed its three brigades along the railway between Dueidar and Al Qantara.

As the Ottomans arrived in the assembly area at Bir el Abd at the end of July, von Kress reorganized his forces from administrative movement echelons into four combined arms tactical groups.[34] The 1st Group, under the command of Colonel Refet, comprised the 31st Infantry Regiment, the German 601st and 604th Machine Gun Companies, the Austro-Hungarian howitzers and the 100mm and 150mm artillery, a medical detachment and an infantry company from the 81st Infantry Regiment. The 2nd Group, commanded by Colonel İbrahim, was composed of the 32nd Infantry Regiment, the 602nd and 605th Machine Gun Companies, a mountain gun battery, an engineer company and a medical detachment. The 3rd Group, under the command of Major Mühlmann, was made up of the 39th Infantry Regiment, 603rd and 606th Machine Gun Companies, a mountain gun battery, an engineer company and a medical detachment. The 4th Group, in reserve under the command of German Major Meyer, comprised a provisional unit of regimental strength composed of the 4th Battalions of the 32nd and 39th Infantry Regiments, the 607th and 608th Machine Gun Companies, a mountain gun battery and a company from the 81st Infantry Regiment.

Von Kress planned to launch the 1st Group against the main defensive line held by the British infantry divisions to fix the enemy in position. He would then conduct a short flanking attack around the British right with the 2nd Group. Both groups were to push through the British outpost line and then attack with bayonets and hand grenades. Finally, Mühlmann's 3rd Group would pass to the south of the 2nd Group and conduct an envelopment deep into the enemy rear. The 4th Group was in reserve but was prepared to support the envelopment. Von Kress intended to move with Mühlmann and establish his command post on a small hill overlooking the southern flank of the British line.[35]

The 1st Group began its movement at 9.00 pm on 3 August and reached its assault positions at 4.00 am in the morning. The 2nd and 3rd Groups left 2 hours earlier and reached their assault positions at the same time. Minor skirmishing between the advancing Ottomans and the British outposts occurred between 2.00 and 4.00 am, when dawn broke on 4 August revealing the attacks. The main Ottoman attacks began at 5.15 am supported by the artillery and several aircraft, which made bombing runs. The British were alert and ready for the enemy attacks and the 1st Group's assault foundered quickly. After several subsequent attacks, Refet's men were done by 10.00 am. The 2nd Group advanced and became involved in a meeting engagement with the Australian Light Horse along Wellington Ridge. At 10.00 am the British 156th Brigade moved up to relieve the Light Horsemen. Fighting continued as the 2nd Group attempted to push forward, but, by 2.00 pm, its attack had collapsed with the British capturing many prisoners from the group's scattered units.[36]

The 3rd Group, now commanded by Major Kâmil, pushed forward to a small hill known to the British as Mount Roystan, where Australian and British cavalry made a determined, but brief, stand. Kâmil seized Mount Roystan at about 10.00 am. Unfortunately for Kâmil, the British commander ordered the New Zealand Mounted Rifles Brigade to advance from Dueidar and flank Kâmil, who was deep inside the British position. At about 11.30 am, Brigadier General Edward Chaytor arrived with the New Zealanders and seeing that Kâmil held Mount Roystan, but was completely unsupported, ordered the brigade to flank the hill.

By 4.30 pm, the 3rd Group was isolated and forced to surrender 2 hours later.[37] Surrendering with Kâmil were over 500 infantrymen, a mountain artillery battery and a machine-gun company, although some parts of the group were able to escape. It was a disastrous end to von Kress's ambitious plan and he ordered a retreat.

As dawn broke on 5 August, the British vigorously began to advance. They rapidly crushed the 2nd Group before it could retreat from Wellington Ridge and another 864 men surrendered. At 6.30 am, the British launched a relentless pursuit and the day deteriorated into a series of rear guard actions while von Kress attempted to disengage and withdraw his main body. Refet and Mühlmann were instrumental in maintaining a cohesive retreat under pressure and the British noted that the Ottomans did not become demoralized and were able to mount disciplined fire.[38] Von Kress lost Katia but reformed a defensive line which held though 6 and 7 August. Von Kress withdrew from this line and, protected by his rear guards, pulled back to the vicinity of Bir el Abd, where he prepared another defensive line. As the British approached on 9 August, von Kress launched a pre-emptive a counter-attack under the tactical command of Colonel Refet. This surprised the British, who took some losses, and then pulled back. This created a tactical pause which allowed von Kress to withdraw his artillery and much of his logistical and medical units.

On 10 August, von Kress continued his retreat, with Colonel Refet again fighting a final rear guard engagement on 12 August. On 14 August, the First Expeditionary Force retreated into the sanctuary of the El Arish fortified position. Colonel Refet with the 31st Infantry Regiment, three machine-gun companies, a mountain artillery battery and an anti-aircraft detachment remained at Bir el Mazar to construct a forward defensive blocking position. Colonel İbrahim took command of the El Arish position with the 32nd Infantry Regiment, three machine-gun companies and the heavy artillery, while the remaining formations were withdrawn to positions near Gaza and Beersheba.

The British made one further attempt to push the Ottomans back. On 16 September 1916, Major General Harry Chauvel organized a large raiding force of two light horse brigades and a number of independent companies. He hoped to surprise the Ottoman garrison at Bir el Mazar and overcome it. Chauvel attacked at dawn on 17 September to find an alert garrison in a well-fortified position. Unable to prevail against well-dug in infantry supported by artillery, Chauvel withdrew his force.

At the time, General Murray estimated Ottoman losses as 9,000 men altogether, while the British and the Turkish official histories claim 'perhaps 6,000' and 4,000 respectively.[39] Belen claimed the Ottomans lost 4,000 men, of whom 1,000 were killed or wounded and the remainder captured or missing. He also noted that von Kress lost 3 infantry battalions, a mountain artillery battery, 2 German machine-gun companies and 2 medical detachments against total British losses of 250 killed and 1,130 wounded.[40] In any case, the failed offensive was a disaster and reflected poorly on von Kress. Not only were Ottoman and German losses severe and hard to replace but the battles encouraged the British to move forward 100km from Romani to Bir el Abd. Moreover, once there, General Murray resumed work on the infrastructure (railways, roads and water pipelines) necessary to bring the war into Palestine in 1917.

The Fourth Army Situation in Late 1916

The Ottoman general staff recognized that the Fourth Army faced a much larger adversary than it was capable of defeating. Furthermore, the staff realized that Cemal faced a war of manoeuvre in the Sinai–Palestine theatre and it determined that reinforcements were necessary to maintain the tactical balance. In September, Enver ordered the Second Army in Caucasia to send the 3rd Cavalry Division and the 7th and 8th Infantry Regiments to Aleppo for assignment to the Fourth Army. Cemal believed these reinforcements were insufficient and requested two additional infantry divisions from Constantinople. In turn, Enver met Cemal in Aleppo on 27 September 1916 to discuss the situation.[41] They agreed on two major points and decided, in view of the Arab Revolt, that two additional infantry divisions should be deployed to Palestine. They also decided that, in order to improve the combat effectiveness of the First Expeditionary Force, Ottoman officers and soldiers needed to be rotated in and out of the German formations in the Sinai, which included machine-gun companies, mortar and grenadier detachments, and bridging and wireless detachments. On 27 October, Enver ordered the 16th Infantry Division from Constantinople to Aleppo and the 7th Infantry Division was alerted for possible deployment as well.[42] On 1 November, the assembled 3rd Cavalry Division in Aleppo began to deploy to Beersheba.

In the Hejaz, the Ottoman high command selected Lieutenant Colonel Necip to command the new 58th Infantry Division, and he began to organize the slowly arriving units on 14 November 1916. Necip and some units of the division saw action against Abdullah's army in mid-December but the 58th Infantry Division was not fully combat capable until 13 February 1917.[43] This illustrates the perennial strategic problem with time and space the Ottoman military had to overcome when deploying forces to distant theatres of operation such as Arabia, Mesopotamia and the eastern Caucasus.

Between 10 June and 22 September 1916 Hussein ibn Ali formed three Arab small armies, only two of which (Feisal's and Abdullah's) figure prominently in the English-language historiography. Reinforced by Emir Feisal, Abdullah's force became known as the Arab Eastern Army later in the year. Feisal's Arabs captured the coastal towns of Jeddah, Rabegh and Yanbu in the period from September 1916 to January 1917. Abdullah's tribesmen then moved northward in December 1916 and captured Wejh on 25 January 1917. These battles secured the central Red Sea coast west of Medina and Mecca for the Arabs and the British.

Murray was not inactive while the Fourth Army was attending to Hussein and his sons. Cemal was increasingly concerned about the extension of British logistics into the Sinai. On 21 November Cemal alerted the Ottoman general staff to the acute danger presented by the British build-up at Bir el Mazar.[44] In reply to queries from Enver, Cemal wrote a long message on 30 November explaining that he had carefully considered preparing a pre-emptive counter-attack employing the incoming 3rd Cavalry Division.[45] In the message he said that he was fortifying Jerusalem and he noted the vast British superiority in infantry, artillery and cavalry. He ended the message by saying that, in the event of a major attack, he would slowly fight a delaying action back to defensive positions he was preparing north of El Arish. Further communications between the Ottoman general staff and Staff Colonel Ali Fuat, Cemal's chief of staff, amplified the Fourth Army's logistical shortcomings as well. The general staff promised to send 100 motorized trucks and combat units from Galicia (in Hungary) when that campaign ended.

Unsatisfied with the support he had been promised, Cemal went to Constantinople and met with Enver on 4 December 1916. Cemal outlined his plans to construct a defensive line from Gaza to Beersheba, a position that offered the most defensible terrain between the frontier and southern Palestine. Enver concurred and they worked out the details creating a position that could withstand the assault of 50,000 men. Enver also promised to increase the amount of supplies going to Palestine and to improve the lines of communications leading from Constantinople to Aleppo.[46]

After these discussions with Cemal, Enver travelled to Germany to persuade the Germans to send a second Pasha II detachment, which would double the number of the existing Pasha I formations in the Fourth Army. When he returned to Constantinople on 22 December, Enver ordered the 7th Infantry Division to Palestine and the 53rd Infantry Division be brought up to full strength. Importantly, Enver also ordered the III Corps headquarters and the 54th Infantry Division to prepare for deployment to Palestine.

The Affair of Magdhaba

The Fourth Army's forward defence of the Palestine–Sinai frontier was not a continuous trench line but, rather, a series of widely separated fortified camps held by the 80th Infantry Regiment. This string of camps ran from El Arish, held by the 1st Battalion, south to Magdhaba, headquarters of the 80th Infantry Regiment and garrisoned by most of the 2nd and 3rd Battalions as well as quick firing artillery battery, thence to Bir Hasene, held by an infantry company, and ended at Kalatünnahil, held by the 4th Battalion and an artillery battery. Von Kress tasked Refet's 3rd Infantry Division to support the 80th but time and distances worked against any reinforcement in real time.

Murray ordered the EEF to push as far forward as possible and in mid-December began to mass forces east of El Arish. Ottoman reconnaissance aircraft spotted the build-up and reported it to Cemal, who surmised that the expected British offensive was about to begin.[47] In accordance with his ideas about the defence of the frontier, Cemal had already decided to withdraw to the Gaza–Beersheba line. Consequently, on 20 December he ordered the evacuation of El Arish and the 1/80th Infantry Regiment withdrew to Khan Yunis. British mounted troops occupied the empty town the next day. The British had intended to push on to Rafah but Major General Philip Chetwode, commander of Murray's Desert Column, was uncertain that it might be held in strength. Chetwode was also concerned about the scarcity of water at El Arish and knew that good wells existed at Magdhaba. Consequently, he cancelled the advance to Rafah and ordered Chaytor and Royston's mounted brigades and Smith's Camel Brigade to seize Magdhaba on 22 December 1916. They conducted a 40km approach march, which was followed by a finely executed encirclement. Towards noon the town was completely cut off and the dismounted enemy began to probe the defences. There was some sporadic fighting but resistance collapsed almost immediately. By mid-afternoon Kadri Bey, commander of the 80th Infantry Regiment, surrendered his force. Over 1,200 Ottoman soldiers, including 2 battalion commanders, went into captivity. The Turkish official history is silent on the cause of the collapse stating that no reports or records were ever recovered from the regiment.[48]

The First Expeditionary Force reestablished a defensive screen by fortifying the towns of Khan Yunis and Hafir el Avce. Under the command of their regimental commanders, von Kress positioned two battalions of the 31st Infantry Regiment, the 1/80th Infantry Regiment and a mountain gun battery in El Arish and two battalions of the 32nd Infantry Regiment, the 4/80th Infantry Regiment, three machine-gun companies, an artillery battery and an anti-aircraft artillery platoon in Hafir el Avce. Von Kress ordered Lieutenant Colonel İsmail Hakkı, 31st Infantry Regiment commander, to hold the town of Rafah with a small detachment of troops. The remainder of the 3rd Infantry Division lay behind these towns in Beersheba and Tel es Sheria. The newly organized 2nd Camel Cavalry Regiment lay in Gaza.

On 28 December 1916, the Fourth Army (the 53rd Infantry Division and 3rd Cavalry Division excluded) had a strength of 192,270 men, 29,482 animals and 17,824 camels from which it could field 40,744 rifles, 62 machine guns and 254 artillery pieces.[49] Von Kress with the First Expeditionary Force disposed 20,818 men, 2,510 animals and 2,215 camels, of which 7,702 were infantrymen. The Hejaz Expeditionary Force disposed 15,165 men including 7,960 infantrymen and the provisional forces guarding the Hejaz railway and the Medina garrison composed 13,767 men of whom 5,900 were infantrymen. The Fourth Army's remaining 142,000 men were assigned to the XII Corps (23rd and 44th Infantry Divisions), the VIII Corps (27th, 41st, and 43rd Infantry Divisions) and the 4th Army Lines of Communications Inspectorate. Additionally, the Fourth Army had a number of independent formations including artillery batteries, volunteer cavalry detachments and army schools detachments.

Conclusion

The year 1916 had been a period of manoeuvre and raiding for the Ottomans but for the British it was a year of steadily pushing the front toward the Sinai–Palestine frontier. The badly outnumbered Ottomans were able to seize the initiative from the British from time to time, which delayed the British advance east from the Suez Canal. At the tactical level, mixed battle groups of Ottoman and German soldiers performed well together, but at the operational level, Cemal and von Kress displayed a tendency to assign missions to tactical forces too small to accomplish them. Ottoman officers with a gift for command began to emerge in the crucible of desert command, notably Colonel Refet and Fahrettin Pasha.

Notes

1. MacMunn and Falls, *Military Operations Egypt and Palestine, From the Outbreak of War with Germany to June 1917*, pp. 97–9.
2. GS Z.33, Sir A. Murray's Appreciation, 15 February 1916, reprinted in MacMunn and Falls, *Military Operations Egypt and Palestine, From the Outbreak of War with Germany to June 1917*, pp. 170–4.
3. Okçu and Üstünsoy, *Sina-Filistin Cephesi, Harbin Başlangıcından İkinci Gazze Muharebeleri Sonuna Kadar*, p. 340.
4. For a comprehensive treatment of the Turkish narrative regarding the operations of TE Lawrence and the effect of the Arab Revolt on the Ottoman Army in the First World War, see Edward J. Erickson,*"Wasp or Mosquito? The Arab Revolt in Turkish Military History"* British Journal for Military History, Volume 4, Issue 3, July 2018.
5. Djemal Pasha, *Memories of a Turkish Statesman 1913–1919*, p. 214.
6. Okçu and Üstünsoy, *Sina-Filistin Cephesi, Harbin Başlangıcından İkinci Gazze Muharebeleri Sonuna Kadar*, p. 338.
7. Djemal Pasha, *Memories of a Turkish Statesman 1913–1919*, p. 223.
8. Okçu and Üstünsoy, *Sina-Filistin Cephesi, Harbin Başlangıcından İkinci Gazze Muharebeleri Sonuna Kadar*, p. 231.
9. Ibid.
10. Headquarters 22nd Division, Order 112, 25 August 1916, ATASE Archive 588, File 107/108, reproduced in Erkal, *Hicaz, Asir, Yemen Cepheleri ve Libya Harekâtı*, pp. 248–9.
11. Headquarters Hejaz General Force, Hejaz Commander to Commander, 22nd Division, Order 330, 22 September 1916, ATASE Archive 588, File 136-139 reproduced as Document 8, Erkal, *Hicaz, Asir, Yemen Cepheleri ve Libya Harekâtı*, pp. 839–40.
12. Erkal, *Hicaz, Asir, Yemen Cepheleri ve Libya Harekâtı*, p. 251.
13. Ibid., p. 179.
14. Ibid., p. 184.
15. Ibid.
16. Ibid., p. 185.
17. Necati Ökse, Nusret Baycan and Salih Sakaryalı, *Türk İstiklal Harbi'ne Kalilan Tumen ve Daha Ust Kademelerdeki Komutanların Biyografileri (Turkish War of Independence, Biographies of Divisional-level Commanders and Above)* (Ankara: Genelkurmay Basımevi, 1989), pp. 98–100.
18. Okçu and Üstünsoy, *Sina-Filistin Cephesi, Harbin Başlangıcından İkinci Gazze Muharebeleri Sonuna Kadar*, pp. 338–9.
19. Ibid.
20. Fahri Belen, *Birinci Cihan Harbinde Türk Harbi 1916 Yılı Hareketleri (The Turkish Front in the First World War, Operations in 1916)* (Ankara: Genelkurmay Basımevi, 1965), p. 204.

21. Ibid., p. 211.

22. MacMunn and Falls, *Military Operations Egypt and Palestine, From the Outbreak of War with Germany to June 1917*, pp. 162–70.

23. Belen, *Birinci Cihan Harbinde Türk Harbi 1916 Yılı Hareketleri*, pp. 205–6.

24. Von Kress orders, 22 April 1916, reproduced in Okçu and Üstünsoy, *Sina-Filistin Cephesi, Harbin Başlangıcından İkinci Gazze Muharebeleri Sonuna Kadar*, pp. 352–3.

25. Ibid., pp. 253–4.

26. Belen, *Birinci Cihan Harbinde Türk Harbi 1916 Yılı Hareketleri*, pp. 208.

27. Okçu and Üstünsoy, *Sina-Filistin Cephesi, Harbin Başlangıcından İkinci Gazze Muharebeleri Sonuna Kadar*, pp. 354–9 and MacMunn and Falls, *Military Operations Egypt and Palestine, From the Outbreak of War with Germany to June 1917*, pp. 167–8.

28. MacMunn and Falls, *Military Operations Egypt and Palestine, From the Outbreak of War with Germany to June 1917*, p. 169.

29. Ibid.

30. Belen, *Birinci Cihan Harbinde Türk Harbi 1916 Yılı Hareketleri*, pp. 216–17.

31. Okçu and Üstünsoy, *Sina-Filistin Cephesi, Harbin Başlangıcından İkinci Gazze Muharebeleri Sonuna Kadar*, pp. 360–1.

32. Ibid., Kroki (Sketch) 27a.

33. MacMunn and Falls, *Military Operations Egypt and Palestine, From the Outbreak of War with Germany to June 1917*, pp. 178–81.

34. Okçu and Üstünsoy, *Sina-Filistin Cephesi, Harbin Başlangıcından İkinci Gazze Muharebeleri Sonuna Kadar*, pp. 374–6.

35. Belen, *Birinci Cihan Harbinde Türk Harbi 1916 Yılı Hareketleri*, Kroki (Sketch) 46.

36. Okçu and Üstünsoy, *Sina-Filistin Cephesi, Harbin Başlangıcından İkinci Gazze Muharebeleri Sonuna Kadar*, p. 384.

37. Ibid., pp. 384–5.

38. MacMunn and Falls, *Military Operations Egypt and Palestine, From the Outbreak of War with Germany to June 1917*, pp. 192–4 and Okçu and Üstünsoy, *Sina-Filistin Cephesi, Harbin Başlangıcından İkinci Gazze Muharebeleri Sonuna Kadar*, pp. 386–7.

39. MacMunn and Falls, *Military Operations Egypt and Palestine, From the Outbreak of War with Germany to June 1917*, p. 199 and Okçu and Üstünsoy, *Sina-Filistin Cephesi, Harbin Başlangıcından İkinci Gazze Muharebeleri Sonuna Kadar*, p. 393.

40. Belen, *Birinci Cihan Harbinde Türk Harbi 1916 Yılı Hareketleri*, p. 216.

41. Okçu and Üstünsoy, *Sina-Filistin Cephesi, Harbin Başlangıcından İkinci Gazze Muharebeleri Sonuna Kadar*, p. 404.

42. Belen, *Birinci Cihan Harbinde Türk Harbi 1916 Yılı Hareketleri*, p. 221.

43. Erkal, *Hicaz, Asir, Yemen Cepheleri ve Libya Harekâtı*, pp. 203–11.

44. Okçu and Üstünsoy, *Sina-Filistin Cephesi, Harbin Başlangıcından İkinci Gazze Muharebeleri Sonuna Kadar*, pp. 415–16.

45. Ibid., Cemal to Enver, 30 November 1916, text reproduced on pp. 419–20.

46. Ibid., pp. 419–21.

47. Ibid., pp. 423–5.

48. Ibid., p. 430.

49. Ibid., pp. 407–8.

Chapter 5

1917
First and Second Gaza

Introduction

In the late fall of 1916, Murray's Egyptian Expeditionary Force began to push east from El Arish toward the frontier. The Ottoman Fourth Army established a defensive line between Gaza and Beersheba. However, Cemal and von Kress believed that a counter-offensive was possible should the EEF move to attack Gaza. In turn, they positioned the Ottoman Fourth Army in a mobile defence rather than a traditional defensive line by mid-March 1917. They defeated the EEF at First Gaza in March 1917. Then rapidly constructing a defensive line, the Fourth Army again turned back the EEF at Second Gaza in April. These twin defeats, after two-and-a-half years of war against the Ottoman Empire, proved how little the British had learned about fighting the Ottomans and were 'Murray's doing'.[1] In the operational pause that followed Second Gaza, Cemal reorganized his army into conventional army corps. This was followed by the activation of the Yildirim Army Group under German General Erich von Falkenhayn and the marginalization of Cemal.

Reinforcements poured into Syria and Palestine as Enver envisioned and planned dramatic offensives by the new army group. By the fall of 1917, Cemal was left in command of Syria and western Arabia. Cemal still had to contend with the Arab Revolt but Ottoman operational command in Palestine passed to German commanders and their Ottoman subordinates. As another British offensive drew near, under General Edmund Allenby, the Yildirim Army Group struggled to establish cohesive defences along the Gaza–Beersheba line.

The Action of Rafah

A small Ottoman detachment remained at Rafah under the command of

Lieutenant Colonel İsmail Hakkı, commander of the 31st Infantry Regiment. Von Kress had recommended that the detachment be pulled back behind Khan Yunis, but Cemal ordered it to remain in place.[2] The detachment was composed of the regimental headquarters, the 1st Battalion, 31st Infantry Regiment, the 6th and 8th Companies of the 2nd Battalion, three heavy machine-gun companies, a camel cavalry company, a jandarma company and the 8th Mountain Battery from the 1st Artillery Regiment. The position was well dug in and there were five strongpoints with good fields of fire. Although strongly held, the 3rd Infantry Division recognized the vulnerability of the exposed and isolated position but Colonel Refet thought that he would be able to reinforce it quickly, if necessary. On 8 January 1917, Ottoman aerial reconnaissance revealed a gathering British force at El Arish and a telegraph message to the detachment the next morning at 7.15 am gave warning of an impending attack.[3] A subsequent message from Refet alerted the Rafah detachment of the possibility that it would have to retreat to Khan Yunis. The division notified the 160th Infantry Regiment in Khan Yunis at 8.00 am that it might be ordered to advance to the aid of the 31st Infantry Regiment.

The British force identified on 8 January was the reinforced Australian and New Zealand Mounted Division, under the command of Major General Philip Chetwode, which began an advance at 1.00 am on 9 January. At 6.15 am Chetwode's men crossed the frontier and began to swing to the east in an envelopment operation. By 10.00 am dismounted troopers supported by artillery began to probe the south-western defences of the Rafah detachment and an hour later the New Zealand Mounted Rifle Brigade had completely cut off Rafah. Chetwode now began a concentric attack on the isolated Ottomans. The last message to the 3rd Infantry Division from Rafah at 10.40 am noted the impending encirclement and reported that large numbers of enemy infantry, cavalry and artillery were about to assault the town.[4]

At about noon Refet ordered the 160th Infantry Regiment to advance to relieve Rafah and at 12.30 pm he ordered the 32nd Infantry Regiment and the Austro-Hungarian artillery at Beersheba to move in support of the 160th. However, this was too little too late because the British had completely surprised the Ottomans with the rapidity and clarity of the envelopment. Ottoman aerial reconnaissance revealed at 1.35 pm that Rafah was surrounded and under attack. At 4.15 pm New Zealand patrols reported the advance of the relief force and Chetwode decided to withdraw. However, Ottoman soldiers began to surrender at about this time and resistance completely collapsed. Rafah was in British hands by 5.00 pm when darkness fell. Chetwode reaffirmed his decision and began to pull back with prisoners and captured artillery. Observing the surrender at long distance, the commander of the 160th Infantry Regiment notified the 3rd Division at 5.45 pm that he was returning to Khan Yunis.[5] The next morning British aircraft confirmed that the Ottomans were making no attempt to reoccupy the town and Chetwode ordered Australian light horsemen take the town.

Unknown to the British, the 6th Company, 2/31st Infantry Regiment and a machine-gun company successfully broke out of the encirclement and reached Khan Yunis. Altogether, the Ottomans surrendered 1,875 officers and men (including 11 Germans), 402 irregulars, 6 heavy machine guns and 4 mountain guns. Additional booty included ½ million rifle bullets, 112,000 machine-gun bullets and 1,489 artillery shells.[6] Chetwode conducted a brilliant operation and the British histories are very critical of Cemal's decision to leave the Rafah detachment so exposed. Like the surrender of Magdhaba, the loss of the detachment in Rafah was preventable.

As a further result of Rafah, von Kress decided to reorganize Staff Colonel Refet's badly battered 3rd Infantry Division. The division's 39th Infantry Regiment had been almost completed destroyed at Romani and the loss of units at Magdhaba and Rafah further depleted the division's combat strength. The unassigned (to an infantry division) 80th and 160th Infantry Regiments were inactivated. The 2nd and 3rd Battalions, 160th Infantry Regiment were re-designated as the 3rd and 4th Battalions, 138th Infantry Regiment and the 1st Battalion, 160th Infantry Regiment became the 3rd Battalion, 31st Infantry Regiment, while the 3rd Battalion, 80th Infantry Regiment became the 3rd Battalion, 31st Infantry Regiment. Finally, the 4/80th Infantry Regiment became the 4th Battalion, 32nd Infantry Regiment. These re-designations brought the division's three infantry regiments up to their authorized strength of four battalions each. Field and mountain artillery formations were also consolidated as the 5th Artillery Regiment (three battalions of two batteries each).

The Withdrawal to the Gaza–Tel es Sheria–Beersheba Line

Initially, von Kress and Cemal intended to construct a defensive line behind the Wadi Gaza, which lay about 10km south of the town of Gaza and then ran south east to the village of Şelale. This became known as the Şelale position and on 15 January 1917 von Kress tasked Refet's

3rd Infantry Division to hold the position. He maintained a tiny screening force at Khan Yunis and a reinforced battalion screening force at Hafir el Avce. Von Kress moved his own headquarters to Jerusalem where he could maintain better communications with Cemal in Aleppo.

On 20 January 1917, the 3rd Cavalry Division, commanded by Colonel Esat, arrived in Beersheba. The cavalry division was composed of the 6th and 7th Cavalry Regiments and supporting arms.[7] Two days later, the 79th Infantry Regiment began to turn Gaza into a fortress and the heavy artillery was turned over to Refet in the Şelale position. In late January, the leading elements of the 16th Infantry Division arrived and on 28 January, Enver alerted the III Corps headquarters and the 41st Infantry Division for deployment to Palestine as well.

In early February the 53rd Infantry Division began to deploy from Dera to Jaffa and on 8 February, Ali Rıza Pasha, his III Corps headquarters and the 54th Infantry Division reached Aleppo. Von Kress sent the 125th Infantry Regiment to Hafir el Avce on 12 February, bringing the force there up to four infantry battalions and several artillery batteries.[8] However, on 20 February, von Kress became concerned that his unsupported forces there could be easily encircled, as had happened at Magdhaba and Refah, and he decided to withdraw them to the Şelale position. Three days later Cemal came by automobile from Damascus and met von Kress at Şelale, where von Kress persuaded him to abandon the Şelale position itself. This was a major change in the operational design for the defence of Palestine, shifting from a linear defensive line to a posture of mobile groups positioned to take the offensive.

In the middle of this operational change, Enver Pasha and Mustafa Kemal arrived in Damascus on 28 February to discuss the deteriorating situation in the Hejaz with Cemal. The discussions turned to the Palestine Front and the relentlessly aggressive Enver became enthusiastic about the opportunity there of regaining the initiative. On 3 March, Enver and Cemal drove by automobile to Beersheba, where they went out to Şelale. At the village, they were met by von Kress, who gave them a detailed tactical briefing and showed them the terrain.[9] Von Kress, who was an advocate of the German general staff's operational concept of Cannae-like encirclement battles of annihilation (as he had done at Katia and attempted to do at Romani), believed it was possible to lure the British into over-extending themselves above Gaza making them vulnerable to encirclement and isolation.[10] He believed that Murray, who had been very successful encircling Ottoman detachments at Magdhaba and Rafah, would repeat his behaviour if offered an opportunity. In fact, on 3 March, British cavalry again encircled a small Ottoman detachment, commanded by Captain Ömer Lütfü, at Khan Yunis before Lütfü could withdraw.[11] Enver and Cemal endorsed von Kress's plan and hoped for a decisive victory.

On 7 March, the 3rd Infantry Division, now under the command of Colonel Edip, began to withdraw to Cemame as the general reserve and von Kress began to move formations in order to create ad hoc tactical groups. Von Kress finalized his thoughts on 18 March and sent Cemal a report outlining his deployments.[12] In the meantime, von Kress moved his own headquarters forward from Jerusalem to Tel es Sheria. By 24 March, von Kress had created four tactical groups. In Gaza, Major Tiller commanded the Gaza Group, composed of the 79th Infantry Regiment and its machine-gun company, the 125th Infantry Regiment and its machine-gun company, the 2nd Battalion, 81st Infantry Regiment and the 267th Machine Gun Company, a cavalry company and a camel cavalry company, the 1st Field Artillery Battery from the 6th Artillery Regiment, the Austo-Hungarian Mountain Howitzer Battalion and a 100mm heavy artillery battery. Tiller's mission was to turn the town of Gaza into a fortress and to defend it.[13] The Cemame Group, commanded by Colonel Edip, comprised the 3rd Infantry Division, less the 138th Infantry Regiment and artillery battery. The Tel es Sheria Group, commanded by Colonel Halil Rüştü, comprised the 16th Infantry Division with its own 47th and 48th Infantry Regiments and the 16th Artillery Regiment, less the 125th Infantry Regiment in Gaza.

In Beersheba, Colonel Esat, commanded the Beersheba Group, composed of his 3rd Cavalry Division, the 138th Infantry Regiment and a machine-gun company. Von Kress ordered Esat to prepare for pursuit operations.[14] This marked an important point of departure for this hitherto purely cavalry division. From early March 1917 until the end of the war, this cavalry division always had infantry attached to it, making it somewhat of a mixed or composite division.[15] Its commander, Colonel Esat, was very successful in forging a well-trained team in which 'infantry and artillery co-operation was very good'.[16] Of note, like men, horses were at a premium in Palestine and the newly arrived 3rd Artillery Regiment was ordered to exchange its horses for camels at a rate of one camel for every two horses (most of which went to the cavalry division).[17]

First Gaza

Murray broke his force down into two tactical elements. His main effort was styled the Desert Column, a mix of the 53rd Infantry Division and two cavalry divisions, which would attack Gaza and encircle it. A supporting effort titled the Eastern Force composed of the 52nd and 54th Infantry Divisions would screen and guard the eastern flank of the Desert Column. To his rear the 74th Yeomanry Division guarded Murray's lines of communications, particularly the vulnerable and important water pipeline and railway. Importantly, overly optimistic British intelligence believed that von Kress did not intend to put up a determined fight at Gaza because his army was demoralized.[18] Murray himself remained in his railway car near El Arish, some 70km to the south of Gaza. His attack began on 26 March 1917.

Murray's attack was no surprise to von Kress or the Ottomans, who observed the British concentration from reports by aerial reconnaissance on 26 March.[19] This was because von Kress directed his airmen, somewhat against their will, to provide him with continual updates of Murray's progress.[20] The deployment of most of the First Expeditionary Force out in the desert away from Gaza was no accident. In fact, British intelligence was correct in its assessment that von Kress did not intend to fight hard for Gaza.[21] However, this was because von Kress intended instead to conduct an immediate counter-attack and encirclement of Murray's advancing army rather than abandoning Gaza. A Fourth Army report to Constantinople on 22 March 1917 outlined von Kress's intent to use the Cemame, Tel es Sheria and Beersheba tactical groups to counter-attack the British right flank with a view towards encirclement and cutting the rail road and water pipeline.[22]

In the week before the battle, von Kress reorganized his meagre forces, gave the Gaza Group orders to dig in and issued the remainder of his forces out in the desert with orders to be prepared to move immediately and attack.[23] In effect, von Kress intended to isolate the British once Murray committed his forces to the main attack. Alerted to the movement of British cavalry around the eastern side of Gaza by his airmen at 9.00 am on 26 March, von Kress had Halil Rüştü's Tel es Sheria Group moving to the west an hour later.[24] He ordered Colonel Edip's Cemame Group to move at noon and Colonel Esat's Beersheba Group to move at 3.30 pm.[25] Altogether, 12,000 out of 16,000 available Ottoman soldiers were moving west to attack Murray's right flank by nightfall on 26 March 1917.[26] (See map 5.1.)

The battle went very much as Murray intended and by 6.00 pm the Desert Column had almost completely encircled Gaza. At this critical point, the battle was probably all but won, however, doubt crept into the

Map 5.1: Ottoman counter-attacks, 1st Gaza, 27 March 1917

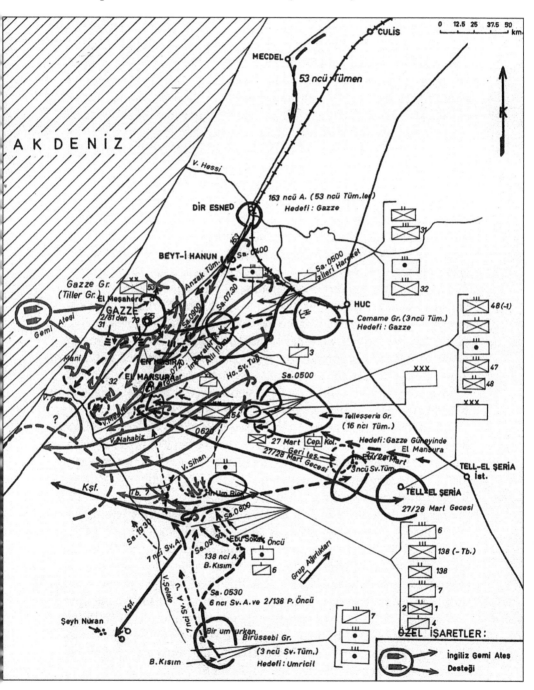

minds of the British command team.[27] Half of Chetwode's Desert Column was ensnared in Tiller's defences and the other half was north of Gaza in an unsupported and vulnerable position. Major General Sir Charles Dobell's Eastern Force was also partially trapped in Gaza and partially spread out along the coast road and wadi. British communications broke down and they were unable to contact Murray for either direction or for encouragement. Moreover, both British commanders knew, from aerial reconnaissance, that some 10,000 Ottoman infantry and cavalry were advancing on their undefended right flank. Consequently, Chetwode and Dobell issued orders that pulled the British cavalry and infantry back to their start lines.

Von Kress called off his envelopment on 27 March 1916, when it became fully apparent that the British had withdrawn to safety. Throughout that day the British continued to retreat until, at dawn on 28 March, the entire force lay behind the Wadi Gaza. When the final rolls were counted, Murray found he had suffered about 2,400 casualties. In an operational sense, von Kress used Gaza simply as a lure to put Murray in a vulnerable position for envelopment. Whether 12,000 Ottomans would have prevailed over the two full-strength British infantry divisions that Murray had positioned for this very contingency is problematic. But, given that the British were not in prepared defences and moving, a meeting engagement might have developed in the desert east of Gaza. Time also appeared to be on Cemal's side because the Ottoman Army's 53rd Infantry Division was arriving as reinforcement from the north and would have added distress to Murray's over extended cavalry.

The defeat at Gaza seemed to indicate that the British Army fighting the Ottomans failed to learn and adapt to the demands of modern war.[28] Certainly, Murray and the staff of the EEF were overly optimistic and badly underestimated the determination of the Ottomans. Murray himself even portrayed his defeat as somewhat of a Pyrrhic victory, noting that the Ottomans lost about 9,000 men while he lost about 4,000 men.[29] Actual Ottoman casualties were 294 killed and 1,078 wounded.[30] British intelligence was weak and contributed to an erroneous picture of the Ottoman force at Gaza. Moreover, British commanders at all levels lacked clear situational awareness and were unable to communicate effectively. And, almost two full years after Gallipoli, co-ordination between the infantry and the artillery continued to remain very weak. It might be argued that Murray's organizational focus in 1916 and early 1917 was largely logistical rather than on improving the tactical effectiveness of the EEF.

The Reorganization of the Fourth Army

By mid-March it was apparent that the growing number of Ottoman infantry divisions in southern Palestine needed greater command and control assets than were currently available on the Sinai front. After messages between Cemal and Enver, the Ottoman general staff authorized the activation of the XXII Corps headquarters on 26 March.[31] However, First Gaza delayed the implementation of this directive and an enthusiastic Cemal ordered a major counter-offensive on 28 March against Murray's army, which now sat in hasty defences behind the Wadi Gaza. Trying to solve all of his challenges at once, Cemel then inactivated the First Expeditionary Force and gave command of the newly forming XXII Corps to von Kress, with the 3rd, 16th and 53rd Infantry Divisions assigned to the corps. Five days later, after discussions with von Kress, Cemal issued his operations plan for an army level counter-offensive.[32] To execute the offensive, Cemal ordered the incoming XX Corps and its 7th and 54th Infantry Divisions south from Remle to the Gaza lines. As envisioned, the XXII Corps would attack the Wadi Gaza east of the town, the XX Corps would attack toward Şelale, and the unassigned 3rd Cavalry Division (under army control) would sweep behind Murray's right flank. The objective of the offensive was to force Murray back to El Arish. However, staff estimates projected that it would take twelve weeks to move all of the formations into their attack positions and to bring forward the necessary munitions and supplies for a deliberate offensive.

Cemal's forces began to flow slowly into the area between Gaza and Beersheba and, by mid-April, constituted a line stretching east from Gaza to Beersheba. In the midst of the offensive preparations, an intelligence report from the German general staff alerted Enver that Murray intended to resume the offensive in April. This caused Enver to examine closely Cemal's proposed offensive and Enver came to the conclusion that, should Murray attack before the Fourth Army had completed its preparations, Cemal's army would be unable to defend itself. Over the next few days, Cemal and von Kress traded messages about the situation with Enver and the Ottoman general staff. In the middle of these deliberations the XX Corps headquarters, deploying from Macedonia and under the command of Abdülkerim Pasha, arrived in Jerusalem. On 11 April, von Kress went to Cemal's Fourth Army headquarters, which Cemal had moved forward to Jerusalem, for consultations. That afternoon, instead of talking, Cemal took his two corps commanders out to Beersheba by automobile. Von Kress argued for an acceleration of the schedule for the offensive, even if all the forces were not in place, and Cemal and Abdülkerim returned to Jerusalem the next day.

By the night of 14 April, Cemal understood that Murray intended to attack Gaza a second time and he fully recognized the danger of his army being caught in the midst of offensive preparations.[33] In view of this, Cemal cancelled all offensive plans and shifted the army to a defensive posture. He ordered the 3rd Infantry Division to man the Gaza fortifications and ordered Esat's 3rd Cavalry Division to Cemame as his immediate mobile tactical reserve. Major Tiller was ordered to Beersheba with the 79th Infantry Regiment with orders to fortify the town. Cemal's intent was to form a defensive line anchored on Gaza and Beersheba. Noting the enemy's artillery concentration, Cemal ordered the construction of bombproof shelters along the line. Cemal also ordered his XII Corps to send forward 3,000 replacements from the 23rd and 24th Infantry Divisions to the front-line divisions.[34] The movement of the British 52nd and 54th Infantry Divisions forward of the Wadi Gaza on 17 April fully confirmed Cemal's intelligence and gave the Ottomans several days to complete their preparations.

Cemal made a final reorganization and reassigned the 16th Infantry Division and Tiller's group to the XXII Corps. The incoming 54th Infantry Division arrived in Mecdel as the army reserve. Von Kress held Gaza with the 3rd Infantry Division, and his 53rd Infantry Division held a line 15km to the east. From there Abdülkerim's 16th Infantry Division held the line to Beersheba, which was in the hands of Tiller's Group. Altogether, Cemal had 14,000 riflemen, 1,200 cavalrymen, 94 machine guns, 99 artillery pieces and 6 aircraft for the defence of the Gaza–Beersheba line.[35] On 17 April 1916, Murray's offensive began but, in the words of the Turkish official history, 'it was not a surprise for the Ottomans'.[36]

Second Gaza

Under intense political pressure to continue his offensive, Murray tried to break the Gaza line once again. Unfortunately for the British, Ottoman reinforcements reached the front in early April 1917 and Murray's best opportunity to break into Palestine had evaporated. For his forthcoming attack, Murray assigned Dobell's Eastern Force of three experienced infantry divisions to attack Gaza. Dobell planned a direct frontal attack on the well-prepared Ottoman defences. Murray's Imperial cavalry and Australian mounted brigades were on Dobell's right flank and were to push and demonstrate against the 53rd Infantry Division.

For the first time in the Middle Eastern war, Murray had 8 tanks and he had 4,000 poison gas shells.[37] Dobell's attack began at 5.30 am on 19 April 1917, with an artillery bombardment that lasted 1 hour and 45 minutes. The British also employed naval gunfire and unleashed their gas shells. The 3rd Infantry Division defended Gaza with the 31st and 32nd Infantry Regiments on the perimeter in the west and east respectively. Refet held his 138th Infantry Regiment in reserve. The attacking British infantry rushed forward towards Gaza only to meet ferocious Ottoman machine-gun and artillery fire from Refet's defending regiments. In mid-morning, Refet committed two battalions and a machine-gun company from his reserve regiment at 9.00 am to reinforce the 32nd Infantry Regiment. A tank attack at 12.20 pm failed when the tanks broke down or were destroyed by artillery.[38] Refet's division restored its defensive perimeter in the mid-afternoon. Casualties in the assaulting British 52nd and 54th Infantry Divisions were particularly heavy.

On the British right flank, the cavalry demonstrations against the 53rd and 16th Infantry Divisions were easily repulsed. Cemal was so encouraged by incoming reports that at 2.45 pm, he ordered Esat's cavalry division forward to Tel es Sheria. At 4.00 pm, Cemal launched the 3rd Cavalry Division through his own defences and 3 hours later, Esat's men were one again threatening the right flank of Murray's army. Tiller's Group was also ordered to move east to support Esat.[39] As night fell Dobell called off the attack, which was reluctantly endorsed by Murray. The British lost 6,444 casualties.[40] Ottoman losses were 2,000 altogether. Murray and Dobell were sent home to England.

Murray's frontal attack was repulsed and the tanks proved surprisingly easy for the Ottoman artillery to knock out.[41] The Ottomans reported that their soldiers fought well. A report from the Ottoman 53rd Infantry Division noted that, 'The English had attacked three times along the entire front and were repelled. Our officers and men displayed the utmost heroism.'[42] Once the battle began, the Ottomans noted that British artillery fire was minimal and was generally ineffective.[43] Moreover, British sea, land and air operations were poorly co-ordinated. As for the British gas attack, the Ottomans noted that 'poison gas was apparently used . . . [but] it failed to reach the resolute Ottoman soldiers'.[44] While it is generally accepted that the gas attack was ineffective, there are conflicting versions with regard to the casualties inflicted, but all agree that casualties from gas were almost non-existent.[45]

An American civilian, working as a secret agent for the American embassy in Constantinople, was present in Jaffa during Second Gaza and was able to interview British prisoners after the battle. A British POW said, 'We were ordered to attack a strongly entrenched position without any artillery preparation.' He also told the agent, 'We certainly had no idea how strong the Ottomans were.'[46]

Once again, two years after Gallipoli, the British demonstrated a lack of understanding concerning the characteristics of the Ottoman Army. In particular, the British artillery was very ineffective. The bombardment was too short and knocked out very few Ottoman guns. Moreover, the Ottoman defences were almost untouched by the bombardment and it proved impossible to knock out the Ottoman machine guns in strongpoints. Murray's Fourth Dispatch places the blame for failure on the shoulders of General Dobell, but other than repeatedly mentioning 'heavy shelling and machine gun fire', virtually ignored the role of the Ottoman Army in the battle.[47] Matthew Hughes rightly called the British assault an 'unsupported infantry attack'.[48] Moreover, the battle was a serious failure in command in that Murray launched his offensive without the preparation and forces that he felt necessary for success.[49] The momentary success in the Sinai against isolated enemy detachments proved to be an illusion of Ottoman weakness and once again, the over confident British were defeated.

In May 1917, the Fourth Army was organized into five army corps, two of which garrisoned the Gaza–Beersheba line. The overall personnel and materiel situation in the Fourth Army was as follows: 174,908 men, 36,225 animals, 5,351 camels, 145,840 rifles, 187 machine guns and 282 artillery pieces.[50] Of course, substantial portions of this strength were scattered along the Levantine coast or garrisoning Arabia. Facing the British on the Gaza line were the XX Corps and the XXII Corps, as well as the 3rd Cavalry Division and the 54th Infantry Division. The XII Corps and VIII Corps were in Adana and Damascus, respectively. The incomplete III Corps was marshalling in Aleppo. By July, the Fourth Army had grown to 151,742 rifles, 354 machine guns and 330 artillery pieces (its highest recorded strength). However, the defensive lines had also been extended, now almost encircling the oasis town of Beersheba, and stretching continuously for almost 50km. Although the opposing Imperial force was greatly increasing its strength as well, the Ottomans (and Enver, in particular) were optimistic.[51]

The Activation of the Yildirim Army Group
It is unclear when and where the idea of forming the Yildirim Army

originated. Although it certainly actualized in the fertile and aggressive mind of Enver, it is unknown exactly how much the Germans had to do with it. In the first two-and-a-half years of war, there had been much profitable discussion and cooperation between the Ottomans and the Germans. In any case, sometime after the fall of Baghdad and before the arrival of von Falkenhayn in Turkey for staff discussions on 7 May 1917, Enver was seized with the idea of retaking Baghdad. He intended to accomplish this by forming the Yildirim Army Group (in Turkish *Yıldırım Ordular Grubunu*; in English Yildirim translates as lightning or thunderbolt). Enver envisioned this force concentrating in upper Mesopotamia, perhaps centred on Mosul. From there, the Yildirim Army Group would conduct a grand offensive to retake Baghdad and then reconquer lower Mesopotamia or perhaps invade Persia. It was strategy on a grand scale and it appealed to Enver's grandiose sense of high drama. In Enver's grand scheme, Halil's Sixth Army in Mesopotamia, would form one component of the Yildirim Group. The second component would be a newly formed Seventh Army. Together with German assistance, these two Ottoman armies would take the offensive. Troops for the new Seventh Army would come from the infantry divisions returning from Galicia, Romania and Macedonia.

The possibilities of retaking the offensive excited Enver and he visited the Palestine Front, which appeared to have stabilized, again in June. He told Cemal that he was contemplating an offensive to retake Baghdad and that he intended to form an army group called the Yildirim Group.[52] Enver also told Cemal that he had decided which divisions would be assigned to this force and that German General Erich von Falkenhayn would command it. On 24 June 1917, Enver convened a meeting in Aleppo to discuss his plans. Joining Enver and Cemal were Ahmet İzzet, commanding the Caucasus Army Group, Mustafa Kemal, commanding the Second Army, and Sixth Army commander Halil. Colonel Bronsart von Schellendorf of the Ottoman general staff, staff officers from the Ottoman general staff and Caucasus Army Group staff, and the chiefs of staff of the Third and the Fourth Armies attended as well. At this meeting, Enver unveiled his plan to create a new Seventh Army on the upper reaches of the Euphrates River using the divisions made available by the conclusion of the European operations. Enver explained that Halil's Sixth Army would attack south along the Tigris River, while the Seventh Army attacked east along the Euphrates River. The British, at Baghdad, would be caught in a pincer movement and would be destroyed.[53]

Cemal was unhappy with this plan and pressed for a revision.[54] Cemal felt that instead of aiming to retake Baghdad, the Ottomans should concentrate their dwindling number of fresh divisions in the vicinity of Aleppo. At Aleppo, Cemal reasoned, this force could act as a centrally positioned strategic reserve and would be able to respond to threats in the Caucasus, in Palestine or in Mesopotamia. He also put forth the idea of maintaining troops in the Adana region as insurance against an amphibious landing by the Entente. Cemal concluded his summary of the strategic situation by stating that an all-out offensive against Baghdad was dangerous for the Ottomans. These divisions were the Ottoman Army's last reserves and could not be replaced. Enver replied that the Ottoman general staff had already decided upon this course of action and had already provided 'the best German general' to put in command.[55] Enver then told Cemal that the Germans would also provide a light division of six infantry battalions, with a large number of machine guns. Ahmet İzzet was also uncomfortable with the plan and recommended that Enver leave a division at Aleppo to act as a reserve contingency force. His appeals also went unheeded. An incensed Cemal cabled the grand vizier directly to express his concerns over this adventure. He received replies that said that the decision had already been made in the council of ministers, and that the grand vizier, personally, had requested the services of von Falkenhayn from the Germans.

Cemal was so incensed about the Yildirim idea that he journeyed to Constantinople in mid-August 1917 to argue against the plan. Erich von Falkenhayn was also having doubts about the feasibility of an offensive strategy and expressed them in a memorandum to the German general staff.[56] Another council of war was held, at which Cemal, Enver, von Falkenhayn, Bronsart von Schellendorf and Cemal's chief of staff, Colonel Ali Fuat, were present. Cemal and his chief of staff presented their appreciation of the weakness of the Fourth Army and concluded that the retention of a theatre reserve was vital to a successful defence. Cemal related that, at this point in the meeting, Enver and von Falkenhayn began conversing in fluent German and began an animated discussion at the map boards.[57] It was apparent to Cemal that he had lost the argument. Afterwards, much to Cemal's surprise, Enver explained that von Falkenhayn agreed with Cemal about the vulnerable condition of the Fourth Army. Furthermore, von Falkenhayn now advocated using the Yildirim Group to throw the British back across the Suez Canal, before attempting to retake Baghdad. Cemal was uncomfortable with this new proposal, preferring instead to simply abandon the Baghdad scheme and maintain a theatre reserve. Cemal was also very uneasy about the Yildirim staff and the new Seventh Army staff deploying into his own operational area. This would inevitably interfere with his authority and autonomy as commander in Palestine.

This strategic dispute at the highest levels continued until Cemal received an invitation from Kaiser Wilhelm to visit Germany, which he promptly accepted. Cemal went to Germany and visited the fleet at Kiel, the Krupp works and the army headquarters at Bad Kreuznach. Everywhere he went, he was feted. However, when he arrived at Bad Kreuznach, a cable from Enver reached him. This cable informed Cemal that he was relieved of command of the Palestine theatre and that von Falkenhayn would take over the war effort there. Cemal fired back a cable predicting catastrophe and then made his way to Constantinople. However, he was too late to affect events. Cemal returned to Syria, taking the title of Commander of the Armies in Syria and Western Arabia. He retained command of a truncated Fourth Army (to be composed of the VIII and XII Corps, and the Hejaz Expeditionary Force), and was also reduced to providing logistical support to von Falkenhayn.[58] Unhappy with this turn of events but willing to continue to serve in a diminished capacity, Cemal settled into a new headquarters in Damascus. There he observed the destruction of von Falkenhayn's army during the next year. Cemal noted later in his memoirs that there were continuous disputes between Mustafa Kemal and von Falkenhayn over command and policy issues in the Yildirim Group. Cemal further went on record in stating that, were it not for von Falkenhayn, the Ottomans could have held the Gaza–Beersheba line for years.[59]

The Germans came to refer to the Yildirim Army Group as Army Group F, and von Falkenhayn took command at the end of July 1917. As originally configured, the staff of the army group would consist of sixty-five German and nine Ottoman staff officers. This scheme was presented to the Ottomans as being easier for von Falkenhayn because the staff would not have to depend as much on translators.[60] It is doubtful that von Falkenhayn, who expressed the highest admiration for the Ottoman *asker* (soldier), ever trusted Ottoman officers to carry out general staff work to German standards. However, the Ottomans were not fooled by this charade and, in any case, were not assigned important staff work, which further cut them out of the decision process. The Germans also sent the 'German Asia Corps', which was actually only a brigade-sized force, to support the new army group. The Ottomans had expected to see some kind of light German infantry divisions and, instead, received three infantry battalions, three machine-gun detachments and three cavalry detachments. Also accompanying the Asia Corps were an artillery battalion, a squadron of aircraft for artillery spotting, two heavy artillery sections, an infantry/artillery coordination section, communications and motor transport. Of particular value was a small air component made up of four detachments of eight aircraft each.[61]

The Reorganization of the Ottoman Armies in Palestine
The marshalling of the new Seventh Army began in earnest and by the month of September, substantial forces were assembling in Aleppo. Previously, in May 1917, the 24th and 26th Infantry Divisions were alerted for service in Palestine and these were put on the road south. On 27 June, Cemal also shifted the Fourth Army's 27th Infantry Division south from Lebanon to Beersheba. In July, the XV Corps headquarters arrived from Galicia. Coming by train from Hungary, its divisions (the 19th and 20th Infantry Divisions) arrived in Constantinople, where they staged for deployment south. Each day, for almost a hundred days, a train carrying elements of the XV Corps departed for Aleppo. By the end of August, the 19th Infantry Division had arrived, and its sister division, the 20th Infantry Division, arrived in September. The III Corps headquarters reached strength and the 50th Infantry Division from Macedonia and the 59th Infantry Division from Aydin were also assigned to it. Four or five trains a day ran south to bring these formations into Syria. However, there were severe problems beginning to appear which indicated a gradually weakening Ottoman Army. In a report to the Yildirim Army headquarters in September 1917, von Kress noted that the 24th Infantry Division from Gallipoli had departed from Hyderpaşa train station with 10,000 men and that only 4,634 arrived fit for duty.[62] In the division 19 per cent were sick, 24 per cent had gone missing and 3 per cent were given permission to return home on leave.

Elements of the German Asia Corps were the last major units to arrive in Syria, having come all the way from their staging area in Neu Hammer in Silesia. Overall, considering the poor state of the Ottoman railroads, the staging of the Seventh Army to Aleppo was a considerable achievement. Once there, the Ottoman general staff planned to move the army east by rail to the end of the railhead. From there, the 400 trucks of the Asia Corps would transport the infantry divisions the last 160km to assembly areas south of Mosul. It was a very ambitious undertaking.[63]

However, in the middle of September 1917, the ambitious plan to retake Baghdad was consigned to the scrap heap. Enver had, at last, made up his mind to take von Falkenhayn's advice and send the Yildirim Army initially to Palestine. He may also have been spurred on by disturbing reports from von Kress concerning the massive British offensive preparations then being observed opposite the Gaza–Beersheba line. Furthermore, Enver was apparently uncomfortable with the lingering influence of Cemal in Palestine and decided to do something about that too. As a result, on 26 September 1917, Enver divided the existing Fourth Army area and he ordered the Yildirim Army Group and the Seventh Army south to Palestine.[64] Cemal was left with Syria and western Arabia and was forced to move the Fourth Army headquarters north to Damascus. In subsequent orders, given on 2 October, Enver activated a new Eighth Army, appointing von Kress to command it. He then assigned both the Seventh and the Eighth Armies to Falkenhayn's Yildirim Army Group. Falkenhayn also retained command and control of the Sixth Army in Mesopotamia.

The Arab Revolt Continues

The Ottoman high command reorganized its forces in the Hejaz by activating the Hejaz Expeditionary Force under the command of Fahrettin Pasha on 30 June 1916.[65] With Galip surrounded in Taif, Fahrettin took command of the defence of Medina and, after Galip's surrender and the loss of Mecca and Jeddah, became the single overall Ottoman commander in the Hejaz in the autumn of 1916. Fahrettin Pasha was an extremely able and aggressive officer and he decided to secure Medina by conducting punishing attacks on Ali's Southern Arab Army, which threatened the town from the south. With the arrival of Colonel Ali Necip's 58th Infantry Division, Fahrettin had an offensive instrument at his disposal. At the Battle of Bir i Derviş, 17–19 March 1917, Fahrettin's men defeated the Arabs and he then sent the 42nd Infantry Regiment south to Bir i Maşi to inflict another defeat on them in a battle, 1–4 April.[66] By conducting these limited tactical offensive operations Fahrettin solidified Medina's vulnerable southern flank on 18 April. These small but important victories enabled Fahrettin to redeploy forces northward in reaction to the growing problem of railway interdiction caused by the Arab's increasing attacks. The fall of Aqaba compounded this problem by creating a direct threat to Maan, which was the northern terminus of the Medina railway.

There were additional problems with supporting the Hejaz Expeditionary Force dealing with logistics. Fahrettin's force was composed of about 20,000 men, of which about 8,500 were infantrymen capable of bring the war to the enemy.[67] Although there was enough food to sustain this number of men for one year, Enver had already directed that some of them be pushed to locations north of Medina where they could be more easily supplied. Fahrettin's staff began working on this and, accidentally, as the situation changed, Enver's decision proved fortuitous.

Because of the difficulty of command and control over the long length of the railway, Fahrettin activated a new headquarters south of Maan called the 1st Provisional Force, which took control of the forces north of Tebuk.[68] Supporting this force, Fahrettin deployed the 1st and 3rd Battalions of Necip's 55th Infantry Regiment north along the railway. However, the headquarters of the 58th Infantry Division remained in Medina and focused on its defence against the increasingly powerful Arab armies of Abdullah and Ali. On 15 March 1917, the 1st Provisional Force grew to include the 1st and 3rd Battalions, 162nd Infantry Regiment, the Maan Mobile Jandarma Battalion and a number of independent artillery and cavalry detachments.[69] The loss of Aqaba to Lawrence and the Arabs on 6 July 1917 seriously damaged the Ottoman operational posture in the Arabian Peninsula by creating a direct threat to Maan. This situation, combined with the increasing number of Arab attacks on the Medina railway (there were fifty separate attacks between August and December 1917 alone in which the Ottomans lost several hundred men killed, wounded and prisoner and had 15 bridges, 3,254 rail ties and 152 telegraph poles destroyed),[70] forced Cemal and Fahrettin to revise the Ottoman command architecture in lower Palestine.

Between 28 August and the end of September 1917, Cemal's VIII Corps took up positions in Maan with 5,000 soldiers. This enabled Fahrettin to shift forces south from Maan, previously stationed there by Enver, linking up with forces moving north from Medina to increase his strength along the railway.[71] As a result, Fahrettin moved the 1st Provisional Force south to El Alâ and activated the 2nd Provisional Force at Tebuk. On 31 October 1917, Allenby drove Cemal's Fourth Army out of the Gaza–Beersheba line, causing the withdrawal of the VIII Corps forces at Maan. This imposed yet another restructuring of his forces on Fahrettin. By November 1917, Fahrettin resumed responsibility for Maan and sent a greatly reinforced 1st Provisional Force there (composed of the 146th Infantry Regiment, a cavalry regiment and numbers of independent detachments) to hold the town and to block an Allied advance from Aqaba. He then expanded the 58th Infantry

Division's area of responsibility north to cover the area formerly occupied by the 1st Provisional Force.[72]

By the spring of 1918, Fahrettin deployed a reinforced regiment in Maan (the 1st Provisional Force), a reinforced regiment in the centre of the Medina railway (the 2nd Provisional force) and the 58th Infantry Division now composed only of a reinforced regiment and a cavalry regiment north of Medina. Forming these provisional forces, which were brigade-sized units, depleted Fahrettin's combat strength, but he accomplished it through economy of force measures by leaving a small holding force facing Ali and Abdullah in the south.

Conclusion

Overall, the first half of 1917 ended positively for the Fourth Army with twin victories over the British at Gaza. Although Murray's EEF was gaining in strength, these were mostly gains in capacity rather than in capability. This led to an inability to compete with von Kress in battles of manoeuvre in which Ottoman tactical ad hoc combat groups seemed to excel. The failure to win battles led to Murray's relief and replacement in the second half of 1917. On the other hand, a strategic surplus of infantry divisions re-deploying from the European fronts enabled Enver Pasha to send badly needed reinforcements and replacements to the Palestine theatre. These assets arrived in time to enable von Falkenhayn to attempt a defence of the Gaza–Beersheba line. One of these reinforcements was the 3rd Cavalry Division under the command of Colonel Esat. This division would become, over the next year and a half, something of a fire brigade and an extremely valuable tactical asset. Its commander, Esat, proved exceptionally able, courageous and had a gift for bringing his division to the right spot at the right time. The presence of this particular division would prove invaluable in subsequent campaigns.

There was a final consequence of First Gaza for the history of the Middle East. On 28 March 1917, Cemal ordered the evacuation of the Jewish and Arab populations of the coastal city of Jaffa as a security measure.[73] Located some 50km north of Gaza, Jaffa sat astride Gaza's lines of communications. Cemal had previously emptied Gaza itself in February for similar reasons. After the relocation was complete, about 10,000 Ottoman Arab, Christian and Jewish citizens had been forced out of Jaffa to camps in the Syrian desert. According to historian Sean McMeekin, the relocation of some 3–4,000 Jews became a *cause célèbre* for the Zionist movement and helped spur support in Britain for the Balfour Declaration.[74]

Notes

1. Matthew Hughes, *Allenby and British Strategy in the Middle East 1917–1919* (London: Frank Cass, 1999), p. 18.
2. MacMunn and Falls, *Military Operations Egypt and Palestine, From the Outbreak of War with Germany to June 1917*, p. 270.
3. Okçu and Üstünsoy, *Sina-Filistin Cephesi, Harbin Başlangıcından İkinci Gazze Muharebeleri Sonuna Kadar*, p. 452.
4. Ibid., p. 453.
5. Ibid., p. 455.
6. Ibid., p. 456.
7. Ibid., p. 480.
8. Ibid., p. 485.
9. Ibid., p. 496. See also Fahri Belen, *Birinci Cihan Harbinde Türk Harbi 1917 Yılı Hareketleri* (*The Turkish Front in the First World War, Operations in 1917*) (Ankara: Genelkurmay Basımevi, 1966), pp. 103–4.
10. ATASE, Proposal from Commander, First Expeditionary Force, Archive 3221, Record H-45, File 1-35, reprinted in Okçu and Üstünsoy, *Sina-Filistin Cephesi, Harbin Başlangıcından İkinci Gazze Muharebeleri Sonuna Kadar* as EK (Appendix) 3,753–6.
11. Okçu and Üstünsoy, *Sina-Filistin Cephesi, Harbin Başlangıcından İkinci Gazze Muharebeleri Sonuna Kadar*, pp. 496–7.
12. ATASE, Thoughts and Proposal from Commander, First Expeditionary Force, 18 March 1916, Archive 3221, Record H-47, File 1-30, reprinted in Okçu and Üstünsoy, *Sina-Filistin Cephesi, Harbin Başlangıcından İkinci Gazze Muharebeleri Sonuna Kadar* as EK (Appendix) 4,75796.
13. Okçu and Üstünsoy, *Sina-Filistin Cephesi, Harbin Başlangıcından İkinci Gazze Muharebeleri Sonuna Kadar*, p. 503.
14. Ibid., p. 15.
15. XX Corps Orders, 7.40 pm, 2 November 1917, reprinted in ATASE. *3ncü Süvari Tümeni Tarihçesi* (*3rd Cavalry Division History*), ATASE Library, Record 26-421 (unpublished staff study), Record 26–421. In these orders, for example, the division was assigned the 125th and the 177th Infantry Regiments and the 16th Artillery Regiment to screen the retreat from Beersheba.
16. ATASE, *3ncü Süvari Tümeni Tarihçesi*, Record 26–421, p. 17. This Esat Pasha (3rd Cavalry Division commander) was a different individual from the III Corps commander at Gallipoli and was a well-known governor and police official in Constantinople. De Nogales described Esat has having 'an abundance of energy and initiative', Rafael de Nogales, *Four Years Beneath the Crescent* (New York: Charles Scribner's Sons, 1926), p. 311.
17. ATASE, *3ncü Topçu Alayı Tarihçesi*, unpublished staff study (Meki Ererthem), ATASE Library, Record 26–413, p. 14.
18. Sheffy, *British Military Intelligence in the Palestine Campaign*, pp. 210–14.
19. Okçu and Üstünsoy, *Sina-Filistin Cephesi, Harbin Başlangıcından İkinci Gazze Muharebeleri Sonuna Kadar*, p. 512.
20. Ibid., p. 506.
21. Sheffy, *British Military Intelligence in the Palestine Campaign*, pp. 209–11.
22. ATASE, Proposed Operations, Fourth Army to Ministry of War, 22 March 1917, Archive 3221, Record H-48, File 1-6, reprinted in Okçu and Üstünsoy, *Sina-Filistin Cephesi, Harbin Başlangıcından İkinci Gazze Muharebeleri Sonuna Kadar*, p. 506.

23. Okçu and Üstünsoy, *Sina-Filistin Cephesi, Harbin Başlangıcından İkinci Gazze Muharebeleri Sonuna Kadar*, pp. 516–17.

24. Ibid., Kroki (Sketch) 40.

25. Ibid.

26. Rafael De Nogales, a Venezuelan soldier of fortune serving with the Ottoman cavalry, thought it was the appearance of the Ottoman 3rd Cavalry Division so far to the south and west of Beersheba that convinced the British to call off the offensive. De Nogales, *Four Years Beneath the Crescent*, p. 331.

27. MacMunn and Falls, *Military Operations Egypt and Palestine, From the Outbreak of War with Germany to June 1917*, pp. 305–13.

28. Hughes, *Allenby and British Strategy in the Middle East*, 18–20.

29. Archibald Murray, *Sir Archibald Murray's Dispatches (June 1916–June 1917)* (London: J. N. Dent & Sons Ltd, 1920), p. 153. Murray's Fourth Dispatch, 28 June 1917, covered the First and Second Gaza battles. Moreover, Murray disguised his defeat by noting that 'my primary and secondary objects were completely attained, but that the failure to attain the third object – the capture of Gaza . . . prevented a most successful operation from being a complete disaster to the enemy'.

30. Okçu and Üstünsoy, *Sina-Filistin Cephesi, Harbin Başlangıcından İkinci Gazze Muharebeleri Sonuna Kadar*, p. 555.

31. Ibid., p. 565.

32. ATASE, Fourth Army Attack Plan, 2 April 1917, Archive 3221, Record H-50, File 1-12, reprinted in Okçu and Üstünsoy, *Sina-Filistin Cephesi, Harbin Başlangıcından İkinci Gazze Muharebeleri Sonuna Kadar*, pp. 569–70.

33. ATASE, Fourth Army to XXII Corps, 14/15 April 1917, Archive 3221, Record H-51, File 1-41, reprinted in Okçu and Üstünsoy, *Sina-Filistin Cephesi, Harbin Başlangıcından İkinci Gazze Muharebeleri Sonuna Kadar*, p. 585.

34. Okçu and Üstünsoy, *Sina-Filistin Cephesi, Harbin Başlangıcından İkinci Gazze Muharebeleri Sonuna Kadar*, p. 585.

35. Belen, *Birinci Cihan Harbinde Türk Harbi 1917 Yılı Hareketleri*, p. 110.

36. Okçu and Üstünsoy, *Sina-Filistin Cephesi, Harbin Başlangıcından İkinci Gazze Muharebeleri Sonuna Kadar*, p. 612.

37. Anthony Bruce, *The Last Crusade, The Palestine Campaign in the First World War* (London: John Murray Publishers Ltd, 2002), pp. 100–1. This was the first time the British used tanks and poison gas on the Ottoman fronts.

38. Okçu and Üstünsoy, *Sina-Filistin Cephesi, Harbin Başlangıcından İkinci Gazze Muharebeleri Sonuna Kadar*, pp. 611–14.

39. Ibid., Kroki (Sketch) 44.

40. Ibid., p. 104.

41. Ibid., pp. 612–13 and 630–1. The Ottoman official history makes the point (several times) of the steadiness of the Ottoman soldiers in the face of these weapons, which were new to the Ottoman theatre of war.

42. ATASE, 53rd Infantry Division to XXII Corps, 4.10 pm, 19 April 1917, Archive 4524, Record H-2, File 1-20, reprinted in Okçu and Üstünsoy, *Sina-Filistin Cephesi, Harbin Başlangıcından İkinci Gazze Muharebeleri Sonuna Kadar*, p. 621.

43. ATASE, 48th Infantry Regiment to 53rd Infantry Division, 11.00 pm, 19 April 1917, Archive 4524, Record H-2, File 1-16, reprinted in Okçu and Üstünsoy, *Sina-Filistin Cephesi, Harbin Başlangıcından İkinci Gazze Muharebeleri Sonuna Kadar*, p. 623.

44. Okçu and Üstünsoy, *Sina-Filistin Cephesi, Harbin Başlangıcından İkinci Gazze Muharebeleri Sonuna Kadar*, p. 631.

45. Yigal Sheffy, 'Chemical Warfare and the Palestine Campaign, 1916–1918', *The Journal of Military History*, Vol. 73, No. 3, July 2009, 10–12.
46. NARA, Comment on the Military Operations at Gaza, 2 May 1917, Special American Agent 'UY2', M 1271, 8544–30.
47. Murray, *Sir Archibald Murray's Dispatches*, pp. 160–3. Murray was kind to Dobell in the Fourth Dispatch by presenting the idea that Dobell, 'who had suffered some weeks previously from a severe touch of the sun, was no longer in a fit state of health to bear the strain of further operations in the coming heat of summer. . . . I felt it my duty to relieve him of his command.'
48. Hughes, *Allenby and British Strategy in the Middle East*, p. 21.
49. Bruce, *The Last Crusade*, p. 104.
50. Merhum Kâmil Onalp, Hilmi Üstünsoy, Kâmuran Dengiz and Şükrü Erkal, *Birinci Dünya Harbinde Türk Harbi IVnü Cilt, 2nci Kısım, Sina-Filistin Cephesi, İkinci Gazze Muharebesi Sonundan Mütarekesi'ne Kadar Yapılan Harekât 21 Nisan 1917–30 Ekim 1918 (First World War, Turkish War, Sinai-Palestine Front, Operations from the Second Gaza Battle to the Mondros Armistice, 21 April 1917–30 October 1918)* (Ankara: Genelkurmay Basımevi, 1986), p. 18.
51. Djemal Pasha, *Memories of a Turkish Statesman 1913–1919*, p. 184.
52. Ibid., p. 183.
53. Belen, *Birinci Cihan Harbinde Türk Harbi 1917 Yılı Hareketleri* , pp. 114–15.
54. Djemal Pasha, *Memories of Turkish Statesman 1913–1919*, p. 183.
55. Ibid., p. 184.
56. Brigadier General F. J. Moberly, *Military Operations: Mesopotamia, Vol IV, The Campaign in Upper Mesopotamia to the Armistice* (London: HMSO, 1927), p. 65.
57. Djemal Pasha, *Memories of a Turkish Statesman 1913–1919*, p. 188.
58. Ibid., pp. 190–2.
59. Ibid., p. 195.
60. Belen, *Birinci Cihan Harbinde Türk Harbi 1917 Yılı Hareketleri*, p. 115.
61. Ibid., p. 116.
62. Ibid., p. 125.
63. Ibid., p. 117.
64. Onalp et al., *Sina-Filistin Cephesi, İkinci Gazze Muharebesi Sonundan Mütarekesi'ne Kadar Yapılan Harekât*, pp. 114–15.
65. Ibid., p. 179.
66. Ibid., Kroki (Sketches) 32–4.
67. Belen, *Birinci Cihan Harbinde Türk Harbi 1917 Yılı Hareketleri*, p. 163.
68. Erkal, *Hicaz, Asir, Yemen Cepheleri ve Libya Harekâtı*, p. 342.
69. Ibid., pp. 344–5.
70. Ibid., p. 354.
71. Ibid., Kroki (Sketch) 37.
72. Ibid.
73. Sean McMeekin, *The Ottoman Endgame: War, Revolution, and the Making of the Modern Middle East 1908–1923* (New York: Penguin Press, 2015), p. 351. McMeekin noted that Cemal had previously deported 750 Russian Jews from Jaffa in 1914 as potential security risks.
74. Ibid., pp. 353, 416.

Chapter 6

1917
Beersheba, Third Gaza and
Jerusalem

Introduction
After the victories at First and Second Gaza, the Ottomans had reason
to be optimistic about their ability to defend Palestine. With the
activation of the Yildirim Army Group and the reorientation of the
empire's strategic priorities, the defence of Palestine came to be seen as
a real possibility. However, the reinforcement of the theatre by fresh
Ottoman formations disguised a gradual weakening of the army and
major problems were beginning to appear in the Ottoman Army in 1917,
the most serious of which was the issue of the eroding supply of
manpower. This was compounded by a terrible attrition from combat
losses, disease and desertion. Morale also became a serious issue for the
army when the deployment of increasing numbers of men in Palestine
overwhelmed the limited logistical capacity of the theatre. Morale
among Arab soldiers was a particular issue that concerned Ottoman
commanders and which directly affected the reliability of tactical units.

The Ottoman Army in Palestine – summer 1917
As a result of the formation of the Yildirim Army Group in June 1917,
the Ottomans began to send substantial forces to Syria and Palestine.[1]
The activities of the newly arriving divisions reflected the will of
commanders who maintained an active interest in preparation for
combat. Incoming formations conducted a myriad of complex activities.
They engaged in multi-echelon combined arms training, organizational
restructuring, presentations on fresh combat methods from the Western
Front and sent officers to local training courses.
    The 7th Infantry Division's experience was typical. When the

infantry regiments of the division arrived in Jerusalem in early May they began company level training immediately.[2] The regiments remained in reserve and trained until late June in battalion and regimental tactics when the division went into the line. During the lulls in fighting, the regiments underwent training in fortification, reconnaissance and counter-reconnaissance. In its first combat action in the new theatre the division conducted a full-scale counter-attack at Yuksek Tepe on 15 July under the command of Colonel Kazım. After the battle, he reminded the division of its history during divisional ceremonies on 6 August when the regimental colours of the 20th and 21st Infantry Regiments were awarded military medals for the Gallipoli Campaign.[3] Tactical innovations from the Western Front were also introduced on a routine basis in Palestine. On 25 October 1917, German Colonel Adolf Hergote, fresh from the Western Front, delivered a presentation to the 21st Infantry Regiment on the principles of assault and battle training, and also on reconnaissance training.[4]

The 7th Infantry Division was simultaneously engaged in a major restructuring of its tactical organizational architecture. After its arrival in Beersheba, the division inactivated the 4th Company of each infantry battalion on 28 June.[5] On 10 August, reflecting the most current tactical thinking, the division activated a machine-gun company, armed with light machine guns, in every infantry battalion.[6] This reorganization was repeated, subject to the availability of equipment, in other Ottoman infantry divisions in Palestine. Although the 7th Infantry Division lost a quarter of its rifle strength it gained offensive and defensive capability by the addition of light machine guns within infantry battalions.[7]

On 17 July 1917, the division activated an assault detachment (*hücüm müfrezesi*) of fifty men (this was the Ottoman version of German *stosstruppen*). This was a local initiative implemented by von Kress, who wanted to introduce the most current Western Front tactical innovations into his army. He assigned German Major Kiehl to supervise the training of the Ottoman assault troops, and this proceeded 'with good results'.[8] Von Kress inspected the companies in September 1917 and noted, 'it is evident that proper training and grooming would bring out the best in these brave, obedient, and humble Anatolian soldiers'.[9] In the absence of written doctrinal information, an unofficial manual on assault troop tactics was written and distributed by the 19th Infantry Division commander, which was based on the experiences of his division in Galicia.[10]

On 1 September 1917, Enver ordered a selective activation of assault troops within the Ottoman Army. Enver directed the XV Corps, the First Army and the Fourth Army to activate the 1st, 2nd and 3rd Assault Battalions respectively.[11] Additionally, he ordered each infantry division in the Yildirim Army Group and in the Fourth Army to activate assault detachments. Enver was very specific that only the best officers, NCOs and men 'from the best units in the division; who were intelligent, healthy and hardy, and not more than 27 years of age' were selected for these elite units.[12] Additionally, the assault units received better rations, a distinctive badge (an embroidered hand grenade) and completed a one-month assault course. Later, the divisional assault detachments matured into assault battalions. The Ottoman armies in Mesopotamia, western Anatolia and Caucasia do not seem to have been required to activate assault troops.

A clear photograph of a platoon of Ottoman Army storm troops in Palestine in the summer of 1918 shows men kitted out in well-fitting uniforms, German style steel helmets, underarm grenade bags with stick grenades, German Mauser rifles and puttee leggings.[13] This unique photograph is important because the men look confident and fit, well fed and are thoroughly equipped – indeed, a picture that is at odds with our historical perception of the Ottoman Army in Palestine. Although it is dangerous to draw a generalized conclusion from a photograph, it is obvious that the Ottomans, at least in one locality, gave a high priority to the selection of men for, and to the maintenance of, its assault troop formations.

The activation of assault battalions (*hücüm tabur*) essentially returned the Ottoman Army in Palestine to the elitist organizational architecture of 1910–14 (in which an infantry division was authorized a non-regimental jäger/chasseur battalion). On paper, infantry divisions with assault troops were authorized three infantry regiments (each of three infantry battalions) and one assault battalion or assault detachment. By design, within the assault unit, there was a high concentration of aggressive and fit officers and men. However, there were never enough qualified infantrymen to fill every division to strength and, as a consequence, manning the assault unit took some of the best men from the line infantry regiments. Unlike the German Army, the Ottoman Army formed no specialized assault or storm troop units at divisional or regimental level.

By the end of 1917 the strategic and operational initiative in Palestine had passed to the British. Consequently, both the practical and technical need of the Ottoman Army to possess assault troops also passed.

Nevertheless, the assault troop battalions of the Ottoman Fourth, Seventh and Eighth Armies were retained, possibly with a view to future offensive operations of the Yildirim Army Group. It should be remembered that until the failure of the Ludendorff offensives in the late spring of 1918, the strategic posture of the Central Powers appeared favourable.

In addition to the unit training described previously, Cemal established some centralized training facilities.[14] The main facility was located at Tel es Sheria and was staffed with German and Austrian instructors. There was a fifteen-day course for commanders and a six-week course for divisional staff officers. These courses taught the most current tactics and weapons mastery based on methods then in standard use on the Western Front, especially machine-gunnery, which was vital to the newly reorganized Ottoman infantry battalions. Ottoman officers with experience on the European fronts (Galicia, Romania and Macedonia) were also brought in to assist with the training. Particular attention was paid to artillery training, which seemed to suffer from inexperienced officers who were using out-of-date methods and tactics.

In 1917 in Palestine, Ottoman unit strength became a significant problem. The 21st Infantry Regiment noted on 26 October 1917 that its infantry companies were at half strength in trained men and that its sick and battle casualties were not being replaced at a rate that would keep up with the losses.[15] The 16th Infantry Division departed from Constantinople in September 1916, with 11,500 officers and men, arrived in Jerusalem in February 1917 and was then heavily involved in the Second Gaza battle.[16] By 15 October, the division numbered only 5,017 officers and men.[17] The 3 infantry battalions in its 78th Infantry Regiment numbered about 400 men each (out of an authorization of about 750 men per battalion).[18]

Morale on the Palestine front was a problem for Ottoman Army commanders. This was mainly a function of logistics and climate; there was little water and food and the climate was terribly hot in the summer. Postal, recreational and health services were particularly deficient and desertion plagued units sent to the desert. And, for the first time in the Turkish official histories, morale among the Arab units was noted as being 'depressed and vulnerable to enemy propaganda'.[19]

The 45 active combat infantry divisions of the Ottoman Army on 3 August 1917 reported shortages of 190,000 men and the Yildirim Army Group reported a deficit of some 70,000 soldiers.[20] But, out of the available 24,000 newly trained conscripts (men of the class of 1900) only 5,000 were sent to the Fourth Army.[21] Altogether the Yildirim Army on the Palestine front received about 27,000 replacement soldiers (from all sources) in 1917 to fill the vacant ranks in the Seventh and Eighth Armies – for a net shortage of some 40,000 men.

Many of the conscripted men from the Fourth Army area of operations were of Arab ethnicity and, by 1917, the Arab Revolt was in full swing. Historian Matthew Hughes has commented on the Arab composition of the Ottoman divisions defending the Gaza line using wartime data from Hüseyin Hüsnü Emir's *Yıldırım*.[22] In the summer of 1917, Captain Hüseyin Hüsnü Emir was assigned as the assistant chief of staff of Falkenhayn's Yildirim Army Group and was in a position to observe directly the staff operations of the Yildirim Army Group. Emir's data is relevant because it highlights the fact that the army group staff maintained such information and speaks of its interest in the reliability of ethnic minorities at this point in the war. For example, of the 2,408 trained infantrymen in the 27th Infantry Division who would defend Beersheba in the forthcoming battle 76 per cent were Arab, 21 per cent were Turks and 3 per cent belonged to another ethnicity.[23]

Other senior Ottoman officers expressed concern over ethnicity. The memoirs of Colonel Ali Fuat (Erden), Fourth Army chief of staff, distinctively identified those battalions that were ethnically Ottoman Turk, which were sent to Palestine and Syria in 1917.[24] General Fahri Belen wrote in 1966 that the Arab units in Syria in 1917 were 'to a certain degree combat ineffective because of British propaganda, disease, and shaken morale'.[25] Before and after Third Gaza, Kress von Kress also expressed concern over his Arab units.

Commentary on the reliability of Arab units was not limited to professional Ottoman staff officers and British intelligence. A 1917 report from the American Army attaché in Constantinople to the United States War Department noted, 'The first line troops in Palestine are composed exclusively of Ottomans . . . they are a hardy, thoroughly reliable body of men whose remarkable staying power and uncomplaining submissiveness make up for their lack of dash and intelligent initiative'.[26] Moreover, the reported continued, 'There are, of course, regiments composed of Arabs, but they are not considered trustworthy, large bodies of them frequently deserting or going over to the enemy.'

Emir's statistics from September 1917 also confirm that every division on the Gaza line fielded operational infantry battalions at about 50 per cent of normal authorized strength. This was in spite of last minute efforts in the summer of 1917 to divert additional replacements to the Palestine front by giving the Fourth Army priority of personnel fill over the Sixth Army in Mesopotamia.[27] Additionally, the Fourth Army's VIII and XII Corps in the quiet Syrian sector and along the coast were continuously ordered to send levies of trained men to the Gaza Front.

One area in which the Ottoman Army in Palestine did not suffer was in its abundant supply of seasoned and capable commanders. Many of the commanders had served against the British in the Sinai or at Gallipoli. Additionally, all were veterans of the Balkan Wars of 1912–13. Of interest is the high density of professionally trained Ottoman general staff officers among the Ottoman leadership in Palestine. All three corps commanders and three of five division commanders were Ottoman general staff officers (graduates of the Ottoman War College).[28] They knew each other well and routinely served together; Asım and Ali Fuat were members of the class of 1905 and overlapped with Fahrettin (1902), İsmet and Selahattin (1906).[29] Kazım and Refet were members of the class of 1912.

Ottoman Plans and Dispositions

The Seventh Army was now commanded by Mustafa Kemal who was not at all happy with the affirmation of an offensive strategy. In a long and strongly worded, but unsolicited, letter sent directly to Enver on 20 September 1917, Kemal advocated a return to a defensive military policy within which every reserve was to be guarded and carefully committed.[30] He based this on the premise that superior British lines of communications (ship and rail) would ensure the continued numerical superiority in any theatre that the Ottomans wished to contest. Therefore, Kemal reasoned, it would be impossible for the Ottomans to gain the initiative with the Yildirim Army anywhere. He also advocated the merging of the Seventh and the Eighth Armies and offered to step down in favour of von Kress. Mustafa Kemal also stressed the importance of strengthening the internal administration of the country so that the army would have the people and the economy solidly behind it. In an emotional but rather poorly thought out conclusion to his letter, Kemal bitterly condemned German influence in Ottoman strategy and expressed his concern that the Ottoman Empire was becoming a 'German colony'. This was singularly blunt criticism of Enver's pro-German war strategy and, moreover, Kemal could not resist exchanging additional angry letters with von Falkenhayn, in which he expressed similar sentiments. Enver and von Falkenhayn were enraged and this led to a scathing rebuke of Kemal by Enver. In turn, Mustafa Kemal resigned his command of the Seventh Army. On 9 October, Brigadier General Mustafa Fevzi took command of the Seventh Army, with Lieutenant Colonel Ömer Lütfü serving as his chief of staff. Mustafa Fevzi (later Fevzi Çakmak) was a War College graduate and general staff officer, who was fluent in seven languages, and who had served as a field army chief of staff during the First Balkan War (1912–13).[31] He served as a corps commander during the Gallipoli campaign and as an army wing commander in Caucasia.

The headquarters elements and the infantry divisions then being concentrated near Aleppo began to move south on 30 September, but not all went south to Palestine. Recognizing the need to reinforce Mesopotamia, Enver sent the 50th Infantry Division to Ramadi. The unfortunate 59th Infantry Division was inactivated and its troops used to fill out the other divisions departing the Aleppo staging area. To make up for these lost forces, Enver ordered the Ottoman Fifth Army at Gallipoli to send the 42nd Infantry Division to Syria and the Ottoman Second Army in Anatolia to send the 1st Infantry Division to Damascus. Enver ordered the Third Army in the Caucasus to send the 2nd Caucasian Cavalry Division as well. However, it would be months before these formations arrived in Syria. By the end of October, only the headquarters of the Seventh and Eighth Armies would actually be in position to participate in combat operations in Palestine. On the ground from Gaza to Beersheba there was little change in the tactical deployment of the Ottoman XXII, XX and III Corps. Von Kress recast his corps staff into the new Ottoman Eighth Army headquarters, which had responsibility over the entire Palestine front. Brigadier General Fevzi remained in Aleppo until 18 October when he began to move his headquarters forward to Halilürrahman, arriving on 23 October.[32]

On 28 October 1917, von Falkenhayn's headquarters issued orders that significantly altered the operational architecture of the Sinai Front.[33] In these orders, Fevzi's Seventh Army assumed operational command of the eastern half of the Ottoman Front, including Beersheba, and he was assigned Staff Colonel İsmet's III Corps headquarters, which commanded the 24th Infantry Division and the 3rd Cavalry Division. İsmet (later İsmet İnönü, president of the Republic of Turkey) was a War College graduate and a general staff officer with experience in combat as a division commander in the Balkan Wars and as a corps commander at Gallipoli. The incoming XV Corps and the 19th and 20th Infantry

Divisions were projected to go to İsmet as well. The Eighth Army remained in control of the town of Gaza and the western half of the front.

The majority of the Yildirim Army Group staff was stationed in Jerusalem, working under Ottoman assistant chief of staff Captain Hüseyin Hüsnü and German Staff Major von Papen, while von Falkenhayn and his chief of staff, Colonel von Dommes, remained in Aleppo. Personal location was a dilemma for von Falkenhayn, who feared that while travelling south to Jerusalem, he might be caught without communications and he decided to remain in Aleppo where he had good telegraphic communications with not only his Seventh and Eighth Armies in Palestine but also with the Sixth Army in Mesopotamia.

The Yildirim Army Group expected the main British attack to be delivered against Gaza and a demonstration or feint against the Beersheba position. The Ottomans knew that Gaza offered the British proximity to logistical bases, support from the Royal Navy, and an adequate road and rail network, which made it easier for them to attack there. Their suspicions were apparently confirmed on 10 October 1917 when an intelligence bonanza dropped in their laps. This was the famous 'lost haversack episode' hatched by Major Richard Meinertzhagen.[34]

Meinertzhagen was an intelligence officer who set up a phoney front-line reconnaissance during which he appeared to drop a haversack while fleeing from Ottoman cavalry. The blood-stained haversack contained personal possessions and letters, sandwiches and false operational documents relating to an impending British attack. Meinertzhagen claimed to have barely escaped with his life, which added a convincing touch to the drama. The false documents were backed up by operational deception measures that made a British attack on Gaza appear imminent. It was brilliant work and Kress von Kressenstein was convinced of the documents' authenticity.[35]

The false operational documents contained the outline of a plan that the British would attack before the muddy winter season, that a small cavalry force would conduct a demonstration against Beersheba, that Anglo-French forces would conduct three amphibious landings north of Gaza and that the main attack would hit Gaza using night assaults and tanks.[36] This played into the intelligence estimates of the Ottoman and German staff officers who believed that the British possessed the logistical capability to move only two divisions (one infantry and one mounted) through the desert to the town of Beersheba.[37] In fact, Meinertzhagen's ruse was so believable that it led directly to changes in the Ottoman operational posture along the Gaza–Beersheba line.

Believing that the British intended to attack Gaza yet again, von Kress focused his attention on the Gaza defences over the course of the next two weeks. He was especially concerned about the vulnerable coastline north of the town. Consequently, as the incoming 53rd Infantry Division arrived in Palestine, von Kress moved it into the front-line positions held by the 7th Infantry Division in the Gaza perimeter. He then pulled the 7th Infantry Division back into coastal defence positions north of the town to guard against the expected amphibious invasions.[38] Von Kress also retained the newly arrived 24th Infantry Division in reserve near Gaza as a counter-attack force against a cavalry encirclement of the town. He also prioritized the strengthening of his defences in Gaza and sent replacements there as well.

While hardening his Gaza defences, von Kress remained concerned about Beersheba. He characterized the 27th Infantry Division, which manned the Beersheba lines, as 'badly trained, badly organised, and composed of Arabs who had to be watched'.[39] He was worried about this division and he recommended that it should be deactivated and its soldiers used as replacements. Furthermore, he also considered diverting the incoming 19th Infantry Division into the Beersheba lines in place of the 27th Infantry Division.[40] Despite these misgivings, but based on the perceived threat to Gaza presented in the captured haversack, von Kress decided that the 19th Infantry Division be held in reserve near Cemame.[41] Von Falkenhayn approved these dispositions, which placed the 19th Infantry Division nearer Gaza than Beersheba, as well as taking the veteran 7th and 24th Infantry Divisions out of the line.

The end result of all of this was that, between 10 and 28 October 1917, the Eighth Army shifted significant Ottoman forces (three experienced and hardened infantry divisions) to reserve positions that supported the retention of Gaza rather than the defence of Beersheba. Beersheba itself remained in the hands of the Ottoman III Corps, composed of the mostly Arab 27th Infantry Division and the two-regiment 3rd Cavalry Division. Von Falkenhayn did, however, reinforce İsmet with the 2nd Infantry Regiment which provided the III Corps with badly needed infantrymen. Without the distraction of Meinertzhagen's ruse, von Kress planned to have the powerful 19th and 24th Infantry Divisions defending Beersheba with the reinforced 3rd Cavalry Division positioned nearby in reserve.[42]

In its final pre-battle deployment, the Yildirim Army Group held the Gaza–Beersheba line with two field armies abreast. On the right flank, holding Gaza, was the Eighth Army, commanded by von Kress, composed of the XXII Corps, with the 53rd Infantry Division in a strongly fortified position around Gaza and the 3rd Infantry Division holding its left flank. Von Kress's XX Corps, with the 54th and 26th Infantry Divisions held the line out into the desert. As of 28 October, Fevzi's new Seventh Army held the Ottoman left and the decisive oasis town of Beersheba. The 16th Infantry Division held the line from the XX Corps to Beersheba and, in Beersheba itself, İsmet's III Corps (the 27th Infantry Division and 3rd Cavalry Division) defended a lightly fortified half-circle position around the south side of the town. On 28 October, the 24th Infantry Division had arrived and was in reserve behind the 16th Infantry Division, and the 19th Infantry Division was detraining in an assembly area 20km behind the lines.[43] The defence was anchored on the well-fortified town of Gaza and the less well-fortified town of Beersheba, both of which were ringed by entrenchments presenting a well-planned defence.

Beersheba

The Battle of Beersheba lasted one day and was fought on 31 October 1917.[44] General Sir Edmund Allenby, who replaced Murray as commander of the EEF, achieved operational surprise with overwhelming force – the 4-division XX Corps and the two divisions of the Desert Mounted Corps against the equivalent of a single brigade (İsmet had 4,400 riflemen, 60 machine guns and 28 artillery pieces).[45] Moreover, the attack was delivered concentrically from three sides denying the III Corps the opportunity of massing effectively its tactical reserves.

Allenby's brigades closed on their assembly areas at about 5.30 pm on 30 October and tactical movement began the next morning. İsmet's 27th Infantry Division occupied trenches on the east and south sides of Beersheba, with the 81st, 67th and 48th Infantry Regiments, in line from north to south and east, defending a 12km line. Each regiment had a battalion in immediate reserve and artillery and machine guns were tied into the defensive plan. İsmet kept Esat's cavalry division on his left flank and and the 1st and 2nd Battalions, 24th Infantry Regiment in general reserve. (See map 6.1.) Beersheba began to receive artillery fire at 5.55 am and by 7.45 am, İsmet was aware of the scale of the attack as cavalry began to sweep around his lightly defended eastern flank.[46] Shortly thereafter, he deployed the two battalions of the 24th Infantry Regiment to establish hasty defensive positions directly east of the town.

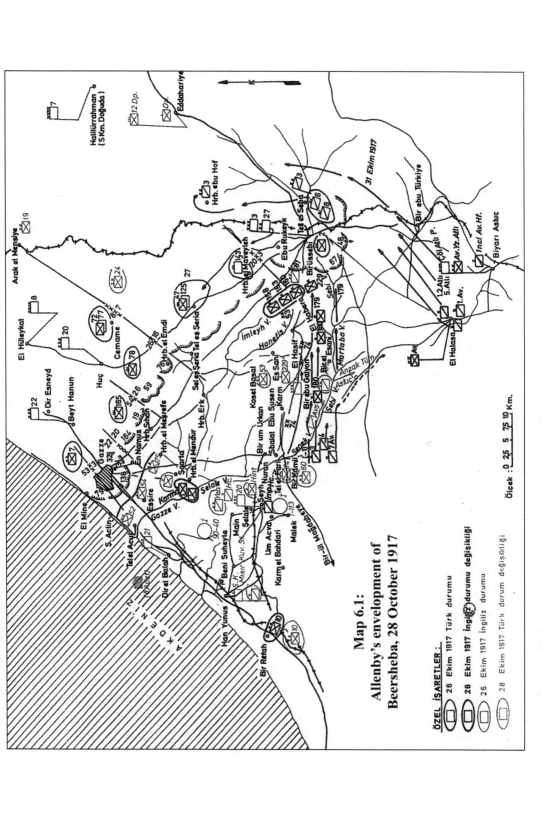

Map 6.1:
Allenby's envelopment of
Beersheba, 28 October 1917

Ölçek : 0 2,5 5 7,5 10 Km.

ÖZEL İŞARETLER :

- 26 Ekim 1917 Türk durumu
- 28 Ekim 1917 İngiliz durumu değişikliği
- 26 Ekim 1917 İngiliz durumu
- 28 Ekim 1917 Türk durum değişikliği

At 9.00 am, İsmet ordered the 3rd Cavalry Division to block the encircling enemy cavalry north east of Beersheba and Esat reported at 10.20 am that the enemy cavalry attack was much stronger than expected. Along the line fighting was particularly heavy in the 67th Infantry Regiment's sector. By early afternoon it was obvious to İsmet that encirclement was all but certain and at 4.00 pm he gave the order for the surviving elements of the III Corps to retreat to the north.[47] However, it was too late to save every soldier and, except for the 3rd Cavalry Division, which conducted a fighting withdrawal through the porous British cavalry screens, over 2,000 Ottoman soldiers were captured. İsmet, a few of his staff officers and twenty soldiers evaded capture and escaped to the north. Australian light horsemen reached the centre of the town at about 6.30 pm, ending the battle.

According to von Kress the battle was lost for four reasons. First, the III Corps units were badly understrength. Second, the state of training and discipline in the 27th Infantry Division was so substandard that it should have been deactivated. Third, the III Corps commander committed his reserves too early in the battle. And fourth, the operations of the 3rd Cavalry Division were ineffective.[48] As a battle fought, Kress von Kressenstein shifted the primary blame for failure onto Colonel İsmet.[49]

Stung by this criticism, İsmet, promptly wrote a twenty-page rebuttal. He noted that his rapid commitment of reserves and his deployment of the 3rd Cavalry Division to the north prevented the encirclement of the Ottoman III Corps by Allenby's Desert Mounted Corps.[50] He also observed that his men were stretched too thin on a 26km front, and in particular, opposing the British XX Corps, he only had 1,400 men and 16 machine guns manning a 7½km front. İsmet also mentioned that von Kress failed to send him reinforcements when he asked for help and noted that on 28 October he had expressed concern that the nearest reserves were 20km from Beersheba. İsmet acknowledged that the town fell more rapidly than expected but he did not highlight Arab soldiers as a contributing factor.[51]

Von Falkenhayn also rendered comments on the loss of Beersheba in an after action report.[52] He accepted the idea that all formations were under strength but noted that the reserves were improperly employed. In particular, von Falkenhayn identified the failure of von Kress to issue instructions properly to reserves and to issue orders rapidly to the III Corps during the battle. Finally, von Falkenhayn noted that the Eighth Army had adequate reserves near Tel es Sheria and should have planned to use them in the event that the attack on Beersheba was more than a simple diversion. Importantly, the Yildirim commander did not highlight Arab ethnicity as a factor in the defeat. Altogether, von Falkenhayn's after action report was a damning indictment of von Kress's management of the battle.

Concerning the issue of Arab reliability, the Turkish official histories do not specifically mention this as a factor in the loss of Beersheba, although the Arab soldiers in the 67th and 81st Infantry Regiments were thought to be notably weak in 'fighting spirit' prior to the battle.[53] However, it is significant that two British infantry divisions took the entire day of 31 October to push the 1,400 men of these Arab regiments out of their trenches. The attack of the British XX Corps was not decisive but it did draw most of İsmet's infantry reserves to the south-western perimeter of Beersheba, thus allowing the famous cavalry charge of the Australian 4th Light Horse Brigade to sweep, almost unopposed, into the town of Beersheba at about 5.00 pm. In any assessment of the 27th Infantry Division's performance, it must be noted that after the battle, the 4 regiments of the division gathered at Tel es Sheria included 124 officers, 2,176 soldiers, 10 machine guns and 7 artillery pieces.[54] That so many broke out of the encirclement with heavy equipment is testament to effective command and control.

The Beersheba defences were manned sufficiently to repel an attack by two divisions largely because the Ottoman Army did not believe that the EEF had the logistical capability to move larger numbers of men around the desert flank. This estimation played into the hands of the haversack ruse. Much of the criticism levelled at von Kress dealt with his perceived tardiness in shifting reserves towards Beersheba to support İsmet's III Corps. In truth, his positioning of the 7th, 19th and 24th Infantry Divisions in reserve positions nearer Gaza than Beersheba, based on the Meinertzhagen ruse, made this impossible in real time. Moreover, the ongoing reorganization of Ottoman command architecture in Palestine certainly hindered his ability to control the battle as well. Brigadier Şükrü Mahmut (later Şükrü Nedim), a retired Iraqi brigadier general who had served in the Ottoman Army, writing in 1965, criticized the new Ottoman command architecture that went into effect prior to the battle.[55] Nedim maintained that the Seventh Army's assumption of tactical control of the Beersheba sector four days prior to a major engagement was a noteworthy error that negatively affected proper control of the battle and he concluded that the 'role of the commander' was undermined in the confusion of the battle.[56]

Nedim's assessment is not entirely correct, von Falkenhayn gave Fevzi's Seventh Army control of Beersheba and the eastern half of the Palestine Front on 28 October. However, on the same day, von Falkenhayn issued supplementary orders providing guidance as to what should occur if the British attacked before the command architecture was in place.[57] In these orders he noted that because of British movements over the last several days, the tactical situation was possibly dangerous. As such, he noted that 'until the new command arrangements are functional, von Kress would command all units on the Sinai Front'.[58] Moreover, von Falkenhayn gave von Kress authority to employ the army group reserves – the 19th Infantry Division and the 74th Heavy Artillery Battalion. While this made sense operationally, it left von Kress in his headquarters at El Huleykat, north east of Gaza and over 40km away from Beersheba. It also left Fevzi and his Seventh Army staff in an uncertain operational position.

It is unclear today exactly which Ottoman headquarters had contact with one another during the day of 31 October 1917. Brigadier General Fevzi was cut off from news from Beersheba at about noon when the telegraph line was cut. Fevzi immediately sent his own Seventh Army chief of staff to Tel es Sheria, headquarters of the 16th Infantry Division, to find out information.[59] In the meantime, Fevzi ordered the nearby 12th Depot Regiment to prepare for combat and he sent fifty armed soldiers from his headquarters to assist the conscripts. Having heard no news from the Eighth Army, at 3.30 pm Fevzi ordered the 12th Depot Regiment to form four improvised combat groups to man positions astride the Beersheba road along the Ebuhof line.[60]

It is clear, however, that at some point in mid-afternoon, von Kress lost communications and operational control of the battle. This is evidenced by the fact that he sent out Colonel Hergote by automobile to find out the situation in Beersheba.[61] He gave Hergote instructions to establish a new defensive line from Tel es Sheria–Ebuhof–Eddahariye if Beersheba had fallen. Hergote made his way to the headquarters of Esat's 3rd Cavalry Division near the Jerusalem road, where he found that Esat's cavalrymen were already entrenching near Ebuhof, the defeated but resilient 27th Infantry Division regrouping to the west of Tel es Sheria, and the conscripts of the 12th Depot Regiment blocking the Jerusalem road near Eddahariye.[62]

Later that night, Fevzi received orders from the Yildirim Army Group that clarified his mission. At 11.30 pm, Fevzi's Seventh Army reassumed control of his original operational area, including all combat units, support units and line of communications troops north of Beersheba.[63] The latter was quite important because the 12th Depot Regiment was now in the line, but remained technically out of Fevzi's control. Fevzi wasted no time in issuing his own orders early on 1 November 1917, which formally directed his units to establish a defensive line.[64] He also moved his headquarters forward to El Halil.

Colonel İsmet actually performed quite well. It is clear today that his reports and requests for assistance to both the Seventh and Eighth Armies never reached their intended destinations, leaving him isolated. Without waiting for direction or instructions, early in the day, he ordered his major corps reserve, the 3rd Cavalry Division, north east to block the Australians on the Jerusalem road. During the battle, İsmet was alerted to the fact that British cavalry had captured the key mound of Telüssebi (Tell es Sabe). Consequently, at 4.00 pm, in spite of his orders to defend the town, İsmet ordered the retreat of his surviving formations from Beersheba.[65] These were important tactical decisions because they ensured the survival of the Ottoman III Corps.

İsmet's total losses, although severe, were limited to about 500 men killed, 2,000 men missing (1,947 were reported as captured by the British) and 13 cannon captured.[66] Importantly, the 3rd Cavalry Division, the only Ottoman cavalry division in Palestine, survived the battle. The 27th Infantry Division, although badly battered as a fighting force, survived the debacle as well.[67] The most important loss to the Yildirim Army Group was loss of the eastern bastion anchored at Beersheba, which doomed the Ottoman position on the Gaza line.

Third Gaza

The Battle of Third Gaza, fought by Bulfin's British XXI Corps, was never intended to be anything more than a way to pin significant Ottoman forces in Gaza while the town was enveloped from the east. Neither Allenby's nor Bulfin's plan envisioned the seizure of anything more than the first line of Ottoman trenches.[68] For this Bulfin's corps employed new infantry tactics, tanks and a new Western Front style artillery organization. Moreover, Allenby authorized a lavish expenditure of hundreds of thousands of shells, including about 10,000 poison gas shells, over the 12-day period of the battle. The shelling began on 27 October and the ground attack on 2 November. But, after three days of fighting, XXI Corps was only able to take portions of the first line of Ottoman trenches, in two locations, but not much more. The British and Turkish official histories are in general agreement on the forces involved with about 11,000 British riflemen with 148 cannon attacking 4,500 Ottoman riflemen, which swelled to 8,000 as the Ottoman reserves were drawn in, with 116 cannon.[69] The British also had substantial naval gunfire support available as well. In any case, it is clear that the British did not enjoy a particularly large numerical superiority at Gaza.

The experienced and capable Staff Colonel Refet was assigned as the XXII Corps chief of staff on 17 August and was moved up to command the corps itself on 9 October 1917. Refet was an experienced general staff officer and had served in Palestine since December 1916 as an infantry division commander. Refet deployed his 53rd Infantry Division as the Right Wing Group. He assigned his 3rd Infantry Division with a dual mission as the Centre Group and the Left Wing Group. In order to do this, Refet detached the 161st Infantry Regiment from the 53rd Infantry Division and assigned it to Colonel Hussein Nurettin's 3rd Infantry Division. Nurettin assigned it and his own 138th Infantry Regiment in the centre sector, and his 31st and 32nd Infantry Regiments in the left sector. Altogether the XXII Corps's two front-line divisions defended a 10km front south of Gaza, while the 7th Infantry Division lay in reserve. Night attacks by British infantry began at 22.45 pm on 1 November, although Refet's front lines had been pounded by artillery and naval gunfire for the previous five days. The main assault, by three British infantry divisions, began at 11.00 am the next day.

The British penetrated in several places but immediate counter-attacks threw them back. Casualties among Refet's defenders were relatively light but Allenby's newly formed counter-battery artillery groups inflicted heavier than usual casualties on the XXII Corps gunners.[70] The attacks died away by early afternoon. On 3 November, a second series of British attacks began at 3.00 am, supported by tanks, but strong Ottoman counter-attacks in mid-morning drove these back as well. These attacks drew in the Ottoman divisional reserves. After nightfall, von Falkenhayn sent a message to Enver that all attacks on Gaza had been repulsed. Another attack followed on 4 November and at the end of the day, the British held several strongpoints.

The Gaza battle favoured the defenders and, by 5 November 1917, they still maintained a solid defensive line, although they had lost some portions of their forward trench system and some strongpoints. According to the defending Ottoman XXII Corps commander, Staff Colonel Refet, the integrity of the Gaza fortress remained intact.[71] However, local success was largely irrelevant when the Yildirim Army Group Operations Directorate notified Refet on 4 November 1917 that the British XX Corps and the Desert Mounted Corps were flanking Gaza from Tel es Sheria. They warned Refet that the XXII Corps should expect orders to retreat. Staff Colonel Refet notified his divisional commanders that day to prepare evacuation plans. To use a modern concept, the loss of Beersheba caused a 'cascade failure' of the Ottoman operational posture in southern Palestine. Although Fevzi and İsmet continued to conduct a fighting withdrawal north from Beersheba, they could never concentrate enough combat power to stop Allenby's enveloping right wing. This forced Staff Colonel Refet to order a night evacuation of Gaza on 6/7 November and the British occupied the abandoned town the next day.[72]

The Turkish official history noted that Gaza never fell to a direct assault but was deliberately evacuated. The official history did not mention any real improvement in British infantry tactics, but it did highlight the effectiveness of the 'Counter-battery Group' (Allenby's Heavy Artillery Groups) and also noted that Ottoman artillery batteries had about 300 shells on hand while the British artillery batteries had about 15,000 shells on hand.[73] Turkish and Ottoman sources do not mention the effectiveness of, nor casualties from Allenby's gas attacks, but Yigal Sheffy, an Israeli military historian, pointed out in 2009 that post-battle British reports indicated that 50 men were killed by gas attacks and another 150 men were incapacitated from British gas in 9 of Refet's infantry battalions and 1 artillery battery.[74]

Writing about Beersheba, Lieutenant Colonel Archibald Wavell noted that although 'the Ottomans were taken completely by surprise, Ottoman guns shot well but infantry did not appear to have put up at stiff fight'.[75] However, writing of Gaza, Wavell commented that although 'Ottoman losses were heavy, stubborn fighting continued' and he also observed that the British advance after the battle was hindered by 'strong rear guards that offered considerable opposition'. At about the same time, Allenby sent London a cable noting that 'the Ottomans are known to be "shaken" because of constant hammering'.[76]

Von Falkenhayn realized that the Yildirim Army Group would be destroyed if it attempted to retrieve the tactical situation which was already lost. Instead, he ordered the Eighth and the Seventh Armies to conduct a fighting withdrawal to a new defensive line about 10km to their rear. It was a dangerous manoeuvre under any circumstances. Very skilfully, von Kress and Fevzi began to disengage their forces, leaving small rear guards when necessary. Many Ottomans died holding the line while larger forces withdrew and much of the movement was done at night. In these extreme circumstances, large numbers of Ottoman soldiers were taken prisoner.[77] The Ottoman 3rd Cavalry Division screened the left flank of the Seventh Army's withdrawal. The British main effort was now clearly identified in the centre and along the coast, and the Eighth Army had great difficulty maintaining control and cohesion in the face of the massive British pursuit. By 9 November, the Seventh and Eighth Armies had fallen back 15km, the headquarters of the Yildirim Army Group retired to Jerusalem and the Seventh and Eighth Army's headquarters retired to Bethlehem and Ramle, respectively.

The Jerusalem Campaign
Allenby relentlessly continued his attack driving the Ottoman divisions north and the British attacks along the coast were very successful. Von Falkenhayn reacted to the defeat by trying to reform the line and create operational reserves. On 7 November, he detached the 53rd Infantry Division from von Kress and withdrew it to the centre of the army group north west of Cemame. However, the battered armies could not hold and continued to retreat. The following day went much the same and von Falkenhayn had to put the 53rd Infantry Division back into the line. Numbers of small battles enabled the Ottomans to wage a fighting withdrawal. On 11 November, von Falkenhayn decided to counter-attack in an attempt to regain the initiative.

Yildirim Army Group orders reached the Seventh Army in the early hours of 11 November and tasked Staff Colonel Ali Fuat's XX Corps to conduct a hasty attack with the 16th, 26th and 53rd Infantry Divisions.[78] Ali Fuat (later Cebesoy) was an experienced general staff officer, who had commanded an infantry division at Gallipoli and in Caucasia. His divisions would attack the open left flank of Allenby's army between Musa Halıl and Zuhuriye (stations on the railway). The 19th Infantry Division and 3rd Cavalry Division were tasked to support the left of the main attack. This massing of strength in the centre left the XXII Corps with only two infantry divisions to hold back the relentless British offensive along the coast. Coordination was almost impossible as Fevzi and Ali Fuat attempted to organize the attack. In spite of this, the divisions marched to their assembly areas and prepared for the assault. For the Yildirim Army Group, the counter-attack was an all or nothing endeavour – if it failed to slow Allenby's advance, there was almost no recovery. Unfortunately for the Ottomans, their infantry divisions were tired and very understrength. The 26th and 53rd Infantry Divisions together, for example, only managed to put 198 officers, 3,823 soldiers and 54 machine guns into the fight.[79]

The assault began at 11.00 am on 12 November. According to the British official history, the Ottoman attack involved some 5,000 men and was 'well-supported by artillery'.[80] In some places the Ottomans pushed the British back 5km and, in some ways, the attack was very successful. At about 6.00 pm, as darkness fell, Ali Fuat halted his advancing divisions and prepared to renew the attack on the following morning. Meanwhile, simultaneously along the coast, heavy British attacks broke the resistance of the XXII Corps' 3rd and 7th Infantry Divisions manning the Su Kerir River line. Von Kress's Eighth Army had been stripped of divisions for von Falkenhayn's counter-attack and was unable to render any assistance to the XXII Corps. Refet's XXII Corps was pushed back about 10km to the Rubin River before the headlong retreat could be halted. In order to salvage the situation, von Falkenhayn decided to halt Ali Fuat's attack. He withdrew the 16th Infantry Division and its headquarters, and two battalions of the 57th Infantry Regiment from Fevzi and assigned them directly to Colonel Hergote, who organized an ad hoc combat group.[81] He sent Hergote's group to reinforce the Eighth Army and officially called off the Seventh Army's counter-offensive.

Allenby now launched an attack aimed at the capture of Junction Station (Sarar İstasyonu) a railway intersection connecting the Jerusalem railway line with the Beersheba–Affule railway line. He began by pushing the battered Eighth Army north toward Remle but wheeling east at El Maghar on 13 November.[82] Fearing encirclement, Fevzi was forced to withdraw once again. In turn, the Ottoman retreat left the XX Corps's right flank exposed, compelling Ali Fuat to pull the 53rd and 26th Infantry Divisions to a north–south line 10km west of Jerusalem. Esat's 3rd Cavalry Division maintained a screen between the left of XX Corps and the III Corps units south of Jerusalem. Junction Station, an Ottoman logistical node with large food stores, repair shops, engines and rolling stock, fell to Allenby in the early dawn hours of 14 November 1917. In addition, the Ottomans lost some 1,800 men, 3 artillery pieces and 17 machine guns.[83] That evening, Enver Pasha arrived in Jerusalem from Damascus by automobile for discussions with von Falkenhayn about the deteriorating situation in Palestine.

After three years of war, Enver was inclined to listen to the opinions of his local commanders and he approved as von Falkenhayn sketched out a new operational concept for the defence of Palestine.[84] Von

Falkenhayn planned to withdraw the Ali Fuat's XX Corps into a fortified perimeter around Jerusalem and move İsmet's III Corps north of the city, thus putting the Seventh Army into a defensive posture. At the same time, he planned to reinforce the Eighth Army and conduct a counter-offensive to relieve enemy pressure on Jerusalem. On 17 November von Falkenhayn moved the Yildirim headquarters and the Seventh Army headquarters north to Nablus. The Eighth Army headquarters moved to Tul Karm to rendezvous with the incoming 20th Infantry Division and the first units of the German Asia Corps, which were coming down from Aleppo. At the same time, von Falkenhayn detached the 19th Infantry Division and the 158th Infantry Regiment from the Seventh Army and moved them by train to a position between Nablus and Tul Karm. These moves created a powerful reserve in the Eighth Army area and left Ali Fuat with the 26th and 53rd Infantry Divisions to hold Jerusalem. The Seventh Army commander reminded Ali Fuat that he was expected to hold Jerusalem as Janina (the city of Yanya in Turkish, which was a fortress in what is now northern Greece) had been held in the Balkan Wars.[85] However, von Falkenhayn quickly pointed out that, unlike Janina, Jerusalem was almost entirely unfortified and he ordered the immediate fortification of the city.

Maintaining his cavalry as a screen, Ali Fuat pulled his scattered infantry formations tighter around Jerusalem and on 19 November, British yeomanry and infantry closed on the 53rd Infantry Division's positions near Beyti Issa and Beyti Sürik. İsmet's 3rd Cavalry Division, reinforced by the 58th Infantry Regiment, squeezed past the enemy and through Jerusalem on the same day to reposition near El Bire, 5km north of the city. From there, İsmet's 24th Infantry Division filled in the line around El Jib while his cavalry screened the gap to the Eighth Army. İsmet's 27th Infantry Division, which remained south of Jerusalem, was detached and assigned to Ali Fuat's XX Corps. Von Kress continued to fight a delaying action along the coast, withdrawing to a line 8km north of the Avca River which depleted his front-line strength. Von Falkenhayn designated the 20th Infantry Division as the army group reserve and also ordered the 15th Assault Battalion and the 50th Assault Company to concentrate in reserve at Mesudiye (10km west of Tul Karm).[86] On 20 November, von Falkenhayn designed the 19th Infantry Division as an army group reserve and ordered it to Tul Karm, while reinforcing the concentration at Mesudiye with the 7th Assault Battalion, the 2nd Battalion, 158th Infantry and the III Corps Engineer Company. The 50th Infantry Division Assault Company arrived in Nablus on 21 November. After assembling these reserves, von Falkenhayn ordered both armies to conduct local counter-attacks as well as ordering the 19th Infantry Division south to Kalkiliya for operations.

On 22 November 1917, the Seventh Army launched a counter-attack at Nabi Samweil, which was held by Allenby's 75th Infantry Division. The main attack by the 72nd Infantry Regiment supported by the 1st Battalion, 27th Artillery Regiment (from the 19th Infantry Division) began at 3.00 am in the southern part of the XX Corps sector. It was supported to the north by the 24th Infantry Division and the 3rd Cavalry Division. By 3.00 pm the Ottomans had seized Nabi Samweil and inflicted heavy casualties on the enemy.[87] Fierce fighting continued along the Nabi Samweil Ridge as the British attempted to seize El Jip. The 72nd Infantry Regiment counter-attacked with the bayonet and the 24th Infantry Division sent two infantry battalions to assist in the battle. The British also reinforced their efforts with the 52nd Infantry Division. These battles raged into 24 November with neither side willing to give in and the bitter fighting caused heavy casualties for both armies with inconclusive results.

The Eighth Army launched a corresponding counter-attack on 25 November in the XXII Corps sector using the 3rd and 7th Infantry Divisions. These divisions punched their way south and recovered several kilometres of ground that included some tactically valuable hills. Casualties were light in both divisions.

On 25 November, von Falkanhayn decided to attempt a another counter-offensive in order to relieve the pressure on Jerusalem and he committed the army group reserves that had been accumulated for the new operation. In concept, the Eighth Army became the main effort in a general counter-offensive along almost the entire front and the 19th and 20th Infantry Divisions were assigned to it for the operation. However, these divisions were not kept together to achieve concentration and, inexplicably, were sent in different directions. On 26 November, the 20th Infantry Division moved south to assembly areas east of the railway station at Wilhelma and went into the line north of the 16th Infantry Division. These units were to attack through Wilhelma towards Jaffa. The 19th Infantry Division moved south east to the far left flank of the Eighth Army and occupied the front between the 54th Infantry Division and the III Corps's right flank 3rd Cavalry Division. Von Falkenhayn was also concerned about the ability of the Seventh Army to hold Jerusalem and he reinforced the city from Maan with the 1st Battalion, 150th Infantry Regiment, the 7th Cavalry Regiment and the 48th Division's Assault Company.[88] The reasons for this wide dispersion of combat strength are not explained in the modern Turkish official history.

The Ottoman units conducted assembly and coordination on 27 November and there was particular attention to mutual support along the seam between the armies. The 19th Infantry Division commander, Lieutenant Colonel Sedat, coordinated operations with Colonel Esat, the 3rd Cavalry Division commander. Each division took half of the opposing British 52nd Infantry Division's sector, with the objective of punching through to Ramle (on the railway) and Latron. The counter-offensive began at 2.30 am on 28 November with the 20th Infantry Division achieving progress at Wilhelma and the 19th Infantry Division pushing through to Şilta and Bürc. Combat seesawed in all sectors and, at midnight, an optimistic von Falkenhayn ordered the attacks to continue the following day. However, the attacking divisions gradually lost strength as the day progressed and there were no more reserves available to renew the attacks. By the end of the day, von Falkenhayn's counter-offensive had collapsed. On 30 November, vigorous British counter-attacks had recovered most of the lost ground and, in the 24th Infantry Division's sector, Colonel İsmet was forced to commit the 50th Division's Assault Company to hold Hill 528, near Beytiur.[89]

How much of the failure was the responsibility of the two army commanders is problematic, given that von Falkenhayn was unable to concentrate his reserves. It is difficult to understand why the Yildirim Army Group failed to mass two first-class experienced infantry divisions and its assault battalions, all of which were in general reserve, for a single decisive blow. Hüseyin Hüsnü asserted that von Falkenhayn's objective was simply to relieve pressure on Jerusalem while reinforcements arrived from the Third Army in Caucasia.[90] In any case, for reasons that are unclear today, von Falkenhayn and Enver Pasha came to an understanding to relieve von Kress from command of the Eighth Army. At 10.30 am on 1 December 1917, von Kress met Brigadier General Cevat at Tul Karm and handed over command of the Eighth Army. Von Kress, who had been in the Palestine theatre since September 1914, was ordered to return to Germany. The new commander, 44-year-old Cevat (later Cevat Çobanlı) was a very experienced and able general staff officer (first in his War College class of 1894), who had successfully commanded the Dardanelles coastal defence fortresses on 18 March 1915 and later the XV Corps in Galicia.[91]

During the next week, the British shifted their main effort towards

Zeki Bey and his staff, 1914.

Cemal Pasha at his field headquarters.

Enver Pasha and Cemal Pasha leaving Fourth Army HQ.

'Little Cemal' Pasha in Jerusalem.

Fahrettin Pasha inspecting troops in Medina, 1917.

Fahrettin Pasha inspecting a fortified position.

Friedrich Kress von Kressenstein.

Erich von Falkenhayn inspecting Ottoman soldiers.

Sureya Bay, Ottoman Camel Corps commander.

Colonel Esat with 3rd Cavalry Division staff.

Otto Liman von Sanders.

Mustafa Kemal Atatürk.

VIII Army Corps encampment.

An infantry column departing for the Suez Front, late 1914.

An infantry column, early in the war.

A hastily prepared infantry defensive position.

Entrenched infantry.

A machine-gun section.

Field artillery with a range finder.

Mountain artillery.

6th Cavalry Regiment.

Infantry and cavalry awaiting attack at Beersheba.

Von Kress inspecting Ottoman assault troops.

German aircraft at Huj.

German Albatross DV fighters at Huj.

German Captain Felmy in his aircraft at Huj.

A labour battalion road building and laying pipe.

A railway dump, Jerusalem, 1917.

Kuseimih Watering Point.

El Arish Watering Station.

the capture of Jerusalem as Allenby massed above the city at the tactical seam between Fevzi's III and XX Corps. On 4/5 December von Falkenhayn pulled the 19th Infantry Division out of the line to reconstitute his general reserve. The next day, the 2nd Battalion, 72nd Infantry Regiment and an assault company were placed in army reserve, while the Seventh Army launched several spoiling attacks in the III Corps sector on 7 December. Reports from the front indicating that Allenby was massing divisions west of Jerusalem poured into Ottoman Army and army group headquarters. Anticipating the British offensive, von Falkenhayn ordered the incoming German 701st Battalion (from the Bavarian 10th Infantry Regiment at Ingolstadt and commanded by Major Staubwasser) and the Ottoman 61st Infantry Regiment to El Bire.[92] He warned Fevzi to expect an attack well before 12 December.[93]

Allenby's much anticipated offensive to seize Jerusalem began on 7 December with his 60th and 74th Infantry Divisions battering the Ottoman XX Corps's lines. Fevzi dispatched one battalion of the 72nd Infantry Regiment and the 15th Assault Battalion to reinforce the 53rd Infantry Division.[94] He also dispatched the 48th Assault Company to reinforce the 26th Infantry Division and he sent the 7th Cavalry Regiment into the line. Thus, late that afternoon, when Allenby launched supporting attacks with his 53rd Infantry Division against the XX Corps's 27th Infantry Division south of the city, Fevzi's Seventh Army had no reserves remaining. At 5.00 pm von Falkenhayn telephoned Fevzi asking about the situation in Ali Fuat's XX Corps.[95] Fevzi told him that Allenby was poised to launch a pursuit and that he needed to order Ali Fuat to withdraw immediately. Fevzi noted that not to do so would result in the loss of the XX Corps' artillery, transport and logistics units. Meanwhile, the XX Corps staff re-established a thin defensive line as night fell and, over the next few hours, Fevzi issued a string of orders that would withdraw the XX Corps behind Jerusalem.

Over the course of 8 December, Ali Fuat's XX Corps pulled its rear elements out of the city to the east and fought a delaying rear guard action as its fighting regiments withdrew. Hundreds of Ottoman soldiers were captured in the retreat as well as a few howitzers, but most of the XX Corps withdrew intact as night fell. Early on the morning of 9 December, Jerusalem fell to units of Allenby's 60th Infantry Division. Allenby himself famously entered the city two days later via the Jaffa Gate. The capture of Jerusalem did not stop Allenby's army, however, which continued to push east of the city over the course of the day.

The abandonment of Jerusalem by the Seventh Army was a foregone conclusion because Ali Fuat's XX Corps had so few soldiers with which to defend the city. In October 1917, the actual strength of the 26th, 27th and 53rd Infantry Divisions averaged about 300 officers, 6,000 soldiers, 30 artillery pieces and 50–60 machine guns per division.[96] However, continuous combat so eroded the strength of the Seventh Army that, by early December, Fevzi's total army strength was 18,350 men and 74 artillery pieces.[97] Reinforcements somewhat balanced losses, but it is doubtful if the XX Corps deployed more than 6–8,000 men and 40 artillery pieces for the defence of the 16km defensive line west of Jerusalem. In any case, the city had no tactical or operational worth, although it certainly had prestige value as a religious and political symbol.

The Ending of the Jerusalem Campaign

Long-awaited inter-theatre reinforcements for von Falkenhayn's army group began to arrive with the 1st Infantry Division headquarters and 70th Infantry Regiment at Nablus and the German 701st Infantry Battalion and Ottoman 43rd Mountain Howitzer Battalion at Mesudiye on 12 December. The remainder of the 1st Infantry Division arrived over the next week and, with the Germans, remained in reserve training for offensive operations. The 2nd Caucasian Cavalry Division (composed of the 1st, 9th and 11th Cavalry Regiments) arrived in Palestine on 15 December and went into reserve positions in the Eighth Army sector. It was so under-strength that it was re-named the 2nd Caucasian Brigade, as it comprised only 112 officers, 1,562 men, 6 machine guns and 4 field artillery pieces. This reinforcement gave the Eighth Army a total of some 1,232 officers, 24,811 men, 203 machine guns and 80 artillery pieces.[98] In the Seventh Army sector, the 3rd Cavalry Division was also pulled out of the line and put into reserve behind the 54th Infantry Division on 16 December.

In the meantime, between 13 and 17 December, Allenby's XXI Corps pushed steadily north from Jaffa while his XX Corps pushed north of Jerusalem. Both Jerusalem and Jaffa remained well within the range of Ottoman artillery and Allenby was determined to push his front lines forward to prevent bombardments, especially in the hinterlands above Jaffa, which was projected to become an important logistical port. Allenby's plans thus led to overlapping offensives by both combatants.

Von Falkenhayn was relentless in his insistence on counter-attacks and on 15 December 1917, he ordered the Seventh Army to prepare an offensive operation designed to push back to Jerusalem. His plan envisioned İsmet's III Corps forming three combat groups composed of the 24th Infantry Division, the 19th Infantry Division reinforced with an assault battalion and the 701st Battalion, and the 53rd Infantry Division (a XX Corps division). The fresh 1st Infantry Division made up the reserve.[99] These forces were to be prepared to attack on 24 December in a multi-corps effort. Fevzi Pasha then asked the XX Corps commander on 19 December for an opinion about the proposed attack, to which Ali Fuat noted that the III Corps had but 8,300 tired men available for the attack, which would take on 2 relatively fresh British infantry divisions on a 9km front.[100]

Allenby's XXI Corps launched a major attack north of Jaffa on 20 December into the lines of Colonel Refet's 3rd and 7th Infantry Divisions. The attack crossed the Avca River and the innovative use of assault bridges by the British was instrumental in achieving success. The Turks call this the Avca Battle, which lasted to 22 December. The weakened Ottoman infantry divisions initially held their positions on a series of hills but soon were forced to withdraw. Prompt action by Cevat threw the fresh regiments of the 2nd Cavalry Brigade, each reinforced by a machine-gun company, into counter-attacks which prevented a British breakthrough. Nevertheless, the battle resulted in the British pushing about 10km north, thus ending the indirect fire threat to Jaffa. In the Seventh Army sector, Allenby's XX Corps pushed north against the 19th Infantry Division on 21 December. While this was occurring, the Ottoman infantry divisions designated to make the attack were making final preparations. Battalions from the 1st Infantry Division rotated into the front line. The shortage of men reached crisis proportions in Ali Fuat's XX Corps and he was ordered on 21 December to inactivate the understrength and weak 27th Infantry Division. The battalions of the surviving 81st Infantry Regiment were transferred to the 19th and 26th Infantry Divisions.

The ongoing struggle north of Jaffa and British attacks on the 19th Infantry Division caused von Falkenhayn to delay his offensive until the morning of 27 December. In the meantime, winter rains turned the attack sectors into a sea of mud.[101] Nevertheless, the Seventh Army began its offensive at 1.10 am, 27 December 1917 with a machine-gun and hand-grenade assault supported by field artillery. Unknown to the Seventh Army, Allenby, who had been alerted to the impending attack by Ottoman and German prisoners, lay in wait. The Ottoman infantry failed to gain any footholds in the British lines while Allenby ordered five British divisions to counter-attack. Allenby's attacking XX Corps smashed into the enemy divisions the next day in a meeting engagement that crushed the Ottoman offensive and sent the erstwhile attackers reeling northwards. By midday on 29 December, the Seventh Army's entire front had been pushed back about 10km. Von Falkenhayn's offensive was an absolute disaster. Moreover, a dangerous gap developed between the Eighth and the Seventh Armies, which was hastily filled by the 3rd Cavalry Division screening and maintaining contact between the two armies.

The New Year found von Falkenhayn's army group battered, but holding a line anchored in the east on the Dead Sea and in the west on the Mediterranean Sea. Strategically and operationally, the Gaza and the Jerusalem campaigns were a significant defeat for the Ottoman Army. However, it must be noted that every Ottoman infantry division, which had begun the fight on 31 October on the Gaza–Beersheba line, was intact and still fighting (with the exception of the inactivated 27th Infantry Division). Behind the Dead Sea and the Jordan River, the Ottomans still held the railway from Dera to Medina, although this line was constantly being harassed and cut by insurgent Arab bands.

To the north, there were changes in the Syria and Western Arabia General Command, located in its Damascus headquarters, when on 27 December 1917, Cemal Pasha abruptly departed for Constantinople. Over the preceding five-month period, Cemal had resisted directives to support von Falkenhayn and he had repeatedly requested permission to return to the capital. According to the official history, Cemal departed 'under a black cloud' and he never returned to Palestine.[102] Von Falkenhayn ordered Ali Fuat to Damascus to take command temporarily until he and Enver could resolve a new command arrangement.

As 1917 came to an end, so too did Allenby's offensive. Exhausted and living on lean logistical support, his army ceased offensive operations. The battered Ottomans earned yet another respite. Casualties had been severe during the period from 31 October to 31 December 1917 for both Yildirim armies. The Seventh Army lost a grand total of 110 officers and 1,886 men killed, 213 officers and 5,488 men wounded, 79 officers and 393 men captured, and 183 officers and 4,233 men missing. Also lost were 1,762 animals, 7,305 rifles, 22 light and 73 heavy machine guns, and 29 artillery pieces. The Eighth Army was harder hit by the British and reported 70 officers and 1,474 men killed, 118 officers and 3,163 men wounded, 95 officers and 5,868 men captured, and 97 officers and 4,877 men missing. The army also reported 700 animals lost and 2,384 wounded.[103] The total casualties for the Yildirim Army Group were 25,337 men killed, wounded, captured or missing. In turn,

Allenby lost about 18,000 men, but these were replaceable whereas the Ottoman losses were not. In the eloquent words of British historian Cyril Falls, 'considering that he [Allenby] had odds of well over two to one in infantry and eight to one in cavalry, his achievement may not seem so remarkable. In fact, it was hard and costly to turn Ottoman troops out of defensive positions in this hilly, rocky, country.'[104] Falls's tribute does not include the massive artillery superiority that Allenby enjoyed, or the huge logistical support that he amassed, nor does it attribute any advantage to the Royal Navy. Considering all of these factors in combination, it is remarkable that, after the fall of Beersheba and Gaza, von Falkenhayn managed to hold on to Jerusalem and the coastal plan for as long as he did.

The statistics concerning the number of men who were reported missing and prisoners also revealed a new and serious problem. In other battles against the British at Gallipoli, in Mesopotamia, and in Palestine, the percentages of Ottoman soldiers reported as prisoner and missing were quite low.[105] But by late 1917, desertion from the army was a significant problem and the higher rates of prisoners may reflect incidents of willful surrender. Moreover, the relative percentage of Ottoman enlisted soldiers who were reported as missing or prisoner is higher than the percentage of Ottoman officers reported in these same categories. Arab soldiers (as well as Greeks, Kurds, Jews and Armenians) serving in the Ottoman Army do not appear to have surrendered in disproportionate numbers, as might have been expected. A British intelligence report tallying the 7,233 Ottoman prisoners and deserters captured between 31 October and 24 November 1917 reported the demographics of the men.[106] The British noted that 64 per cent of the prisoners were Turks, 27 per cent were Arabs and 9 per cent were Greeks, Armenians and Jews. Comparable statistics contained in Hüseyin Hüsnü Emir's 9 September 1917 report on the ethnic composition of infantry divisions were 66 per cent Turkish, 26 per cent Arab and 8 per cent of the other races.[107] It appears that the British captured enemy soldiers in numbers almost directly reflecting the ethnic composition of the Ottoman Army in Palestine.

In any case, to an army that suffered from acute shortages of trained manpower, the loss of 25,000 combat arms soldiers was a significant blow that far exceeded the loss of territory and political prestige resulting from the fall of Gaza and Jerusalem. Making matters worse, replacements within the immediate combat theatre were never sufficient and the movement of men from other parts of the empire was a process that took months. For example, on 27 December, a draft of 2,450 conscripts arrived and the army group assigned 844 and 1,566 to the 1st and 24th Infantry Divisions, respectively. But in neither division did the number of replacements balance the number of losses.

Conclusion

This period in the First World War in Palestine was characterized by tactical and operational manoeuvre that had not been seen previously in that theatre. Mistakes were made by both sides but, on balance, Allenby proved a master of the operational environment. At the operational level, he was able to advance on multiple axes of attack, which forced von Falkenhayn into a posture of fragmenting his forces in a reactive manner. It is difficult to criticize Allenby's plans and operations in the late fall of 1917. Reciprocally, von Falkenhayn continually planned counter-attacks and counter-offensives that were severely under-resourced. Often, when offered the opportunity to concentrate his scarce reserves, von Falkenhayn did not and chose instead dispersion. In such a situation, von Falkenhayn might have been better served by deliberate economy of force operations that would have enabled him to pull back and concentrate elsewhere. In this way he might have been able to employ the small number of high-quality forces he had at his disposal, notably the assault battalions and companies as well as the first-class 19th and 20th Infantry Divisions, in a more effective fashion.

Notes

1. See Erickson, *Ordered To Die*, pp. 166–72 for a comprehensive treatment of the strategy and formation of the Yildirim Army Group.
2. Lüfti Doğancı, *20nci Piyade Alay Tarihçesi* (*20th Infantry Regiment History*), unpublished staff study, ATASE Library, Record 26-326, pp. 53–7.
3. Ibid., p. 21.
4. Meki Ererthem, *21nci Piyade Alay Tarihçesi* (*21st Infantry Regiment History*), unpublished staff study, ATASE Library, Record 26-361, p. 28.
5. Ibid., p. 21. The tactical reorganization of the Ottoman Army in 1917 mirrored the ongoing tactical reorganization of the German Army.
6. Ibid., p. 21.
7. German, French and British divisions underwent similar reorganizations in 1917.
8. Friedrich Kress von Kressenstein, *Zwischen Kaukasus und Sinai* (Berlin: 1921), p. 268.
9. Ibid.
10. Ahmed Sedad, *Hücum Kıtaatının Talim ve Terbiyesi* (Istanbul: Erkaa-ı Harbiye Matbaası, 1336 (1920)). The author is indebted to Mesut Uyar for bringing this manual to his attention.

11. NARA, Near Eastern Intelligence Report, 27 February 1918, AEF G-2, RG 120, NH 91, Entry 187, Box 5828.

12. Ibid.

13. David Nicolle, *The Ottoman Army 1914–1918* (Oxford: Osprey Press Ltd, 1994), p. 23. The same photo may be seen in Bryan Perrett, *Megiddo 1918, The Last Great Cavalry Victory* (Oxford: Osprey Press, 1999), p. 30. Nicolle credited the photo to the Imperial War Museum (Q80044).

14. Perrett, *Megiddo 1918*, p. 23. The material for the following paragraph comes from this source. The Ottoman Army noted that many of the divisional officers in Palestine were extremely young and were also deficient in the Ottoman language.

15. ATASE, *21nci Piyade Alay Tarihçesi*, 28, Record 26-361.

16. ATASE, *16nci Piyade Tümeni Tarihçesi* (*16th Infantry Division History*), ATASE Library, Record 26-441 (unpublished staff study), pp. 40–5.

17. Hüseyin Hüsnü Emir (Erkilet), *Yildirim* (Ankara: Genelkurmay Basımevi, 2002), reprint of the May 1921 edition, Ek 21 (Document 21), '8th Army Infantry Strength, 15.10.1917'.

18. ATASE, *16nci Piyade Tümeni Tarihçesi*, Record 26-411, p. 49. The inactivation of the 4th Company of Ottoman Army infantry battalions in the summer of 1917 cut 250 men from an authorization of 1,012 men.

19. Ibid., pp. 23–4.

20. Ibid.

21. Ibid.

22. Hughes, *Allenby and British Strategy in the Middle East*, p. 47.

23. Hüsnü, *Yildirim* (Ek-16), p. 346.

24. Erden, *Birinci Dünya Harbinde Suriye Hatiraları*, pp. 315–18, 341–2.

25. Belen, *Birinci Cihan Harbinde Türk Harbi 1917 Yılı Hareketleri*, p. 100.

26. NARA, Report on the Ottoman Army in Syria, 2 May 1917, Special American Agent 'UY2,' M 1271, 8544-29.

27. Onalp et al., *Sina-Filistin Cephesi, İkinci Gazze Muharebesi Sonundan Mütarekesi'ne Kadar Yapılan Harekât*, p. 49.

28. See Edward J. Erickson, *Defeat in Detail, The Ottoman Army in the Balkans 1912–1913* (Westport, CT: Praeger, 2003), pp. 56–7 for a summary of the Ottoman War College's selection criteria and curriculum.

29. Ökse et al., *Komutanların Biyografileri*, pp. 67, 98, 113, 127, 165, 216.

30. Letter from Commander, Seventh Army to Acting Commanding General, Belen, *Birinci Cihan Harbinde Türk Harbi 1917 Yılı Hareketleri*, Document 2 and Moberly, *Mesopotamia*, Vol. IV, Appendix XLII, pp. 348–51. Belen gives the date of this letter as 20 September 1917 and Moberly gives the date as 30 September 1917. It is possible that Belen used the Ottoman date instead of the Western date.

31. Ökse et al., *Komutanların Biyografileri*, pp. 55–8.

32. Ibid., p. 119.

33. ATASE, Summary Yildirim Army Group Orders, Jerusalem, 28 October 1917, Archive 3704, Record H-1, File 1-1, reprinted in Okçu and Üstünsoy, *Sina-Filistin Cephesi, Harbin Başlangıcından İkinci Gazze Muharebeleri Sonuna Kadar*, pp. 119–20.

34. See Sheffy, *British Military Intelligence in the Palestine Campaign*, pp. 272–4, for a vivid explanation of this episode.

35. Hüsnü, *Yildirim*, pp. 102–3. This is also confirmed in the Ottoman official history and in Kress von Kressenstein's memoirs.

36. 'Summary of Contents of the Haversack', reprinted in Onalp et al., *Sina-Filistin*

Cephesi, İkinci Gazze Muharebesi Sonundan Mütarekesi'ne Kadar Yapılan Harekât, p. 120. The Ottoman official history contains the only full description in print of the false operational documents themselves, which were in Meinertzhagen's haversack. A general list of the haversack's contents may be found in Meinertzhagen's memoirs. See R. Meinertzhagen, *Army Diary 1899–1926* (London: Oliver and Boyd, 1960), Appendix A, pp. 283–7.

37. Hüsnü, *Yildirim*, pp. 124–5.

38. Onalp et al., *Sina-Filistin Cephesi, İkinci Gazze Muharebesi Sonundan Mütarekesi'ne Kadar Yapılan Harekât*, pp. 125–7.

39. Eighth Army Report to Yildirim Army Group Headquarters, 17 October 1917, reprinted in Hüsnü, *Yildirim*, pp. 121–2.

40. Ibid.

41. Onalp et al., *Sina-Filistin Cephesi, İkinci Gazze Muharebesi Sonundan Mütarekesi'ne Kadar Yapılan Harekât*, p. 129.

42. ATASE, *19ncü Piyade Tümeni Tarihçesi* (*19th Infantry Division History*), ATASE Library, Record 26-349 (unpublished staff study), p. 27. The Ottoman general staff then regarded the 19th Infantry Division as the most powerful infantry division in the Ottoman Army's order of battle. This stemmed from its service in Galicia and from its unusually powerful artillery component.

43. Onalp et al., *Sina-Filistin Cephesi, İkinci Gazze Muharebesi Sonundan Mütarekesi'ne Kadar Yapılan Harekât*, p. 128.

44. See, for example, Cyril Falls and A. F. Becke, *Military Operations Egypt and Palestine, From June 1917 to the End of the War* (London: HMSO, 1930), Part II, pp. 25–105 and Bruce, *The Last Crusade*, pp. 111–53.

45. Hüsnü, *Yildirim*, p. 113.

46. Onalp et al., *Sina-Filistin Cephesi, İkinci Gazze Muharebesi Sonundan Mütarekesi'ne Kadar Yapılan Harekât*, pp. 140–1.

47. Belen, *Birinci Cihan Harbinde Türk Harbi 1917 Yılı Hareketleri*, p. 132.

48. ATASE, Report on the Loss of Beersheba, To Yildirim Army Group Commander from Von Kress, 17 November 1917, Archive 3712, Record 15, File 1-44, reprinted as Document 2 (Ek 2), Onalp et al., *Sina-Filistin Cephesi, İkinci Gazze Muharebesi Sonundan Mütarekesi'ne Kadar Yapılan Harekât*, pp. 783–4.

49. İsmet İnönü had a distinguished career in the War of Independence and later became President of the Ottoman Republic. He was an artillery officer and graduated from the Ottoman War College in 1906. Prior to Beersheba, he had commanded IV and XX Corps, served as chief of staff of the Ottoman Second Army in Caucasia and served as the Chief of Operations of the Ottoman General Staff. Ökse et al., *Komutanların Biyografileri*, pp. 216–18.

50. ATASE, Report on the Loss of Beersheba from the III Corps Commander, undated, Archive 3712, Record 15, File 1-17, reprinted as Document 3 (Ek 3), Onalp et al., *Sina-Filistin Cephesi, İkinci Gazze Muharebesi Sonundan Mütarekesi'ne Kadar Yapılan Harekât*, pp. 785–816.

51. Hüseyin Hüsnü noted that the Ottoman III Corps staff felt that the town of Beersheba could be held for 36 hours against two British divisions. Hüsnü, *Yildirim*, pp. 124–5.

52. ATASE, After Action Report on the Loss of Beersheba, To Enver Pasha from the Yildirim Army Group Commander, 24 November 1917, Archive 3712, Record 15, File 1, reprinted as Document 4 (Ek 4), Onalp et al., *Sina-Filistin Cephesi, İkinci Gazze Muharebesi Sonundan Mütarekesi'ne Kadar Yapılan Harekât*, pp. 817–18.

53. Belen, *Birinci Cihan Harbinde Türk Harbi 1917 Yılı Hareketleri*, p. 130.

54. Ibid., p. 134.
55. Şükrü Mahmut Nedim, *Filistin Savasi (1914–1918)* (Ankara: Genelkurmay Basımevi, 1995), *passim*.
56. Ibid., pp. 75–6.
57. ATASE, Yildirim Army Group Orders, 28 October 1917, Archive 3704, Record H-1, File 1, reprinted in Onalp et al., *Sina-Filistin Cephesi, İkinci Gazze Muharebesi Sonundan Mütarekesi'ne Kadar Yapılan Harekât*, p. 129.
58. Ibid.
59. Onalp et al., *Sina-Filistin Cephesi, İkinci Gazze Muharebesi Sonundan Mütarekesi'ne Kadar Yapılan Harekât*, p. 148.
60. Ibid., p. 148.
61. Ali Fuat Cebesoy, *Birussebi – Gazze Maydan Muharebei ve Yirmici Kolordu* (Istanbul: Askeri Matbaa, 1938), p. 69.
62. Belen, *Birinci Cihan Harbinde Türk Harbi 1917 Yılı Hareketleri*, pp. 132–3.
63. Ibid., extract of Yildirim Army Orders, 2300 hours, 31 October 1917, quoted on p. 149.
64. ATASE, Seventh Army Orders, 0300, 1 November 1917, Archive 3704, Record H-1, File 1-14 and 1-15, reprinted in Onalp et al., *Sina-Filistin Cephesi, İkinci Gazze Muharebesi Sonundan Mütarekesi'ne Kadar Yapılan Harekât*, p. 149.
65. Belen, *Birinci Cihan Harbinde Türk Harbi 1917 Yılı Hareketleri*, p. 132.
66. Onalp et al., *Sina-Filistin Cephesi, İkinci Gazze Muharebesi Sonundan Mütarekesi'ne Kadar Yapılan Harekât*, p. 140 and Falls and Becke, *Military Operations Egypt and Palestine, From June 1917 to the End of the War*, Part II, pp. 51, 59.
67. Fahri Belen noted that on 2 November 1917, the 27th Infantry Division (near Ebuhof) returned strength reports of 124 officers, 2,176 men, 1,361 rifles, 10 machine guns and 7 cannon. Belen, *Birinci Cihan Harbinde Türk Harbi 1917 Yılı Hareketleri*, p. 134.
68. See Falls and Becke, *Military Operations Egypt and Palestine, From June 1917 to the End of the War*, Part II, Appendices 8 and 11 (operations plans).
69. Ibid., Part I, p. 76 and Onalp et al., *Sina-Filistin Cephesi, İkinci Gazze Muharebesi Sonundan Mütarekesi'ne Kadar Yapılan Harekât*, p. 162. Falls noted that 10,000 British riflemen attacked 4,500 Ottoman riflemen, which swelled to 8,000 as the enemy reserves were drawn in. Likewise, the Ottomans claim that British XXI Corps had 11,000 riflemen and 148 cannon, while the Ottoman XXII Corps had 8,000 riflemen and 116 cannon.
70. Onalp et al., *Sina-Filistin Cephesi, İkinci Gazze Muharebesi Sonundan Mütarekesi'ne Kadar Yapılan Harekât*, p. 169.
71. ATASE, After Action Report, Evacuation of Gaza, XXII Corps to Yildirim Army Group, 18 January 1918, Archive 3712, Record 15, File 3-2, reprinted in Onalp et al., *Sina-Filistin Cephesi, İkinci Gazze Muharebesi Sonundan Mütarekesi'ne Kadar Yapılan Harekât*, p. 177. Colonel Ibrahim Refet (later Bele) was a War College graduate (1909) and served at Gallipoli in command of the 3rd and 23rd Infantry Divisions. Prior to commanding the XXII Corps (17 August 1917), he commanded the 53rd Infantry Division in Palestine. Ökse et al., *Komutanların Biyografileri*, pp. 98–100.
72. ATASE, Combat Orders, XXII Corps, 1700, 6 November 1917, Archive 3712, Record 15, File 1-6, reprinted in Onalp et al., *Sina-Filistin Cephesi, İkinci Gazze Muharebesi Sonundan Mütarekesi'ne Kadar Yapılan Harekât*, p. 175.
73. Onalp et al., *Sina-Filistin Cephesi, İkinci Gazze Muharebesi Sonundan Mütarekesi'ne Kadar Yapılan Harekât*, p. 163.

74. Sheffy, 'Chemical Warfare and the Palestine Campaign, 1916–1918', 20–2.
75. TNA, Notes on Operations on the Palestine Front, Lt. Col. A.P. Wavell, Liaison Officer, 17 November 1917, WO 106/718.
76. TNA, GOCinC Egypt to CIGS (Cipher 45777), 16 November 1917, WO 106/718.
77. Onalp et al., *Sina-Filistin Cephesi, İkinci Gazze Muharebesi Sonundan Mütarekesi'ne Kadar Yapılan Harekât*, p. 222. From 31 October to 7 November, the XX Corps alone lost 932 killed, 4,444 wounded, 2,177 prisoner and 108 missing. In equipment, the corps lost 45 cannon, 7 mortars and 50 machine guns.
78. Ibid., pp. 269–70, 280.
79. Falls and Becke, *Military Operations Egypt and Palestine, From June 1917 to the End of the War*, Part I, pp. 146–8.
80. Ibid., p. 280.
81. Ibid., pp. 148–51.
82. Onalp et al., *Sina-Filistin Cephesi, İkinci Gazze Muharebesi Sonundan Mütarekesi'ne Kadar Yapılan Harekât*, p. 281.
83. See 'The Action of Maghar' in Falls and Becke, *Military Operations Egypt and Palestine, From June 1917 to the End of the War*, Part I, pp. 162–5.
84. Belen, *Birinci Cihan Harbinde Türk Harbi 1917 Yılı Hareketleri*, p. 144.
85. Hüsnü, *Yildirim*, p. 218. Hüsnü makes the point that, in 1914 at Sarıkamış, Enver was undisciplined and insisted on reckless offensives despite the advice of his generals but after three years of war, he had learned restraint.
86. Onalp et al., *Sina-Filistin Cephesi, İkinci Gazze Muharebesi Sonundan Mütarekesi'ne Kadar Yapılan Harekât*, p. 313. Esat Pasha had heroically and successfully held the fortress city of Yanya (Janina, Greece) for seven months during the First Balkan War. Like Plevna, the siege of Yanya was something of a data point in Ottoman military history.
87. Ibid., p. 333.
88. Falls and Becke, *Military Operations Egypt and Palestine, From June 1917 to the End of the War*, Part I, pp. 207–12 and Onalp et al., *Sina-Filistin Cephesi, İkinci Gazze Muharebesi Sonundan Mütarekesi'ne Kadar Yapılan Harekât*, pp. 340–1.
89. Onalp et al., *Sina-Filistin Cephesi, İkinci Gazze Muharebesi Sonundan Mütarekesi'ne Kadar Yapılan Harekât*, pp. 358–65.
90. Hüsnü, *Yildirim*, p. 244.
91. Ibid., p. 254. See also Falls and Becke, *Military Operations Egypt and Palestine, From June 1917 to the End of the War*, Part I, p. 236.
92. Ökse et al., *Komutanların Biyografileri*, pp. 20–1.
93. Obergeneralarzt Dr (first name not listed) Steuber, *'Jildirim' Deutsche Streiter auf heiligem Boden* (Oldenburg/Berlin: Gerhard Sialling, 1926), p. 62.
94. Onalp et al., *Sina-Filistin Cephesi, İkinci Gazze Muharebesi Sonundan Mütarekesi'ne Kadar Yapılan Harekât*, p. 409.
95. The official history does not identify the assault battalion but the author believes it was the 15th Assault Battalion, which was placed in general reserve at Mesudiye earlier.
96. Onalp et al., *Sina-Filistin Cephesi, İkinci Gazze Muharebesi Sonundan Mütarekesi'ne Kadar Yapılan Harekât*, p. 428.
97. Hüsnü, *Yildirim*, Ek (Appendix) 20, 8 Army General Situation Chart, 350-351.
98. Ibid., Ek (Appendix) 25, 7 Army General Situation Chart, 356.
99. Onalp et al., *Sina-Filistin Cephesi, İkinci Gazze Muharebesi Sonundan Mütarekesi'ne Kadar Yapılan Harekât*, pp. 452–3.

100. Yildirim Army Group orders to Seventh Army commander, 15 December 1917, reprinted in Onalp et al., *Sina-Filistin Cephesi, İkinci Gazze Muharebesi Sonundan Mütarekesi'ne Kadar Yapılan Harekât*, pp. 454–5.

101. XX Corps report to Seventh Army commander, 19 December 1917, reprinted in Onalp et al., *Sina-Filistin Cephesi, İkinci Gazze Muharebesi Sonundan Mütarekesi'ne Kadar Yapılan Harekât*, pp. 468–9.

102 Ibid., p. 490.

103. Ibid., pp. 491–2.

104. Cyril Falls, *The Great War* (New York: G. P. Putnam's Sons, 1959), p. 326.

105. In the other campaigns against the British, the percentage of Ottoman soldiers taken prisoner or reported as missing in action averaged less than 1 per cent of the total force. See Erickson, *Ordered To Die*, Appendix F, Table F.1 (Ottoman Battle Casualties), pp. 237–9.

106. NARA, Near Eastern Intelligence Report, 21 January 1918, AEF G-2, American Expeditionary Force Papers, RG 120, NH 91, Entry 187, Box 5828.

107. Hüsnü, *Yildirim*, p. 346.

Chapter 7

1918
Jordan Valley Operations

Introduction

In Palestine, torrential rainstorms in the last week of 1917 and an ever-hardening Ottoman defence brought Allenby's offensive to a halt north of Jerusalem. Entering 1918, the Yildirim Army Group enjoyed a period of relative calm after a series of powerful British offensives. The stabilization of the front by mid-December 1917 was due primarily to the EEF's lack of logistics as it pushed north into Palestine. Unlike its Ottoman adversary, Allenby's army was highly dependent on a rich logistical support base that had difficulty supporting the tempo of the advance. The absence of supplies degraded the effectiveness of the EEF, which allowed the Ottomans to solidify and construct defensive lines that stretched from the coast to the Jordan River and then south into the Judean hill country. Once the Ottomans had re-established their defensive lines, positional warfare reasserted itself in Palestine. (See map 7.1.)

The Capture of Jericho

Von Falkenhayn and his army commanders spent the beginning of 1918 reorganizing their forces. On 11 January 1918, the army group ordered the inactivation of the 3rd Infantry Division, which combat had reduced to a cadre strength of 62 officers, 960 men and 201 animals.[1] The surviving men and equipment were transferred to the 16th Infantry Division, which enabled the division to allocate four machine guns to each infantry battalion and to bring the regimental machine-gun companies up to an authorized strength of six guns each. On 18 January, after communications with von Falkenhayn, Enver Pasha ordered the inactivation of the General Command of Syria and Western Arabia and reassigned the Fourth Army to the Yildirim Army Group. He gave

Map 7.1: Operational situation at the end of 1917

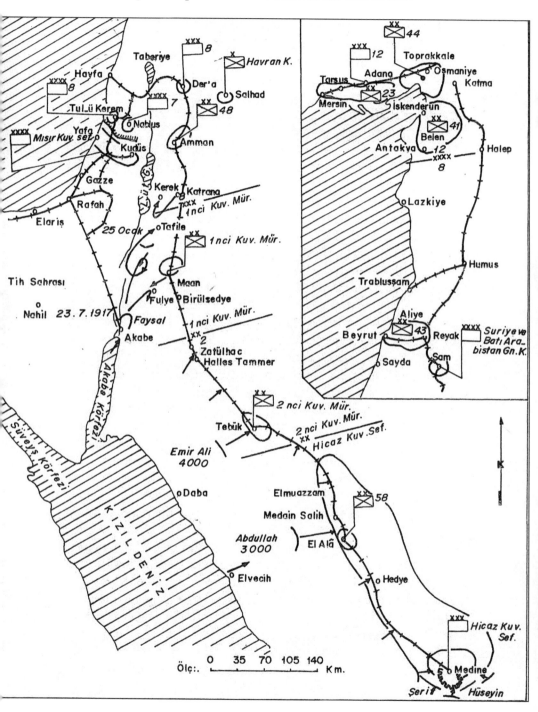

command of the Fourth Army to Brigadier General Cemal Mersinli (also known as 'Little Cemal'), who had been in command of the VIII Corps and in Palestine from the beginning of the war. The scope and mission of the Fourth Army was little changed from the previous general command, and included the VII Corps in Yemen, the Hejaz Expeditionary Force, the 1st and 2nd Provisional Forces, as well as the VIII, XII and XV Corps. Moreover, von Falkenhayn ordered the Fourth Army headquarters to Amman where Little Cemal could control operations more effectively.

Compounding this was a renewal of offensive operations by Faisal's northern Arab armies north of Maan. After capturing the railway station at Jurf al Darawish, Sherif Nasir captured the important farming town of Tafile (Tafila in what is now Jordan) in mid-January 1918. Faisal sent Emir Zeid and T. E. Lawrence to hold the town and recruit volunteers for an advance north. Tafile lay in the 48th Infantry Division's sector (Katrana–Maan) and the division commander, Lieutenant Colonel Hamit Fahri, determined to retake the town.[2] Hamit Fahri led the effort south from Kerak with a force of 600 infantry and an artillery half-battery. He reached a ridgeline overlooking Tafile on 25 January and attacked the Arab lines at midday. Heavy fighting broke out but the Arab line held. Lawrence then led a cavalry envelopment that trapped Hamit's force while Zeid's Arabs conducted a frontal attack. The Ottoman force collapsed, with about 200 men escaping to retreat to Kerak. Hamit Fahri, who had been badly wounded, died the next day. Lawrence reported capturing 200 men, 2 mountain howitzers and 16 machine guns.[3] Lawrence's exploits, well known in the English language narrative, are scarcely mentioned in the Ottoman-Turkish narrative. In fact, the memoirs of an Ottoman artillery officer, who served in Palestine in the Ottoman Army but defected to the Arabs and claimed to know Lawrence personally, asserted that Lawrence was nothing more than a paymaster who 'did nothing to foment the Arab revolution nor did he play any part in the Arab military tactics'.[4]

The EEF entered 1918 with a sense of optimism borne of victory. Guy Dawnay, BGGS, EEF (Brigadier General, General Staff or the equivalent of the army chief of staff) was encouraged by the deteriorating condition of the Ottoman Army. Dawnay noted that, 'the Turk will also be fully aware that his own force proved then, and will probably prove again, insufficient to meet forces of the same strength'.[5] He also observed a general collapse of morale among the enemy and that 'they no longer think of themselves as impervious to our attacks as no doubt they were inclined before their present defeats'.[6] On 9 February General Chetwode forwarded his plan for the capture of Jericho to Allenby for approval, which envisioned the 60th Infantry Division seizing the town while, on the right, the Australian and New Zealand Mounted Division would cut off the enemy close up on the Jordan River.

Chetwode was opposed by Ali Fuat's 53rd and 26th Infantry Divisions (from north to south). The British attack began at 6.00 am, 19 February and made rapid progress taking the Ras et Tawil hilltop held by the 53rd Infantry Division. Difficult terrain held up the advance the next day as the British pushed the 26th Infantry Division off the Cebel Qruntul hill mass. Casualties were light but on the night of 20/21 February Ali Fuat ordered his divisions to break contact and withdraw behind the Jordan River. Chetwode's men captured the abandoned town of Jericho on 21 February. Like Jerusalem, Jericho had no tactical value to the Ottomans and abandonment was a foregone conclusion.

The Relief of von Falkenhayn

February 1918 also brought an important change in the command structure of the Yildirim Army Group – the relief of von Falkenhayn. Over the preceding four months, the Ottomans, at all levels, had become increasingly dissatisfied with the advice and command of General Erich von Falkenhayn. His direction and dispositions were thought to have resulted in the debacles at Gaza and Beersheba. Part of von Falkenhayn's troubles was caused by his high-handed contempt for Ottoman officers and by his refusal to allow Ottoman staff officers to participate in planning combat operations. The reputation for success and credibility in multinational combat operations that von Falkenhayn had built in Romania proved to be a disappointment in the eyes of Enver Pasha and the Ottoman general staff. The Yildirim Army Group commander found himself remembered for his direction of Verdun and for his failure to hold the Gaza–Beersheba line, rather than for his success in Romania.

On 6 February, Enver sent his first assistant chief of staff, German Major General Hans von Seeckt, to visit von Falkenhayn's headquarters. Von Seeckt conducted discussions with the staff and notified Enver that he believed it was not possible to halt Allenby using von Falkenhayn's tactics.[7] As a result, Enver Pasha lost confidence and became determined to relieve von Falkenhayn.[8] After consulting with von Seeckt, there were several possible replacement commanders available in Constantinople, particularly General Otto von Lossow, chief of the German Military Mission, and General Liman von Sanders Pasha (having been awarded this honorific after the successful Gallipoli Campaign), who was then commanding the Ottoman First Army. Enver notified the German general staff about his concerns and he received a reply that he was free to relieve von Falkenhayn and, furthermore, could choose whichever German general he wanted. In spite of their great differences in opinion about Ottoman strategic direction of the war, Enver retained great respect for the fighting abilities of Liman von Sanders. On 19 February 1918, Enver approached Liman von Sanders with an offer to command the Yildirim Army Group. Liman von Sanders, tired of being idle in Ottoman Thrace, eagerly accepted Enver's offer. In addition to changing army group commanders, Enver took the opportunity to overhaul massively the command architecture in Palestine. On 24 February 1918, the Ottoman general staff issued orders stating the following:[9]

1. By order of the German General Staff, Marshal von Falkenhayn is recalled and is assigned to other duties. Marshal Liman von Sanders is assigned as commander of the Yildirim Army Group.
2. The officers of the First Army headquarters will embark from Bandirma (for departure with Liman von Sanders) and the Fifth Army will reorganize itself to assume the responsibilities of the First Army.
3. The First Army is hereby inactivated and all assets and units will herewith fall under the control of the Fifth Army.
4. The Second and Sixth Armies are reassigned to the control of the Ottoman General Staff.
5. The Second and Sixth Armies, and the Euphrates Group are relieved from assignment to the Yildirim Army Group.
6. The Fourth Army will insure that it coordinates operations with the Seventh and the Eighth Armies.
7. Under the authority of paragraph 1, Marshal Liman von Sanders will report when he has assumed command. Paragraphs 2 through 4 will take effect on 1 March 1918.

This order had several far-reaching consequences. First, by dissolving the First Army staff and by sending these officers with Liman von Sanders, Enver ensured that the composition of the Yildirim Army Group staff would become predominately Ottoman. Second, the wording in paragraph one of the order transferred the onus of Falkenhayn's relief to the German general staff, which would assuage any residual bad feelings resulting from von Falkenhayn's relief. Third, the order decoupled the Mesopotamian theatre (the Ottoman Sixth Army) from the Yildirim Army Group, which streamlined and simplified its responsibilities. Finally, the order firmly put forth the idea that the Fourth Army was included in and would coordinate its operations with the Yildirim Army Group. This insured that the Syrian-Palestine theatre was once again brought under the control of a single commander. Overall, these revisions were very carefully orchestrated and put to rest several organizational problems that had afflicted the defence of Palestine.

Liman von Sanders turned over his responsibilities for the defence of Thrace to the commander of the Fifth Army and departed immediately for his new posting. He took with him his chief of staff, Staff Colonel Kazım Bey, and his headquarters staff. After a two-day train journey, he arrived at Samah station, south of Lake Tiberius on 1 March. He was met there by the Seventh Army chief of staff, German Major Falkenhausen, and where he received reports from the subordinate armies. Liman von Sanders arrived at his new headquarters in Nasıra (Nazareth) on 8 March and personally took control of the army group headquarters. There he consulted with von Falkenhayn about the defensive strategy for Palestine. Von Falkenhayn was an advocate of the active defence and had set up a flexible defence, which allowed for both retreat and for the surrender of ground.[10] Liman von Sanders, based on his unyielding defence of the Gallipoli Peninsula, held to an opposite theory of tactical defence – that of refusing to give up an inch of ground by compelling formations to defend terrain at all costs. In these meetings he discovered that the average strength of his infantry battalions numbered 120–50 men (out of the mid-1917 authorization of about 750 men).[11]

The effect of the change in command was immediate. Liman von Sanders issued his first orders from Samah station on 3 March 1918, directing the Seventh Army commander to restore the defensive line from the Jordan River to the Eighth Army. He also ordered Fevzi to establish combat detachments holding posts along the east bank of the Jordan River to prevent the establishment of enemy bridgeheads.[12] He then reinforced the III Corps and ordered the 1st Assault Battalion to join the army group reserve at Nablus. In response to Liman von Sanders's orders Fevzi formed the Lütfü Müfrezesi (the Lütfü Detachment under the command of Major Ömer Lütfü) composed of the 78th Infantry Regiment, an infantry battalion from the 48th Division and several artillery batteries and cavalry companies, in order to cover the Jordan River bridges and fords. Notably different from von Falkenhayn, who sent his orders in French, Liman von Sanders had his orders translated into Ottoman Turkish. Several days later, he assigned Brigadier General Ali Rıza, the erstwhile and under-employed XV Corps commander, as the commander of the Jordan Group, which assumed tactical responsibility for the Jordan River Front and the city of Amman. In this manner, Liman von Sanders solidified command and control along the Jordan River.

From 8–20 March, Allenby maintained pressure on the Seventh Army by conducting local attacks in the EEF's centre sector. This forced Fevzi to commit the 26th Infantry Division, which had been pulled into reserve, into a counter-attack that failed to restore the front. Additionally, a second smaller detachment was formed on 12 March to cover the gap between the Jordan River and the 53rd Infantry Division. The Fourth Army headquarters remained in Damascus while the VIII Corps headquarters moved to Katrana. Importantly, as will be seen subsequently, Fevzi decided to reorganize and reposition the 48th Infantry Division. He ordered the division headquarters to move from Katrana to Amman where it joined the 126th Infantry Regiment, the German 703rd Infantry Battalion, the 1st Battalion, 46th Infantry Regiment and a miscellaneous collection of artillery and tribal cavalry.[13] Fevzi assigned his own army chief of staff, Staff Lieutenant Colonel Asım (later Asım Gündüz, a general staff officer, who had spent two years in Germany training with the German Army) as the division commander with Major Mehmet Nuri as the division chief of staff. Positioning this division in Amman would prove to be a prescient decision when Allenby launched his trans-Jordan offensive operations.

From Amman, Asım moved forward to Es Salt and conferred with Lütfü about the defence of the Jordan Valley. Recognizing the danger, Asım sent the 2nd Battalion, 59th Infantry Regiment and three machine-gun companies to Tel Nimrin (Shunet Nimrin), which is about 10km east of the Jordan River ford at Goraniye (Ghoraniye) on 18 March 1918. Two days later he sent two German infantry companies with machine guns there as well.

The First Battle of the Jordan (The First Trans-Jordan Raid)

Shortly after Liman von Sanders' arrival, the British conducted a limited offensive, aimed at establishing a bridgehead on the east bank of the Jordan, which is known in the British histories as the 'Trans-Jordan Raid'.[14] This offensive was co-ordinated with Arab attacks on the Dera–Hejaz railway and was preceded by diversionary attacks across the entire front. Allenby launched his attack on 21 March with a reinforced infantry division and a mounted division (commanded by Major General Chaytor), which were tasked to break through the Jordan River line. Allenby's intent was to seize Amman and cut the Dera–Hejaz railway (also outflanking the strong Turkish main defensive lines), and then 'probably withdraw'.[15] The attack began with river crossing at midnight on 21 March and by morning 22 March, the British had secured a small bridgehead. However, Lütfü's detachment retained control of the ford at Goraniye and held the British off until noon on 23 March. The next day, Major General J. S. M. Shea ordered an advance to seize Es Salt, but progress was slowed by Ottoman and German rear guards and poor roads. By nightfall, 25 March, Shea's men reached a position a mile from Es Salt but torrential rains forced another delay.

Jordan Group commander, Ali Rıza, and Lieutenant Colonel Asım met in Es Salt on the evening of 24 March to discuss the situation. They were concerned about the highly mobile British encircling the small Ottoman detachments and decided to conduct a fighting withdrawal to Amman. Both then left for that city to organize its defence. There were few units available, but the 48th Infantry Division comprised the 126th Infantry Regiment, a battalion of the 191st Infantry Regiment, the German 703rd Infantry Battalion, two artillery batteries, an engineer company and the 46th Assault Company. Additionally, there were about thirty survivors of the 2nd Battalion, 59th Infantry Regiment, which had been fighting the rear guard actions for a week. On 26 March, Little Cemal brought his Fourth Army headquarters, as well as the VIII Corps headquarters, into Amman, relieving Ali Rıza, who returned to Damascus.[16] At this point, the Fourth Army took over the defence of the Jordan River front but could not prevent the fall of Es Salt on 27 March.

Meanwhile, the British deployed most of the 60th Infantry Division north of Es Salt to cover the left flank while its 181st Brigade, the Australian and New Zealand Mounted Division and the Camel Brigade pushed on toward Amman. The mounted force reached the city's outskirts on 28 March and Chaytor ordered an attack at 1.00 pm. This attack went in on time but quickly failed against Asım's 703rd Infantry Battalion and the 126th Infantry Regiment. Counter-attacks by the 3rd Assault Company assisted the 703rd. On the flanks, the Lütfü Detachment in the north and the Sait Detachment in the south ensured the integrity of the city's defences.[17] The 46th Assault Company was held in army reserve at the Amman train station but on 30 March, Cemal released it to Asım, who attached it to his right wing for the final push.[18]

Subsequent British attacks the next day were similarly unsuccessful and Chaytor decided to withdraw on 1 April. It had been raining for several days and the British withdrawal was difficult.

Failure in front of Amman was not the only problem facing Allenby. Seventh Army commander, Brigadier General Fevzi, formed three ad hoc combat groups and sent them against Chaytor's left flank. The first, under Major Galip, composed of the 143rd Infantry Regiment, several cavalry troops, an artillery platoon and some machine guns crossed the Jordan on 26 March and the next day had firmly planted itself in a blocking position along the Wadi Ebyas. On 27 March, he sent Colonel Esat (3rd Cavalry Division commander) with the 145th Infantry Regiment and the 6th Cavalry Regiment across the Jordan with orders to retake Es Salt. On 30 March, he dispatched the 24th Assault Battalion and the 8th Cavalry Regiment across the river as well.[19] Thus by 31 March, a divisional equivalent of Ottoman troops was poised to push over to the Jordan River crossings and isolate Chaytor's force. This threat also contributed to Chaytor's decision to pull back from Amman and he retreated to a bridgehead around the ford at Goraniye.[20]

For the counter-attacks that followed on 4 April, Lieutenant Colonel Asım was also given the 24th Assault Company as well as the 3rd Battalion, 145th Infantry Regiment (both from the 24th Infantry Division). As the battle developed, Asım launched a pursuit of the British and teamed the 24th Assault Company with the 8th and 9th Cavalry Regiments.[21] After the battle, the 46th Assault Company was withdrawn from the 48th Infantry Division and held in corps reserve. Interestingly, at the same time, the Seventh Army formed a provisional cavalry regiment by combining the organic cavalry companies from the 11th, 24th, 48th and 53rd Infantry Divisions.[22]

On 3 April, the 7th Cavalry Regiment joined Lütfü's detachment, making it into the Lütfü Provisional Division and, on the same day, VIII Corps commander Colonel Ali Fuat began planning a counter-attack to crush the British bridgehead. His main effort composed the 48th Infantry Division (now comprising the 23rd and 191st Infantry Regiments, and the 48th Artillery Regiment) in the north, as well as Lütfü's Provisional Division (the 152nd Infantry Regiment, the 1st Battalion, 146th Infantry Regiment and supporting arms including an artillery battalion) in the south. Esat's 6th Cavalry Regiment was to screen the right (northern) flank, while his 7th Cavalry Regiment screened the left (southern) flank. The 8th Cavalry Regiment remained in the north to cover the tactical seam between the Fourth and Seventh Armies. On the west bank of the Jordan River, the XX Corps was ordered to launch a supporting attack. The divisions moved into their assembly areas on the night of 10/11 April 1918 and launched their attacks at dawn on 11 April. The attacks were insufficiently supported by artillery and made progress in some places but by mid-afternoon British counter-attacks had restored the front. Casualties were heavy as the Fourth Army called off the attack.

The difficulties of the Fourth Army's battles along the Jordan River quickly overloaded the army staff and it was apparent that the scope of its geographic area was a problem. In order to simplify command responsibilities in Syria-Palestine, the Ottoman general staff ordered the augmentation of operational headquarters in theatre. This was possible because the Treaty of Brest-Litovsk in January had created an operational pause for the Ottoman forces fighting in Caucasia against the Russians. As a result the general staff felt able to inactivate the Caucasian Army Group thereby creating excess capacity in that theatre. Some Caucasian divisions had already arrived in Palestine and the general staff ordered the Second Army headquarters to Palestine. In April 1918, the Second Army headquarters arrived in Adana, where it was assigned to take over the defence of the Adana and Levant coast and hinterlands, thus allowing the Fourth Army to focus on the defence of the Jordan River. In addition, the II Corps headquarters was ordered to Amman as well. More German reinforcements (the 11th Jäger Battalion and the 146th Infantry Regiment) were on the way to Palestine and were designated to go to the Fourth Army as much-needed reinforcements.

The Second Battle of the Jordan (the Second Trans-Jordan Raid)
The Second Battle of the Jordan began on 30 April 1918, with the British again launching an attack from their bridgehead across the Jordan toward Amman by way of Es Salt. Allenby's intelligence staffs knew that the Ottoman position on the east bank of the Jordan was weak, with the Ottoman VIII Corps fielding only two divisions. In the words of the British official historian, 'held by the motley collection of troops now known as the VIII Corps'.[23] Although the VIII Corps was only able to put 371 officers, 7,387 men (of whom 4,382 were riflemen), 31 machine guns and 35 artillery pieces on the Tel Nimrin ridge overlooking the Goraniye bridgehead, it is wrong, however, to characterize the corps as 'motley'. Against this small force, Allenby launched the Australian and New Zealand Mounted Division, the 60th Infantry Division, the Imperial Service Cavalry Corps and the 6th Mounted Brigade. These units moved into assembly areas on 29 April and prepared to attack the following morning.

The personnel of the VIII Corps headquarters at the Suayyip bridge, just 5km behind the Tel Nimrin ridge, awoke at 3.00 am, 30 April to the sounds of heavy artillery fire from the British bridgehead. Asım's 48th Infantry Division soon reported that it was under heavy attack by the British 60th Infantry Division and this news was sent to Cemal's Fourth Army headquarters in Es Salt. However, the Yildirim Army Group did not learn of the British attack until 7.30 am, because Arab guerrillas had cut the telephone and telegraph lines.[24] The army group chief of staff, Colonel Kazım, immediately requested an aircraft and flew to Amman seeking information from Little Cemal, and from there he went to the Fourth Army headquarters in Es Salt. At 8.30 am, Fevzi Pasha telephoned Liman von Sanders to report that his 24th Infantry Division was prepared for action. The Ottoman and German infantry on the Tel Nimrin ridge held their positions but on the VIII Corps right flank, Australian mounted regiments pushed the Ottoman 11th Cavalry Regiment screen back and broke out to the north.

The Australian advance threatened Es Salt where, in the late morning, Cemal and Kazım organized an ad hoc battalion of Ottoman and German soldiers, which they sent to a hill 3km west of town to delay the enemy. This bought the army headquarters enough time to escape to Sevilah before the Australians swept into Es Salt at 6.20 pm. At Sevilah the Fourth Army headquarters staff re-established tactical control 2 hours later and received new orders from the army group. The plan was aggressive and Liman von Sanders ordered the adjacent Seventh Army to attack the enemy's exposed left flank with the 24th Infantry Division and the 3rd Cavalry Division on 1 May.[25] Supporting the Seventh Army's main effort, the Fourth Army would conduct a demonstration attack toward Es Salt after receiving reinforcements from Amman. However, moving the two XX Corps divisions east across the Jordan River and reorganizing them for combat took much longer than expected, which delayed the attack.

The first XX Corps formation across the Jordan was Colonel Esat's 3rd Cavalry Division, which, in addition to the 6th and 8th Cavalry Regiments, had the 2nd Infantry Regiment and two artillery batteries assigned. The cavalry division pushed towards Es Salt and fought a minor battle at Cereyan Tarzı. The 24th Infantry Division, now composed of the 143rd Infantry Regiment and one battalion each from the 32nd, 58th, 146th and 150th Infantry Regiments (as additional forces, the 24th Assault Battalion and two artillery batteries were also assigned to the division) crossed the river and pushed down the unguarded left bank of the Jordan. This caused a crisis forcing the British to pull back units on 2 May to plug the gaps and protect their left flank. A provisional brigade, built around the 66th Infantry Regiment, the survivors of Cemal's provisional battalion, and an Arab tribal cavalry troop pushed east in demonstration operations from Suvelah and stopped a British effort to take that town. This provisional brigade was commanded by Lieutenant Colonel Kemal Bey.

On 2 May, VIII and XX Corps continued to attack aggressively and Colonel Esat, the brilliant 3rd Cavalry Division commander, was badly wounded. (See map 7.2.) The division chief of staff, Staff Colonel Mahmut (later Mahmut Hendek), took command of the division and continued the fight. The day went badly for the British, who were fixed in front of the heights at Tel Nimrin and whose left (northern) flank was being pressed hard by XX Corps. Moreover, their position at Es Salt was

Map 7.2: Second Battle of the Jordan, 2–4 May 1918

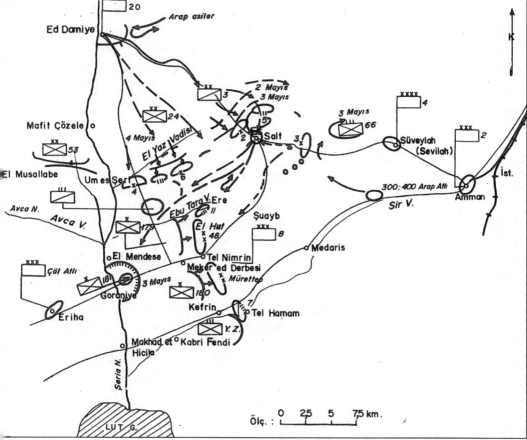

now being attacked from the north and from the east. It appeared to the British that the Ottomans might punch through along the river and trap two British divisions and on 3 May, Allenby himself came to confer with the tactical commander Lieutenant General Harry Chauvel.[26] They decided to call off the operation and conduct an orderly withdrawal from Es Salt back into the original Jordan River bridgehead. The evacuation took place on 4 May and it was completed by 6.30 pm. The British lost some 1,649 men (214 killed) while the Ottomans lost 786 men (196 killed) and had 981 men (including 44 Germans) taken prisoner.[27]

This brought Allenby's offensive operations to a halt, although simultaneous operations along the coast by Allenby's XXI Corps aimed at taking a portion of the Ottoman defences and capturing significant numbers of troops and guns were likewise unsuccessful.[28] The bright predictions that Allenby would push the Ottomans out of Palestine by summer proved to be an illusion.

The Last Ottoman Offensive in Palestine
There was a renewal of Arab attacks in the late spring of 1918, when in April, Lawrence and his Arab allies attacked a number of railway stations near Maan. These were timed in conjunction with Allenby's trans-Jordan raids. Then between 1 and 19 May, Lawrence and the Arabs destroyed twenty-five bridges on the Damascus–Medina railway. However, these were repaired quickly by the Ottoman Army's railway engineers and labour battalions. On 30 May, the Arabs captured the town of Elfifre and held it for a week before retreating. Cyril Falls asserted that these attacks were significant since the 12,000 men assigned on the ration strength of the provisional division on the railway and Hejaz forces would have been 'invaluable to Liman von Sanders'.[29] This is problematic at best since the actual combat forces along the Hejaz numbered not more than a few thousand infantrymen. Moreover, as 1918 progressed, the Ottoman logistics system in Palestine deteriorated to the point where it was almost impossible to keep larger numbers of men supplied with food and ammunition. By the summer of 1918 having more Ottoman soldiers in Palestine did not equate to having a more powerful army.

In late May, the German 146th Infantry Regiment began to arrive in Es Salt from Macedonia. Although the German general staff had concerns that these troops, accustomed to the mountains, would have difficulty acclimatizing to the intense heat in Palestine, it informed Liman von Sanders that more German reinforcements would be sent to his command. In fact, the last German reinforcement, elements of the 11th Jäger Battalion, arrived in Mesudiye station on 1 June and went into army group reserve. On 10 June, the German General Staff notified Enver that it wanted the battalion returned to Constantinople. The Ottomans traded cables with the Germans for ten days. On 21 June, Liman von Sanders learned that the German general staff wanted to send the Jägers to Georgia and he was ordered to move the battalion north. However, two days later the Germans relented and one Jäger company was allowed to remain in Palestine, where the summer temperatures now exceeded 55 °C.

In late June the army group staff began to contemplate a limited offensive on the west bank of the Jordan River in order to take some high ground and straighten out a salient in the lines. Liman von Sanders issued orders to this effect on 4 July 1918. He intended that the XX Corps conduct the main attack to take the Musallabe hill and then take the Ebututl (Abu Tulul) hill, while the VIII Corps conducted a smaller supporting attack on the El Hinu ford. Liman von Sanders notified the Seventh Army that it would receive the army group's German reserves – the 146th Infantry Regiment, the 702nd and 703rd Infantry Battalions, and the remaining Jäger company. Meanwhile, on 8 June the 7th Infantry Division along the coast repelled a local attack by an Indian Army brigade and retook some ground that had been lost by conducting a counter-attack. However, this did not distract the aggressive army group commander who remained focused on his Jordan River left flank.

On 11 July, Liman von Sanders issued formal attack orders to the Seventh Army, which in turn, sent detailed attack orders to the XX Corps the next day.[30] The main attack would be made by the 53rd Infantry Division's 58th and 163rd Infantry Regiments and the 3rd Cavalry Division's 32nd Infantry Regiment, which would be augmented by the 143rd Infantry Regiment and the German 146th Infantry Regiment (as well as the two Asia Corps battalions and the Jägers). The XX Corps retained the 2nd Infantry Regiment and the two German Asia Corps battalions in immediate tactical reserve. The main attack would be made by the 53rd Infantry Division on the right and the 3rd Cavalry Division on the left.

The XX Corps attack began at 3.00 am, 14 July 1918 and, by midday, the Musallabe hill had been taken and the attackers were pushing up the Abu Tulul hill. At the same time, the Fourth Army launched a supporting attack using the 8th Cavalry Regiment, the 63rd Infantry Regiment, the 1st Battalion and 66th Infantry Regiment, supported by an artillery battalion against the left (northern) shoulder of the Goraniye bridgehead. The supporting attack foundered against well-led Indian Army cavalry. Reports went up at midday to Liman von Sanders, who believed that the attack was poised on success and, at 3.00 pm, he ordered the attack to continue. He also ordered the 2nd Infantry Regiment and the 702nd and 703rd Infantry Battalions to reinforce the 58th and 146th Infantry Regiments, respectively.[31] This put the weight and mass of the attack in the centre of the XX Corps assault zone and was intended to be the main effort. The Germans broke through late in the afternoon onto the Abu Tulul hill, but the adjacent Ottoman battalions made no progress. Unsupported, the Australian defenders crushed the Germans and pushed the survivors back down into the valley. The attack collapsed and Liman von Sanders called it off that night.

The Musallabe Battle or the Affair of Abu Tulul (as the British named it) was a tactical disaster that resulted in over a thousand casualties in the combined Ottoman and German regiments. It proved to be the last offensive operation conducted by the Ottoman armies in Palestine. All sources agree that the extreme heat – 55 °C – contributed significantly to the failure.

The Ottoman Army in Palestine – Summer 1918
The Ottoman Army in Palestine grew progressively weaker in terms of military manpower as 1918 progressed. For example, by summer, the 9 infantry battalions of the 16th Infantry Division ranged in effective strength from 100 to 250 men each (or the equivalent of a British infantry company).[32] Mustafa Kemal's famous 19th Infantry Division reported that infantry battalions, which had 500–600 men each at Beersheba, now had only 150–200 men assigned.[33] Many of the losses were from disease and desertion. The 7th Infantry Division was in a similar condition and its 21st Infantry Regiment reported that the 'weak replacement system failed to keep up with the losses and this resulted in weak companies at the front'.[34] To compensate for this, the regiment attempted to keep the 1st Company in each of its three battalions up to strength, so that at least a portion of its combat strength was at authorized levels.[35] Of course, this dramatically weakened the other two companies in each battalion.

The physical condition of the men also began to deteriorate dramatically at this point in the theatre. The memoirs of the participants, both Turkish and German, speak of the terrible problem of eroding manpower. They also speak of the deplorable conditions experienced by

Ottoman soldiers in Palestine. Liman von Sanders observed that many soldiers and officers had no shoes and rags for clothing.[36] Food and fodder were, likewise, in short supply. On 1 February 1918, the Ottoman Eighth Army had 155 tons of flour on hand but by 1 September, this had dropped to 14.5 tons of flour on hand (for an army whose ration strength was 39,783 men).[37] Ottoman soldiers in Palestine were given the barest rations, which frequently included the husks of oats and barley in lieu of the grain itself. The war diary of the 21st Infantry Regiment noted an 'excellent situation' in the late spring of 1918 because the regiment's soldiers received the following daily ration: 825g bread, 250g meat, 150g flour, 100g olives, 50g yoghurt and 40g soap. Notably the animals received a kilo of grain on the same day.[38] What makes this entry unusual is that this ration matched the pre-war daily ration of 3,149 calories authorized for Ottoman soldiers (the point here is that when regiments in Palestine received their actual authorized allowances of food it was a noteworthy event).[39] The normal daily ration in Palestine was 'invariably 125 grams of bread and boiled beans in the morning, at noon, and at night, without oil or any other condiment'.[40] Other commentaries from the men stationed in Palestine during these difficult times frequently focus on the declining amount of food actually received, as well as postal services and weapons training.[41]

Despite the deplorable conditions that the Ottoman Army in Palestine endured in the last year of the war, it continued to train and to prepare its men for combat. The 48th Infantry Division, for example, while holding the line on the Jordan River, organized and conducted training courses on battle tactics and the employment of machine guns, hand grenades and flame throwers.[42] At regimental level, the 20th Infantry Regiment underwent intensive training in early February in day and night fortification and battle drill.[43] At individual level, soldiers from the newly arriving 37th Infantry Division (from the Caucasus) received a two-week course near Nablus in the use of stick grenades.[44]

Of note was the effort that the Ottoman Army put into organizing and training its assault troops, which by 1918 had become an important part of the Ottoman Army's tactical capability in Palestine. Additional assault troops were organized into combined arms assault detachments of company strength. For example, the assault detachment of the 23rd Infantry Division was composed of 1 infantry company (about 100 men), 1 engineer (pioneer) platoon (1 officer, 4 NCOs and 30 men) and 7 light machine-guns teams.[45] The officers assigned to the assault detachments were hand-picked from within the division by the division staff.[46] The assault detachment was given a four-week course in German-style storm-trooper tactics, to which the division sent an additional one officer and five NCOs.[47] Eventually, the assault detachment was expanded into the 23rd Assault Battalion, giving the division additional combat capability.

There appear to have been variances in the composition of the assault detachments and battalions. In the 16th Infantry Division, the 47th Infantry Regiment was tasked to form its first assault detachment of 140 men and 2 machine-gun teams.[48] The 19th Infantry Division, which had deployed to Palestine from Galicia, arrived with its assault battalion already formed and, in this division, each regiment also had its own organic assault platoon.[49] In the absence of Ottoman divisional or corps level offensive operations, the assault troops became somewhat of a 'fire brigade' for both corps and divisional operations.

In late July, the newly arriving Second Army established its headquarters in Aleppo under the command of Major General Nihat Pasha. However, on 1 August, the Seventh Army commander, Fevzi Pasha, fell sick and departed for Constantinople. Nihat Pasha assumed temporary command of the Seventh Army until the arrival of a new commander. On 7 August, Enver Pasha appointed Major General Mustafa Kemal to command of the Seventh Army. Also in the Seventh Army, German Major von Papen, the army chief of staff, went sick and was replaced by German Major von Falkenhausen. On 12 August 1918, the first regiment of the 37th Infantry Division, the 109th Infantry Regiment, arrived from the Caucasus. This regiment went into the army group reserve for training and acclimatization.

In August, Liman von Sanders decided to consolidate the German units in Palestine in the Eighth Army's Left Wing Group, commanded by Colonel von Frankenberg. To accommodate this he moved the 702nd and 703rd Infantry Battalions and the 146th Infantry Regiment from the Jordan Front to Azun and consolidated these units with the German Asia Corps. Liman von Sanders then placed the entire Left Wing Group under the command of Colonel Gustav von Oppen.

The 'Indianization' of Allenby's Army

With the exception of some brief fighting in mid-summer, the Palestine Front was relatively quiet during the late spring and summer of 1918. The principal reason was that the gigantic Ludendorff Offensives in France during the spring of 1918 forced the Imperial general staff to tap Allenby's army for vitally needed reinforcements. Allenby was forced to send to France, beginning in March, 2 infantry divisions, 9 yeomanry (cavalry) regiments, 23 British infantry battalions, 5 heavy artillery batteries and 5 machine-gun companies (in all some 60,000 men).[50] Making matters worse, he had to disband ten infantry battalions to use as reinforcements for his depleted formations. In return, Allenby received several Indian Army infantry divisions from Mesopotamia, and a number of Indian cavalry regiments and infantry battalions. Effectively, Allenby lost a significant portion of his trained and experienced British Army combat power, and in return received less well-trained Indian Army troops. This turn of events forced Allenby to spend the summer engaged in a complete reorganization and retraining of his army.[51] The British were still left with seven infantry divisions in Palestine, but the national character of these formations had changed significantly. Only a single all-British infantry division remained, four others being three-quarter Indian (each brigade containing one British and three Indian battalions), and the final two were Indian Army infantry divisions (which were also three-quarter Indian and one-quarter British). Only in mounted strength did Allenby's situation actually improve, gaining one division, for a total of four cavalry and mounted divisions (of which two were Indian Army as well). Nevertheless, Allenby still commanded a large and well-equipped army with which to renew the offensive against the Yildirim Army Group. Turkish intelligence estimated Allenby's effective and mobile combat strength at 56,000 riflemen, 11,000 cavalry and 552 artillery pieces.[52]

To oppose this collection of Imperial strength, in August 1918, the Yildirim Army Group disposed 40,598 front-line infantrymen, who were armed with 19,819 rifles, 273 light and 696 heavy machine guns.[53] The number of machine guns available to the Yildirim Army Group, in comparison with other campaigns, seems unusually high and reflected the Ottoman Army's new tables of organization and the machine-gun components of the German Asia Corps. The Ottomans ordered these soldiers into twelve under-strength divisions to defend a 90km-plus front.

Over the summer, Liman von Sanders and his subordinate commanders worked feverishly to prepare the defence to receive what was expected to be a major British offensive. In early September 1918, the signs of an impending British offensive were undeniable, but Liman von Sanders and his staff were unable to pinpoint the exact area where Allenby would strike. This was due to the superb tactical deception measures that Allenby used. Consequently, the Yildirim Army Group remained spread along the entire front in static defensive positions. The only formations available for reserve duty at the operational level were the 2nd Caucasian Cavalry Brigade in the Eighth Army area and the 3rd Cavalry Division in the Fourth Army area. In the event of a major British breakthrough, the Yildirim Army Group had few reserves and even fewer options. However, Liman von Sanders's faith in the fighting qualities of his well-dug-in Turkish infantry remained high.[54]

Allenby's Plans

Sir Edmund Allenby intended to inflict 'a decisive defeat on the enemy and driving him from the line Nablus-Samaria-Tul Karim-Caesarea'.[55] To accomplish this he concentrated five of his seven infantry divisions into a restructured XXI Corps to break through the Ottoman lines adjacent to the sea. Immediately after which, his Desert Mounted Corps (three cavalry or mounted divisions) would 'pass round the left of the XXI Corps . . . to cut the enemy's railway communications and to block his retreat in the northerly and north-easterly direction'.[56] In doctrinal terms, Allenby intended to execute a single envelopment of the Ottoman Seventh and Eighth Armies. Once again, his operational intent was clear and lucidly stated for his subordinate commanders.

Allenby was determined to ensure that his plan remained shrouded in secrecy and the EEF conducted elaborate deception measures to mislead Liman von Sanders. These are well documented in the extant English language historiography and included active demonstration operations by Chaytor's force along the Jordan River, air superiority operations to deny enemy aerial observation, phantom wireless units, elaborate dummy positions and installations, and exceptional operations security measures within the EEF.

At corps level much thought was given to the execution of Allenby's intent. The orders of the XXI Corps emphasized the importance of rapid tactical movement, accurate and constant reports, and the proper marking of lanes for the oncoming cavalry.[57] Importantly, the XXI Corps plan included the use of an 'advanced XXI Corps H.Q.' that when opened and operational would control combat operations (all other functions, such as intelligence, logistics, personnel, etc. would remain in, or be routed to, the main XXI Corps headquarters) – this arrangement remains in use today and is called the corps forward command post.[58] In establishing this, Lieutenant General E. S. Bulfin, the corps commander, made certain that he could remain in close proximity to his advancing divisions and could maintain constant command and control. The corresponding Desert Mounted Corps operations order dovetailed neatly into Bulfin's operation and is especially noteworthy in its road and transportation instructions that included priorities, as well as routes.[59] The principal technical difference between these orders published in September 1918 and the earlier counterpart orders (Beersheba and Gaza) published in October 1917 is in the selection of Allenby's objective – the decisive defeat of the Ottomans versus the driving him out of his lines.

Historical opinion on whether or not it was Allenby himself who was the brain behind the plan is changing. Cyril Falls, the author of the official British history of the campaign, in his *Armageddon 1918* written in 1964, maintained that Allenby, returning from a morning ride in late August 1918, changed what could be called 'the short envelopment' to 'the long envelopment' ('to the astonishment of his corps commanders', according to Falls).[60] Jonathan Newell, writing in 1991, took a more reasoned approach and stated 'it is simplistic and misleading to state so categorically that the plan was solely Allenby's creation, on the contrary, there is strong evidence that it was not drawn up in some kind of vacuum but rather under the influence of earlier assessments of how most effectively British forces could advance to complete the conquest of Palestine and Syria'.[61] Certainly, the activities of the EEF from May to August 1918 lend credence to Newell's thinking.

Yildirim Defensive Plans – September 1918

Liman von Sanders had twelve under-strength infantry divisions (and one cavalry division) with which to defend a 90km front. According to Ottoman Army doctrine in 1918, an infantry division would ordinarily be assigned a front of 5km – thus Liman von Sanders should have had eighteen divisions in the line.[62] Moreover, Ottoman Army doctrine maintained that each corps and army would have a regiment or a division in reserve (depending on terrain and roads) – making a grand total of somewhere in the region of twenty-five infantry divisions as the minimal doctrinal requirement to hold the Ottoman line.[63] These doctrinal templates were based on divisions at full strength and Liman von Sanders's army fielded infantry divisions operating at less than 20 per cent of authorized strength. This meant, in real terms, that Liman von Sanders attempted to defend his lines with about 15 per cent of the doctrinal requirement necessary according to the Ottoman Army's tactics. Moreover, when counting the required reserves, which would total altogether some twenty-five infantry divisions, the tactical situation was far worse – the Yildirim Army Group had less than 10 per cent of the forces required to defend a 90km front.

The defensive plan was simple and required the infantry to fight for their positions without giving up any ground.[64] Any ground lost would be retaken by immediate counter-attacks by reserves. The depleted infantry divisions manned their lines and retained, in most cases, a single battalion in reserve.[65] Even at corps and army level, Liman von Sander's armies mostly retained only a single battalion in reserve. The sole exception was Cevat's Eighth Army, which retained the entire 46th Infantry Division in reserve, the only army (of three) permitted to do so. Cevat positioned the 46th Infantry Division in the centre of the Eighth Army sector, near Tul Karm.

The coastal sector where Allenby's main blow would fall was the responsibility of Cevat's Eighth Army and Cevat placed the XXII Corps on the coast and positioned a provisional army corps named the Von Oppen Group inland to link with the Seventh Army. The XXII Corps disposed the 7th Infantry Division and the 20th Infantry Divisions from west to east respectively. As mentioned earlier, Cevat retained the 46th Infantry Division in army reserve, 12km from the front in the centre of his sector.

The defensive frontages of the two front-line divisions in Cevat's XXII Corps were among the shortest in the entire Yildirim Army Group. The 7th Infantry Division held a front of 7km while the 20th Infantry Division held 5km of trenches. In the adjacent Von Oppen Group and on the 20th Division's left flank was the famous 19th Infantry Division, which held a front of 10km. In fact, at the point where Allenby struck the Ottomans themselves achieved a fair degree of concentration of their scant resources – the 20th Infantry Division actually being within the doctrinal 5km template required by contemporary Ottoman tactics. Of course, the crippling levels of reduced operating strength essentially negated any usefulness of doctrinal planning by the Ottoman Army.

At the operational level, there were no secondary lines of defence nor were there any fall-back positions in the event of a retreat. Liman von Sanders intended that the Yildirim Army Group fight to the finish. At the tactical level, the Ottoman defences consisted of a primary line of trenches with a support trench. Although the Ottomans had been on this line for about eight months, it was incomplete and weak in many locations. Fortification and building materials were in very short supply.[66] This was particularly true of barbed wire, concrete and wooden beams (for overhead cover). Even sandbags, which the army had in some numbers, were routinely used to repair soldier's uniforms and shoes instead of for their intended purpose. These shortages mostly affected the construction of strongpoints and bunkers, which were crucial in defensive planning in 1918.

There was an acute awareness of the weaknesses of the Ottoman position in Palestine at almost every level of command. Several days before Allenby's attack Cevat Pasha expressed grave concern about the lack of adequate reserves in a letter to Liman von Sanders.[67] Because he was expecting an enemy attack, Cevat also requested permission to withdraw from his forward lines to avoid high losses. The Seventh Army commander, Mustafa Kemal, was also a thorn in the side of both Liman von Sanders and the Ottoman general staff and frequently dispatched letters recommending the abandonment of Palestine and the creation of large strategic reserves. The previous Seventh Army commander, Fevzi Pasha, had noted serious problems with the inefficient lines of communications and had also that the 'supply and recruiting Zone [was not] proportionate with the strength and situation of the army'.[68] He meant, of course, that there were not enough conscripts in the theatre provinces to sustain the strength of the army. Moreover, Fevzi mentioned that there were combat skills proficiency problems caused by the inability of his under-strength army to withdraw front-line units for training in the rear areas (with the exception of the assault battalions and machine-gun detachments).

Ottoman Morale

By late 1918, confidence levels were exceptionally low and this accelerated the problem of poor morale that afflicted the Ottoman Army in Palestine. This point is very well covered in the literature in English and many of the details need not be reiterated here.[69] Allenby's divisions captured hundreds of prisoners a month during the summer and early autumn of 1918 and came to rely on them as an important source of intelligence. Almost universally, Ottoman prisoners complained of low morale, bad logistics, especially food and clothing, and a generalized lack of support for the war itself. There were other factors at play as well.

One issue that worked its way around the Ottoman Army in Palestine was the withdrawal of some of the German units to the Caucasus. This concerned Liman von Sanders and it also troubled many Ottoman soldiers. A British report summarized the issue: 'a serious blow has been dealt to the morale of the Turkish army in Palestine by the departure of a large proportion of the German combat units'.[70] This kind of thinking was accompanied by contemporary newspaper reports of Allied successes on the Western Front in the late summer of 1918. The cordial relationships developed between Ottomans and Germans over three years were frayed badly by the last year of the war.[71]

Another problem involved replacements – not simply that there were not enough of them – but rather the quality of men that the Yildirim Army Group was receiving by 1918. Since the number of draft-age young men was insufficient to maintain the strength of the army, the Ottoman Empire was compelled to draw on other sources of manpower that included deserters, convalescents and men who had been previously rejected for active service. In Palestine, the Base Details Branch at Jerusalem, part of the 12th Depot Regiment, was responsible for collecting deserters, convalescents, men returning from leave and men who had either avoided or been exempted from service.[72] The branch sent the deserters to the local prison for courts martial and imprisonment, whereupon release they were posted to active units.[73] For example, heavy casualties rendered the 2nd and 3rd Battalions of the 59th Infantry Regiment (assigned to the 19th Infantry Division) combat ineffective and they were rebuilt in early 1918. The battalions received drafts of men from Kurdish labour battalions from the Tarsus district and replacements from the Jerusalem depot, most of whom were former deserters.[74] British intelligence noted that the Ottoman Army's divisions in Palestine were becoming much weaker in the quality of manpower compared with combat divisions previously encountered in Anatolia, the Caucasus and Europe.[75]

Finally, relations between officers and men, sometimes tenuous in the Ottoman Army, were becoming increasingly strained. War weariness, at least in Palestine, had set in making many of the soldiers 'broken in spirit and tired out'.[76] British intelligence observed that 'the morale of the Turkish prisoners is not nearly as good as in the Dardanelles Campaign' and that 'Arabs were especially unhappy'.[77]

Conclusion

British operations across the Jordan River were designed as campaigns of opportunity and Allenby hoped for large returns for minimal tactical investments. The offensives toward Amman were turned back twice and Allenby was left with a small bridgehead on the east bank of the Jordan River. Much of the Ottoman Fourth Army's success in dealing Allenby these defeats rested with the Ottoman Army's continuing capability to create ad hoc battle groups, which were immediately combat effective. This was multiplied by the army's ability to work tactically with its German ally and interchange units and commanders. Moreover, the presence of highly trained and aggressive Ottoman assault troops in the battle groups was value added in the tactical sense. Finally, for those who have never seen the terrain from the Jordan River east to Amman, the author was shocked in 2008 when he visited the area. The rugged and commanding high ground going up from the Jordan River toward Amman is a tremendous military obstacle to operations advancing from the river valley. Most parts of the area are steeper, more rugged and much higher in altitude than Second and Third Ridge on the ANZAC perimeter at Gallipoli, which may give the reader a sense of the geographic difficulties that Allenby's 'raids' encountered on the uphill route to Amman.

Notes

1. Onalp et al., *Sina-Filistin Cephesi, İkinci Gazze Muharebesi Sonundan Mütarekesi'ne Kadar Yapılan Harekât*, p. 519.
2. Belen, *Birinci Cihan Harbinde, Türk Harbi, 1918 Yılı Hareketleri*, p. 22.
3. Murphy, *The Arab Revolt*, pp. 61–5.
4. Sarkis Torossian, *From Dardanelles to Palestine* (Boston, MA: Meador Publishing Company, 1929), p. 197.
5. TNA, CGS Appreciation by BGGS G. Dawnay, 13 December 1917, WO 158/611.
6. Ibid.
7. Onalp et al., *Sina-Filistin Cephesi, İkinci Gazze Muharebesi Sonundan Mütarekesi'ne Kadar Yapılan Harekât*, p. 537.
8. Ibid., p. 536.
9. Ibid., p. 538.
10. Ibid., p. 540.
11. Ibid., p. 541.
12. Yildirim Army Group Orders to Seventh Army, 3 March 1918, reproduced in Onalp et al., *Sina-Filistin Cephesi, İkinci Gazze Muharebesi Sonundan Mütarekesi'ne Kadar Yapılan Harekât*, pp. 547–8.
13. Belen, *Birinci Cihan Harbinde, Türk Harbi, 1918 Yılı Hareketleri*, p. 29.
14. The word 'raid' does not appear in any orders associated with these events. It is only well after the war that Cyril Falls bestowed the term 'raid' on Allenby's operations in March 1918. Falls and Becke, *Military Operations Egypt and Palestine, From June 1917 to the End of the War*, Part I, pp. 328–49.
15. XX Corps Operations Order to 60th Division, 16 March 1918, reprinted as Appendix 20 in Falls and Becke, *Military Operations Egypt and Palestine, From June 1917 to the End of the War*, Part II, pp. 705–7.
16. Onalp et al., *Sina-Filistin Cephesi, İkinci Gazze Muharebesi Sonundan Mütarekesi'ne Kadar Yapılan Harekât*, pp. 573–5.

17. Belen, *Birinci Cihan Harbinde, Türk Harbi, 1918 Yılı Hareketleri*, pp. 40–4. The total strength of the 48th Infantry Division on 28 March 1918 was 130 officers, 2,307 men, 1,841 rifles, 34 machine guns and 8 artillery pieces (or about the strength of a British brigade).

18. Ibid., p. 50.

19. Ibid., pp. 36–8 and Kroki (Sketch) 10.

20. The British official history attributed the British reverses as a function of the enemy bringing up substantial reserves, which offset the numerical advantage of the British. However, the author believes that Allenby hoped to catch the Turks napping and break open the front. In late February, Allenby hoped 'to cross the river, and get to the Hedjaz railway; joining hands with the Arabs, and really breaking the line'. Allenby to Robertson, 23 February 1918, LHCMA, Robertson Papers 7/5/86, reprinted in Hughes, *Allenby and British Strategy in the Middle East*, p. 133.

21. Ibid., p. 60.

22. Ibid., p. 68.

23. Falls and Becke, *Military Operations Egypt and Palestine, From June 1917 to the End of the War*, Part I, p. 366.

24. Onalp et al., *Sina-Filistin Cephesi, İkinci Gazze Muharebesi Sonundan Mütarekesi'ne Kadar Yapılan Harekât*, p. 585.

25. Yildirim Army Group orders, 30 April 1918, reproduced in Onalp et al., *Sina-Filistin Cephesi, İkinci Gazze Muharebesi Sonundan Mütarekesi'ne Kadar Yapılan Harekât*, p. 586.

26. Falls and Becke, *Military Operations Egypt and Palestine, From June 1917 to the End of the War*, Part I, pp. 386–7.

27. Onalp et al., *Sina-Filistin Cephesi, İkinci Gazze Muharebesi Sonundan Mütarekesi'ne Kadar Yapılan Harekât*, pp. 593–4.

28. XXI Corps Operations Order, 1 April 1918, reprinted as Appendix 21 in Falls and Becke, *Military Operations Egypt and Palestine, From June 1917 to the End of the War*, Part II, pp. 707–9.

29. Ibid., p. 407.

30. XX Corps Combat Orders, 12 July 1918, reprinted in Onalp et al., *Sina-Filistin Cephesi, İkinci Gazze Muharebesi Sonundan Mütarekesi'ne Kadar Yapılan Harekât*, pp. 602–3.

31. Ibid., pp. 605–6.

32. ATASE, *16nci Piyade Tümeni Tarihçesi*, Record 26-441, p. 53.

33. ATASE, *19ncu Piyade Tümeni Tarihçesi*, Record 26-349, p. 33.

34. ATASE, *21nci Piyade Alay Tarihçesi*, Record 26-327, p. 28.

35. Ibid.

36. Otto Liman von Sanders, *Five Years in Turkey* (London: Bailliere, Tindall & Cox, 1928), pp. 259–60.

37. ATASE, Ration Stockages, Eighth Army, 1918, Archive 1247, Record 472, File 4-2, reprinted in Koral et al., *Idari Faaliyetler ve Lojistik*, p. 557.

38. ATASE, *21nci Piyade Alay Tarihçesi*, Record 26-327, p. 31. See War Diary entry for 18 March 1918.

39. Selâhattin Karamatu, *Türk Silahli Kuvvetleri Tarihi, IIIncu Cilt 6ncu Kisim (1908–1920) 1nci Kitap (Turkish Armed Forces History, 1908–1920)* (Ankara: Genelkurmay Basımevi, 1971), p. 358. Ottoman soldiers were authorized 3,149 calories per day. The recommended daily ration consisted of 900g bread, 250g meat, 150g bulgar, 20g olive oil, 20g salt and 9g soap.

40. NARA, Turkish Military Information, 18 February 1918, AEF G-2, RG 120, NH 91, Entry 187, Box 5828.

41. Sami Yengin, *Drama'dan Sina-Filistin'e Savaş Günlüğü* (Ankara: Genelkurmay Basımevi, 1967), pp. 74–105.

42. M. Neş'et, 'Büyük Harpte "Suriye" Cephesinde 48. Piyade Fırkası', *Askeri Mecmua*, No. 18, 1 July 1930 (Istanbul: Askeri Matbaa, 1930), 89.

43. ATASE, *20nci Piyade Alay Tarihçesi*, 1977, Record 26-326, p. 55.

44. LC, Interview with S. Dilman, undated, Box TU 01 tape 46.

45. ATASE, *23ncu Piyade Tümeni Tarihçesi*, unpublished staff study, ATASE Library, Record 26-412, p. 28.

46. Ibid., p. 29. The 23rd Infantry Division staff selected Captain Zeki (3/68th Infantry Regiment), Lieutenants Ahmet Hikmet (69th Infantry Regt) and Adayı Asım (2/68th Inf Regt) and a senior NCO from the 69th Infantry Regiment as the leadership for the division assault detachment.

47. Ibid., p. 28.

48. ATASE, *16nci Piyade Tümeni Tarihçesi*, Record 26-441, p. 48.

49. ATASE, *19ncu Piyade Tümeni Tarihçesi*, Record 26-349, p. 27. These were the very first assault troops introduced into the Ottoman Army. The men were hand-picked and had been sent to courses in hand grenades, the assault crossing of barriers and assault tactics and firing.

50. Ibid., p. 421.

51. This subject will be covered in detail later in this chapter.

52. Onalp et al., *Sina-Filistin Cephesi, İkinci Gazze Muharebesi Sonundan Mütarekesi'ne Kadar Yapılan Harekât*, p. 615. However, many of these troops were deployed along the coast or along the lines of communications and unavailable on the front.

53. Ibid., p. 617.

54. Falls makes the point that the 'policy of Falkenhayn was defence by manoeuvre; that of the Liman defence by resistance in trenches'. Falls and Becke, *Military Operations Egypt and Palestine, From June 1917 to the End of the War*, Part I, p. 311.

55. Force Order No. 68, 9 September 1918, reprinted as Appendix 23 in Falls and Becke, *Military Operations Egypt and Palestine, From June 1917 to the End of the War*, Part II, pp. 713–15.

56. Ibid.

57. XXI Corps Order No. 42, 17 September 1918, reprinted as Appendix 24 in Falls and Becke, *Military Operations Egypt and Palestine, From June 1917 to the End of the War*, Part II, pp. 715–18.

58. Ibid., p. 718.

59. Desert Mounted Corps Operation Order No. 21, 12 September 1918, reprinted as Appendix 26 in Falls and Becke, *Military Operations Egypt and Palestine, From June 1917 to the End of the War*, Part II, pp. 720–3.

60. Cyril Falls, *Armageddon: 1918* (Philadelphia, PA: J. B. Lippincott Company, 1964), p. 36.

61. Jonathan Newell, 'Allenby and the Palestine Campaign', in Brian Bond (ed.), *The First World War and British Military History* (Oxford: Clarendon Press, 1991), pp. 199–200.

62. Onalp et al., *Sina-Filistin Cephesi, İkinci Gazze Muharebesi Sonundan Mütarekesi'ne Kadar Yapılan Harekât*, p. 618. Pre-war Ottoman doctrinal templates assigned an infantry division a defensive front of 3.5km, but by 1918 (with additional machine guns and artillery) this had increased to 5km. See T. C. Genelkurmay Başkanlığı,

Türk Silahlı Kuvvetleri Tarihi (1908–1920), p. 312 for pre-1914 defensive frontages.
63. Ibid.
64. Onalp et al., *Sina-Filistin Cephesi, İkinci Gazze Muharebesi Sonundan Mütarekesi'ne Kadar Yapılan Harekât*, pp. 616–18 and Belen, *Birinci Cihan Harbinde, Türk Harbi, 1918 Yılı Hareketleri*, Kroki (Overlay) 15.
65. ATASE, *21nci Piyade Alay Tarihçesi*, Record 26-327, p. 32.
66. Onalp et al., *Sina-Filistin Cephesi, İkinci Gazze Muharebesi Sonundan Mütarekesi'ne Kadar Yapılan Harekât*. See Koral et al., *Idari Faaliyetler ve Lojistik*, pp. 745–72.
67. ATASE, Letter to Yildirim Army Group from Eighth Army, 17 September 1918, Archive 3787, Record H-37, File 11, reprinted in Onalp et al., *Sina-Filistin Cephesi, İkinci Gazze Muharebesi Sonundan Mütarekesi'ne Kadar Yapılan Harekât*, p. 621.
68. NARA, Letter, Fevzi to von Falkenhayn, 15 February 1918, AEF G-2, RG 120, NH 91, Entry 187, Box 5836.
69. See, for example, Sheffy, *British Military Intelligence in the Palestine Campaign 1914–1918*, pp. 300–7.
70. NARA, Military Situation in Turkey, 30 August 1918, AEF G-2, RG 120, NH 91, Entry 187, Box 5836, Case 43-3.
71. This problem was exaggerated by the worsening relationship between Germany and the Ottoman Empire caused by Enver's aggressive expansion into Georgia in May 1918 (in violation of the Treaty of Brest-Litovsk). See Erickson, *Ordered To Die*, pp. 186–7.
72. NARA, Near Eastern Intelligence Report, 18 February 1918, AEF G-2, RG 120, NH 91, Entry 187, Box 5828.
73. Ibid.
74. NARA, Near Eastern Intelligence Report, 27 February 1918, AEF G-2, RG 120, NH 91, Entry 187, Box 5828.
75. NARA, Turkish Military Notes, 21 January 1918, AEF G-2, RG 120, NH 91, Entry 187, Box 5828.
76. Ibid.
77. Ibid.

Chapter 8

1918
Megiddo and Syria

Introduction

Allenby's EEF endured the brutally hot Palestinian summer in the fixed lines it had occupied since the spring and, in order to provide men, organizations, and equipment for the main theatre in France, underwent relentless 'Indianization' and multi-echelon training. While the EEF grew stronger in capability and capacity, the Yildirim Army Group grew progressively weaker. On 19 September 1918, Allenby unleashed a carefully crafted, deliberate and ambitious offensive that ruptured the Ottoman lines and led to a catastrophic breakthrough. The breakthrough was followed by a cavalry envelopment of the Ottoman Eighth Army, which forced the army group to abandon the defensive lines it had held successfully for six months. These were known to the British as the Battle of Megiddo and the Battle of the Nablus Plain to the Ottomans. Overall, Allenby's final campaigns in the Palestine theatre were rapid, decisive and can be characterized as campaigns of manoeuvre.

After Megiddo, Allenby swung his cavalry over the Jordan River attempting to trap the Seventh and Eighth Armies. However, a magnificent tactical performance by Mustafa Kemal and his Seventh Army enabled his army and the remnants of the Eighth Army to retreat across the Jordan River to the safety of the east bank. Allenby then pushed his cavalry north of Lake Tiberius and drove on Damascus using his cavalry in a pursuit operations in an attempt to trap pockets of the retreating Yildirim Army Group south of the city. Once again, brilliant manoeuvring by Mustafa Kemal ensured that most of the surviving Yildirim formations escaped destruction. Forced to retreat from Damascus, Kemal's sure tactical grip made it possible for the surviving Ottoman and German forces to withdraw to Aleppo. While many historians consider Mustafa Kemal's performance at Gallipoli as his finest hour, arguably it was his ability as a practitioner of manoeuvre warfare while being pursued that stands out as his most significant military achievement. At the armistice on 30 October 1918, the greatly reduced and battered Yildirim Army Group was still in the field and capable of resistance. It was a remarkable accomplishment under any circumstances.

Ottoman Intelligence and Operational Surprise

It is commonly held that the Ottomans had expected a major British offensive for some time but were unable to pinpoint its location. Cyril Falls wrote in 1930 that, 'the enemy was thoroughly deceived, wholly unaware of the devastating blow that was about to be dealt to him'.[1] Subsequent English language historians have repeated this theme consistently and it has become part of the Allenby legend.[2] Allenby's plan involved an elaborate deception scheme designed to focus the Turks on the Jordan Valley and fool them into thinking that it was there that he intended to attack. Much of the operational beauty of Allenby's attack involved the skilful concentration of troops hidden by a complicated ruse. The dramatic and surprisingly easy breakthrough of the Ottoman lines on 19 September appeared to vindicate the totality of Allenby's planning effort. In fact, the success of Allenby's deception operation has never been seriously questioned and the assumption that it was a major contribution to his victory detracts from the tactical accomplishments of Allenby's XXI Corps.

The official Turkish military history relates that on 17 September 1918, Ottoman Army intelligence placed five infantry divisions and a French detachment in the west opposite the Eighth Army.[3] Moreover, Ottoman intelligence reckoned that two divisions faced the Seventh Army and two mounted divisions were on the Jordan River Front. Brigadier General Cevat, the Eighth Army commander, was especially concerned about the threat to his front and requested permission on 17 September 1918 to reorganize his defensive arrangements with a view to pulling back from his vulnerable front-line positions.[4] This point is mentioned by Falls in a footnote referring to an Indian Army deserter captured by the Turks on the same day (17 September) who revealed that a major British attack was scheduled for 19 September.[5] However, Falls concluded that Liman von Sanders thought the desertion was a ruse and denied Cevat's request. It should be noted that, in his memoirs, Liman von Sanders did not mention that he was, in any way, surprised by Allenby's attack, either in location, time or intensity.[6] While Allenby's offensive was sudden and unannounced by a long preliminary artillery bombardment, it was not a revelation at either the operational or tactical levels.

The objective evidence supporting is that there were no Ottoman troop movements in reply to Allenby's deception plan. In theory, Ottoman reserves should have been drawn to the Jordan River Front; in fact, exactly the reverse happened. At the theatre level, Liman von Sanders's only incoming reinforcement, the 2nd Caucasian Cavalry Brigade, was routed to the Eighth Army sector and began to arrive at Tul Karm on 16 September.[7] At the operational level, the entire 46th Infantry Division, in reserve near the Eighth Army's headquarters at Tul Karm, was moved 13km to the south west on 17 September to a new reserve position at Tire – directly behind Cevat's threatened Ottoman XXII Corps on the coast.[8] Furthermore, at the tactical level, Ottoman regiments on the front lines were alerted that a major attack was imminent.[9]

In studies of the last two years of the First World War, much can be understood about intentions and priorities by examining where the heavy artillery was positioned.[10] This was true for both offensive and defensive operations because counter-battery artillery operations (using heavy guns and howitzers) had become such an essential part of battle tactics. In Palestine in mid-September 1918, the 'majority of the (Yildirim) army's heavy artillery was deployed in the XXII Corps area'.[11] In fact, three of five Ottoman Army heavy artillery battalions (the 72nd, 73rd and 75th) available in Palestine were deployed in the Eighth Army sector.[12] The remaining two heavy artillery battalions were assigned to Mustafa Kemel's adjacent Seventh Army amd these were positioned close to the Eighth Army boundary (rather than towards the Jordan Valley). Significantly, Liman von Sanders did not assign any heavy artillery battalions to the Fourth Army on the Jordan River Front, although an Austrian heavy artillery battery served there.

The infantry divisions on the threatened front were some of the most highly regarded fighting formations in the Ottoman Army – reflecting the strategic priority of the coastal plain. The 7th and 19th Infantry Divisions were part of Esat Pasha's III Corps at Gallipoli and had earned fine reputations there. The 20th Infantry Division was a pre-war active army division that was raised and stationed in Palestine and it could be called an 'Arab' division. But, as a matter of record, the division had fought well in the latter phases of Gallipoli and was so highly regarded that it was selected for deployment to Galicia for a year of combat against the Russians in Eastern Europe. When the 20th Infantry Division was sent to Palestine in 1918, it was regarded as one of the best divisions in the Ottoman Army.[13]

Altogether the evidence indicates that the Yildirim Army Group was not surprised by Allenby's deception plan and Ottoman commanders were well aware of the strength and location of the impending attack. The few reserves and reinforcements that were available to Liman von Sanders were shifted to the west and not to the east, as desired by Allenby. Moreover, the important coastal plain was heavily weighted by both experienced infantry divisions and by the army's heavy artillery making that area the most strongly defended sector of the Ottoman Front.

The Operational Balance

Beginning in March, Allenby sent the equivalent of over six infantry divisions plus supporting arms to France.[14] In return, he received several Indian Army infantry divisions and a number of Indian cavalry regiments and infantry battalions leaving his army with seven full-strength infantry divisions in Palestine. In mounted strength Allenby's army improved, gaining one division, for a new total of four mounted divisions. Allenby still commanded a large army of some 56,000 riflemen, 11,000 cavalry and 552 artillery pieces.[15]

The Yildirim Army Group disposed 40,598 front-line infantrymen, armed with 19,819 rifles, 273 light and 696 heavy machine guns.[16] For the 90km-plus-wide front, Liman von Sanders had twelve under-strength infantry divisions, a cavalry division and a cavalry brigade available for the defence. Cevat's Eighth Army defended the coast with the XXII Corps (7th and 20th Infantry Divisions) and the provisional Left Wing Group, a corps-sized formation commanded by German Colonel Gustav von Oppen (16th and 19th Infantry Divisions, and the German Asia Corps). A significant asset for the Ottomans returned in the person of Mustafa Kemal, who took command of the Seventh Army on 17 August. The line continued with Mustafa Kemal's Seventh Army of the III Corps (1st and 11th Infantry Divisions) and the XX Corps (26th and 53rd Infantry Division). Cemal's Fourth Army hooked south with the VIII Corps (48th, a provisional division, and the division-sized Şerştal Group), the Şeria Group (3rd Cavalry Division and 24th Infantry Division) and the II Corps (62nd Infantry Division). Available for reserve duty were the 2nd Caucasian Cavalry Brigade in the Eighth Army area and the 3rd Cavalry Division in the Fourth Army area.

Allenby's plan was the operational reverse of the Gaza–Beersheba plan of 1917. Instead of feinting near the sea and attacking inland as he had done at Beersheba, in 1918 Allenby chose to feint near the Jordan River (scene of his spring and summer offensives) and then to smash his way through the Ottoman defences on a narrow avenue next to the sea. After achieving a breakthrough, Allenby intended to pass his cavalry corps through the breach and rupture the Ottoman lines of communications. This being accomplished, Allenby sought to envelop the remaining Ottoman forces. It was operational art on a grand scale.

British offensive began with the Arabs and Lawrence conducting railway-cutting raids between Dera and Amman on 16 September. On 17 and 18 September, Allenby's XX Corps began a diversionary attack in the left centre of the Ottoman Front. These operations were designed to fix the Ottomans in place and to deceive them as to the true location of the main attack. At 4.30 am on the morning of 19 September, Allenby attacked with XXI Corps (reinforced) on a narrow 20km-wide sector adjacent to the sea. Here, he concentrated 35,000 infantry, 9,000 cavalry and 400 guns (60 per cent of his infantry, 80 per cent of his cavalry and 72 per cent of his artillery) against the 8,000 infantry and 120 guns of the Ottoman Eighth Army.[17] What the British would call the Battle of Megiddo and the Ottomans would call the Battle of the Nablus Plain had begun.

The Battle of the Nablus Plain (Megiddo)
The two weak and poorly supported Ottoman Army infantry divisions facing Allenby's XXI Corps absorbed his main effort on 19 September 1918. This day was critical because, like the fall of Beersheba during the previous year, the destruction of these divisions caused a rupture of the Ottoman lines resulting in a complete failure of the Yildirim Army Group's operational posture. The official Turkish military history provides little insight into this catastrophe and yields only a scant seven pages on this day of battle (Cyril Falls used twenty-three pages in his official British history).

The main attack of four British infantry divisions (60th, 75th, 3rd Indian and 7th Indian) fell on Cevat's Eighth Army hitting the two divisions of Colonel Refet's XXII Corps. These were the 7th Infantry Division, commanded by Lieutenant Colonel Nasuhi, and the 20th Infantry Division, commanded by Lieutenant Colonel Veysel. Neither the British nor the Turkish official histories address the actual numerical superiority achieved by Allenby in this critical sector. The most commonly accepted

Map 8.1: Allenby's Megiddo offensive, 19–21 September 1918

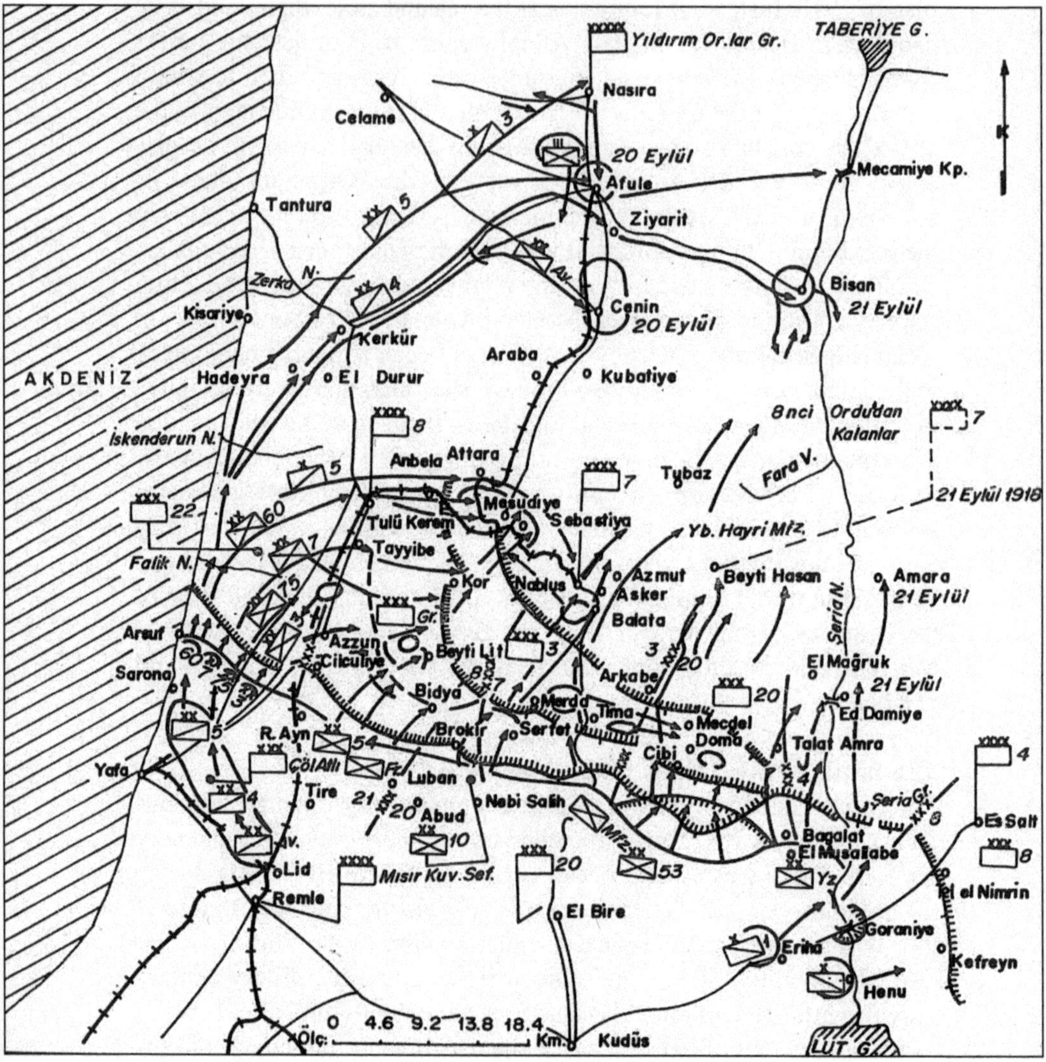

figures are that Cevat's 8,000 infantry and 130 guns faced Allenby's 35,000 infantry, 9,000 cavalry and 383 guns.[18] However, these figures do not clearly define the immense concentration of effort that Allenby actually achieved because they do not separate clearly the Ottoman XXII Corps, the Von Oppen Group or the army reserves. Writing in 1967, retired General Fahri Belen, who was a participant in the Palestine Campaigns, listed the strength of the Ottoman XXII Corps as 3,000 infantry, 134 machine guns and 94 guns.[19] Belen also listed the strength of the 46th Infantry Division as a mere 500 infantrymen in two regiments, of which one regiment was 'Arab'. Assuming that each of the 8 British brigades attacking the XXII Corps contained about 3,000 infantrymen, about 24,000 Indian and British infantry (supported by almost 400 guns) attacked 2,000 Ottoman infantry (supported by 100 guns) near daybreak on 19 September 1918. These figures do not count the four British infantry brigades in reserve, the 53rd Infantry Division or the three cavalry and mounted divisions.

In Lieutenant Colonel Nasuhi's 7th Infantry Division sector British artillery shelling began at 4.35 am, 19 September 1918, and the attack was in full swing by 7.30 am. The division reported that 'the front cracked' at 8.30 am.[20] At regimental level, the division's 20th Infantry Regiment also reported heavy shelling at 4.35 am, noting that it was especially heavy in the adjacent sector (its sister 21st Infantry Regiment) and 'within minutes our communications were broken'.[21] Moreover, the accuracy of the shelling indicated that it was registered effectively and then at 5.10 am, the main weight of the shelling shifted onto the 20th Infantry Regiment itself. This was followed by an immediate infantry attack and at 5.35 am the headquarters command post of the 20th Infantry Regiment came under direct enemy rifle fire.[22] Shortly thereafter, 'English infantry and cavalry began to mop up.'[23]

Nasuhi's 21st Infantry Regiment suffered a similar fate. Shelling began at 4.30 am and the enemy infantry attacked at 4.50 am.[24] At 6.15 am, the regimental headquarters reported that the enemy had penetrated completely through its lines and had broken into the second line of defences held by the 19th Infantry Regiment.[25] News from the other units was equally bleak, but despite the disaster, Ottoman commanders attempted to restore the tactical situation. At about 7.30 am, the 20th Infantry Regiment sent its reserve company to the aid of the collapsing 21st Infantry Regiment.[26] However, this was too small a force to stop the two full-strength British infantry divisions that were pouring through the ruptured lines. In the adjacent sector the regiments of Lieutenant Colonel Veysel's 20th Infantry Division received a similar pounding.[27]

Although wire communications were cut almost immediately, runners carried word of the debacle to Colonel Refet and the staff of the Ottoman XXII Corps in El Tire. At 8.00 am, Refet committed his last reserve, the 17th Engineer Battalion, which he sent forward.[28] At the same time, the Eighth Army notified Colonel Refet that it had released the army reserve, the 46th Infantry Division, to the XXII Corps. In the next hour the corps staff sent reports to the army staff outlining the criticality of the situation and explaining the fact that it was attempting to organize a withdrawal.[29] At 8.50 am, Cevat's Eighth Army headquarters sent a dismal report to Liman von Sanders at the Yildirim Army Group outlining the situation:

> I am in great difficulty because of the terrible situation on the right wing. The 7th Division is out of the fight. The XXII Corps is retreating from El Tire and most of its artillery is lost. The corps is working to preserve itself, but its commander is worried about encirclement. The enemy has broken through our lines in spite of our counter-attacks. The 19th Division is retreating toward Kefri Kasim. Without assistance operations are impossible.[30]

It appears that Cevat's report failed to reach the army group headquarters. In his memoirs Liman von Sanders asserted that communications with the Eighth Army ceased at about 7.00 am on 19 September 1918.[31] He also claimed not to have known about the breakthrough in the western coast sector until later except through the reports of Colonel von Oppen. In any case, the Turkish official history and Liman von Sanders' memoirs coincide in their description of his attempts to repair the tactical situation by noting that he ordered the Seventh Army to organize a relief force comprising one battalion from the 110th Infantry Regiment and one battalion from the Depot Regiment for operations near El Tire.[32] He also ordered that the force be composed of fresh troops and should include as many cavalry detachments as possible.

In the adjacent sector of the von Oppen Group, the 19th Infantry Division was attacked by the all-British 54th Infantry Division. The mission of the 54th Infantry Division was to push forward and act as the pivot for Allenby's encircling left wing. Although this attack was not as strong as those on the divisions of the XXII Corps, the 19th Infantry Division was shelled heavily and subjected to similar infantry assaults. Falls asserted that the 54th Infantry Division broke through the Ottoman lines. In fact, although badly battered, most of the 19th Infantry Division managed to withdraw successfully, however 700 soldiers, 9 guns and 20 machine guns were captured by the British.[33] Importantly for Cevat, both of von Oppen's divisions, the 19th and 16th Infantry Divisions, were intact and retreating under his orders.[34]

The 16th Infantry Division, commanded by Colonel Rüştü (later

Rüştü Sakarya), was the least engaged of the four front-line divisions of the Eighth Army and was attacked by part of the 54th Infantry Division and the French DFPS (a brigade-sized force of colonial and Armenian troops). Unusually, this division reported that it was expecting the attack and held itself in readiness during the night of 18/19 September.[35] Rüştü deployed his 47th and 48th Infantry Regiments holding the front line and he maintained the strongest local reserve of any division on the Palestine Front, composed of the 1st Battalion, 125th Infantry Regiment, a platoon of the 48th Infantry Regiment's machine-gun company and the divisional assault, engineer and cavalry companies. Rüştü's division was also attacked at 4.50 am on 19 September and his situation reports flowed freely upward to von Oppen over telephone lines that had remained intact.[36] Due to the open terrain, the soldiers of Rüştü's forward regiments could clearly see the British assault and they could also see the difficulties of the adjacent 19th Infantry Division. At 10.00 am, Rüştü committed the 1/125th Infantry Regiment and the cavalry troop, and he learned at the same time that the adjacent XXII Corps was in retreat. According to Rüştü, 'Heavy enemy rifle and artillery fires made the tactical situation difficult but manageable.'[37] By 5.00 pm Rüştü had committed all of his remaining reserves but was still holding his positions. About an hour later Rüştü decided to retreat under pressure only because of the disastrous situation on his right threatened to expose his flank.

By noon, Cevat at Eighth Army headquarters was aware that enemy cavalry was near Afule and was advancing on his headquarters at Tul Karem.[38] Concerned about the prospect of capture, he considered moving his headquarters into the hills to his north. By 4.30 pm, he knew that El Tire had fallen but he determined to stay in place for as long as possible in order to maintain effective command. But as darkness fell on 19 September, Cevat recognized that he was completely cut off from news and reports from his subordinate units and he began to move his headquarters north east.[39]

According to Liman von Sanders, the 7th and 20th Infantry Divisions 'completely disappeared' on 19 September. However, this was retrospective, and he claimed not to have known it at the time and he assumed that they 'were falling back to the prepared positions in the rear'.[40] In fact, small groups of survivors did manage to fall back and continue fighting. The cadre of the 7th Infantry Division's staff, for example, fell back to Mesudiye, where it re-established the division headquarters.[41] The British attacked this group the next day and by

2.00 pm, the survivors were completely scattered and had 'melted away'.[42] The division's hard-hit 20th and 21st Infantry Regiments, likewise, were pounded into remnants on 21 September.

The Von Oppen Group's 16th Infantry Division had much better luck than the other Ottoman infantry divisions on the line that day but its situation deteriorated rapidly in the days that followed. This division conducted a fighting retreat on 20 and 21 September, during which it lost most of its artillery.[43] However, by 22 September it too was reduced to less than 480 officers and men.[44] By 24 September, the battered division reported that there were 'enemy horse units everywhere and that it was relying on machine guns to keep them at bay'.[45] Later that day, the division headquarters, now co-located with the surviving headquarters elements of the 19th Infantry Division, came under heavy rifle fire from Indian cavalry at ranges of less than 150m. Both headquarters were overrun and captured.[46] The 2nd and 3rd Battalions, 125th Infantry Regiment and the combined assault/engineers company survived the debacle and fought a delaying action to Damascus, where they finally were captured on 1 October 1918, ending the story of this division.

In the Seventh Army's sector, Allenby's 53rd Infantry Division artillery began to shell the XX Corps' 26th Infantry Division at 10.00 pm, 18 September in the vulnerable salient around the town of Samiye. The 163rd Infantry Regiment reported that the enemy artillery was using gas shells (this report proved to be false).[47] The division commander, Lieutenant Colonel Mehmet Hayri (later Mehmet Hayri Tarhan), released his reserve, a battalion of the 63rd Infantry Regiment, and sent it forward. The adjacent III Corps sector remained quiet. Concerned of an impending attack, XX Corps commander, Ali Fuat, alerted his army reserves, the 2nd Battalion, 109th Infantry Regiment and the 3rd Corps Assault Battalion at Mecdel beni Fadıl. Mustafa Kemal also placed his army reserves, the 7th Army Assault Battalion and the 1st Battalion, 110th Infantry Regiment, co-located with his own headquarters in Nablus, on alert as well. Six British aircraft bombed Kemal's Nablus headquarters at 5.00 am at the same time as a general assault opened up on his army front. Communications between the army headquarters and the subordinate corps and divisions then broke down rapidly thereafter because British aircraft targeted the key communications nodes and headquarters command posts.[48]

There was less enemy pressure on İsmet's III Corps but the British 53rd Infantry Division made rapid progress in the seizure of the XX Corps' salient at Samiye. Ali Fuat decided at about 1.30 am to commit his army reserves at Mecdel beni Fadıl and ordered both battalions to counter-attack. However, these attacks failed to halt the oncoming enemy. In the late afternoon a message from Liman von Sanders reached Mustafa Kemal asking if he could hold his lines in accordance with the army group directives. Kemal answered that the situation was exceptionally dangerous and that he had already given orders to conduct a fighting retreat.[49]

The 19 September 1918 was a disaster for Liman von Sanders and ranks as one of the most decisive single days in the First World War. Allenby's XXI Corps (composed of 4 infantry divisions in the main effort) alone reported capturing about 7,000 prisoners and some 100 guns.[50] More importantly, the entire right wing of the Ottoman Eighth Army had been destroyed and Chauvel's Desert Mounted Corps, composed of two cavalry divisions and the Australian and New Zealand Mounted Division, was unleashed into the army group's rear area. Chauvel pushed his troopers relentlessly in a cavalry exploitation that made any Ottoman reaction, other than immediate withdrawal, irrelevant. In one day Allenby's men had advanced over 20km at cost of some 1,500 casualties and put the Ottomans in an untenable operational position. In addition to the massive number of POWs taken, Allenby's men probably killed and wounded another 3,000 Ottomans and Germans.[51] (See map 8.1.)

Early on 20 September British cavalry took Nazareth, almost capturing a surprised and sleepy Liman von Sanders at 4.30 am that morning. Heavy attacks also developed against the III Corps at 10.00 am on 20 September and İsmet recognized the acute danger to his right flank. İsmet's 1st Infantry Division was able to hold out in its lines but had to abandon them by midday. After escaping to Nablus, Liman von Sanders ordered the 1st Assault Battalion to Der Şeraf and also ordered the Fourth Army to send a cavalry regiment to the aid of the Seventh Army.[52] Late that day, Mustafa Kemal received a report that enemy cavalry had seized Afule and Cenin. He immediately ordered his corps commanders to fall back to a line from Surra through Akrebe to Mafit on the Jordan River.[53] These orders oriented the III Corps facing west to block Allenby's cavalry while XX Corps maintained a fighting withdrawal north toward Beyti Hasan. Ali Fuat was instructed to keep contact with the Fourth Army as he fell back toward the Jordan River bridge at Eddamiya. Kemal's orders were dispatched to İsmet and Ali Fuat at 1.45 pm by telephone. Kemal's prompt and decisive action on 20 September enabled the remnants of the Eighth Army to survive while at the same time prevented an even worse disaster from overtaking the Yildirim Army Group.

Also on the afternoon of 20 September, Kemal formed the provisional Hayri Bey Detachment (Hayri Bey Müfrezesi), under the command of Lieutenant Colonel Hayri, the chief of the army's intelligence directorate (*Ordu 2nci Şube Müdürü*).[54] He assigned Hayri the 3rd Assault Battalion and the 2/109th Infantry Regiment, as well as the army's cavalry squadron and a few unassigned officers, and ordered Hayri's detachment to Beyti Hasan to serve as a fresh tactical reserve. Kemal then sent his chief of staff and aide-de-camp to Beyti Hasan to re-establish his headquarters there and take control. At 6.00 pm, Kemal began to move the main elements of the Seventh Army headquarters from Nablus to Beyti Hasan. In a matter of hours Mustafa Kemal had formulated a tactical plan to save his army, consolidated his reserves under centralized command and repositioned his headquarters in a safer location. This was a remarkable achievement given that his command posts were subjected to constant bombing by British aircraft throughout the day.

On 21 September, the pieces of the surviving Eighth Army divisions, the 16th, 19th and 46th Infantry Divisions, withdrew to the area around Nablus. At 3.00 pm on 21 September, Cevat, the Eighth Army commander, who had asked to withdraw in the anticipation of a heavy attack, got in his automobile and departed Nablus.[55] He made his way to the sanctuary of Mustafa Kemal's Seventh Army headquarters, accompanied by his chief of staff and several staff officers, while his surviving infantry made their way north east to an assembly area between Tubas and Cerze. Mustafa Kemal's Seventh Army, on 21 September, conducted a withdrawal to a line centred on Beyti Hasan.

Attacks by Chaytor's Force on the Fourth Army began in earnest on 20 September and the VIII Corps forces, the 48th Infantry Division, the provisional division and cavalry group, holding the Guraniye bridgehead began to unravel under enemy pressure. Moreover, in the Fourth Army's rear, the 62nd Infantry Division of Colonel Şevket's II Corps (headquartered in Amman) was engaged fighting the Arabs between Tafile and Maan, creating a dangerous situation.[56] That evening, Little Cemal had a telephone discussion with Liman von Sanders's operations staff, who authorized him to break contact and withdraw from the Jordan River line. By the evening of 21 September, Little Cemal had withdrawn his 24th Infantry Division east across the Jordan River bridge at Eddamiye, while the 48th Infantry Division retreated toward Es Salt. In order to ensure tactical unity of command, he formed the forces converging at Es Salt into an ad hoc combat group under the command of German Colonel Hunger. On the Fourth Army's left flank the provisional division and the cavalry withdrew toward Amman. Importantly, Little Cemal pulled Esat's (who was now recovered from his wounds) 3rd Cavalry Division out of the collapsing line and sent it north along the east bank of the Jordan River.

At the beginning of 22 September the Desert Mounted Corps held Cenin and Afule, with brigades moving north toward Nasıra and east toward Bisan. Moreover, Allenby's infantry divisions were pushing steadily from Nablus toward Tubas and Beyti Hasan. Liman von Sanders ordered the Eighth Army and the remnants of the 16th and 19th Infantry Divisions and the German Asia Corps north from Tubas to block the road south of Bisan. He also detached the 3rd Cavalry Division, which had made its way to Selhiyat, from the Fourth Army and placed it under the operational command of the Seventh Army.

Mustafa Kemal ordered Lieutenant Colonel Hayri to defend the Beyti Hasan 'chokepoint' (*Beyti Hasan Boğazı*) because it was the key crossroads where the elements of his retreating army would have to pass through to avoid capture.[57] At the same time, he ordered İsmet's III Corps to defend the town of Tubas and he sent orders to Esat to push his 3rd Cavalry Division north along the east bank of the Jordan to block the British cavalry which had forded the river east of Bisan. In this manner, Mustafa Kemal created a secure perimeter on the west bank of the Jordan into which the Seventh and Eighth Armies could compress themselves and then withdraw over the river to the east.

The Battle of the Nablus Plain ends here in the Turkish official histories and the battle ranks with Ludendorff's 'Black Day' of the German Army in the effect that it had on the consciousness of the Ottoman general staff. It was now apparent to all but the most diehard Young Turks that the Ottomans were finished in the war. In spite of the great concurrent victories in Armenia and in Azerbaijan, the Ottoman Empire was now in an indefensible condition, which could not be remedied with the resources on hand. It was also evident that the disintegration of the Bulgarian Army at Salonika and the dissolution of the Austro-Hungarian Army spelled disaster and defeat for the Central Powers. From now until the armistice the goal of Ottoman strategy in the Middle East would be to retain as much Ottoman territory as possible while preserving the army.

Liman von Sanders could be criticized for not withdrawing the

Eighth Army to a more defensible position, as suggested by Cevat. In theory this might have preserved the army to fight another day. However, transport and animal services were in as bad a condition as the human element of the army. Liman von Sanders made the point that in mid-1918 'there was a gradual failing of the draft and pack animals'.[58] This was the result of inadequate grain supplies, poor pastures and lack of good water. While Cevat's infantry and machine-gunners may have been able to conduct some kind of deliberate withdrawal or fighting retreat, the artillery, ammunition trains, service support units and hospitals were reduced to an almost static posture by September 1918. This point is confirmed by the Turkish official history.[59] The resulting lack of tactical mobility meant that the Yildirim Army Group was compelled to remain in its lines and attempt to fight the British using the bravery and determination that had made the Ottoman Army such a deadly adversary in the past.

Why had Liman von Sanders's front collapsed so quickly? He had, after all, the highest ratio of artillery and machine guns yet seen by an Ottoman army available to support his entrenched infantry. There were three basic reasons, none of which had anything to do with the fighting attributes of the Ottoman soldiers themselves. First, the terrain was favourable for the attack, at least in comparison with the Jordan River Valley and the Judean hills. Second, there was scope at the operational level for Allenby to shift corps-sized formations around the battlefield for deception and concentration. Third, the British Army had made mighty improvements in its organization and training and was very capable in the most current tactical methods. Whether the outcome of these battles would have been different had Liman von Sanders employed Falkenhayn's concepts of flexible defence is problematic. However, it is likely that a more flexible Ottoman defence would not have resulted in the total destruction of division-level Ottoman formations. While surely the British would have advanced in any case, the survival of the infantry divisions on the Ottoman right flank might have prevented the ruptured lines that enabled the great British cavalry breakthrough leading to the disaster.

Allenby's Pursuit to Aleppo

Allenby's cavalry swept north capturing the coastal cities of Haifa and Acre as well as the town of Meggido. On 23 September, Mustafa Kemal pulled the III Corps east to Malih screening Ali Fuat's XX Corps, which withdrew east of the river at the Dir el Amar ford. Lieutenant Colonel Nasuhi commanded İsmet's rear guard and fought a successful fighting withdrawal. The remnants of the Eighth Army fought a delaying action against Chauvel's 4th Cavalry Division before finding fords across the river just south of the Wadi Yabis. To the north of the wadi, Esat's 3rd Cavalry Division screened the Eighth Army's withdrawal across the river. After crossing the river the cadre of the 16th Infantry Division's 125th Infantry Regiment plus the division's assault company and its engineer company deployed to assist Esat's troopers protect the fords.[60]

From his headquarters in Beyti Hasan, Mustafa Kemal reacted equally swiftly and ordered his units due east to cross the river. With the remnants of the Eighth Army to his north most of Kemal's forces made it safely across the Jordan River on the night of 23/24 September. On 24 September, İsmet withdrew his III Corps over the Dir el Amar fords to the east bank of the Jordan, losing only the 1st Battalion, 71st Infantry Regiment, which was captured. So precipitous was the retreat that most of the withdrawing units were forced to abandon their stocks of ammunition and food.

The Fourth Army abandoned Amman on 25 September and Little Cemal split his mobile forces into two main groups for the retreat north. He ordered the Hunger Group, commanded by German Colonel Hunger and composed of the German 146th Infantry Regiment and an Ottoman regiment, to withdraw from Es Salt north though El Ceba toward Dera. He also ordered the VIII Corps, composed in the main of the 48th Infantry Division, to withdraw along the railway to Mafrak and thence toward Dera. In this way, the Fourth Army blocked both avenues of advance from Es Salt–Amman to Dera. On the Little Cemal's right flank, Mustafa Kemal put together a similar fighting withdrawal.[61] He ordered the III Corps to withdraw to Müzeyrib (north west of Dera) and the XX Corps to withdraw to Dera itself, where it rendezvoused with the German Asia Corps. Both corps were ordered to prepare a defence not later than the evening of 26 September.

On 26 September, these movements were in progress, but the advance of Australian cavalry toward the III Corps's route of withdrawal forced Kemal to block it with the 3rd Cavalry Division. Esat's cavalry fought off the Australians east of Erbid successfully screening and securing the withdrawal. Unfortunately for the Ottomans, Esat's cavalrymen could not hold Erbid, which was a principal logistics centre containing huge quantities of barley, wheat and other cereals.[62] The main elements of the VIII Corps and XX Corps occupied positions around Dera on 26 September and the leading elements of the III Corps occupied Müzeyrib as planned.

The retreat to Dera put all three army headquarters in close proximity to each other and on the night of 26 September the three army commanders and their chiefs of staff met in Dera to co-ordinate their operations. They decided, as a consequence of the destruction of the Eighth Army which now possessed virtually no operational combat forces, that further operations should be undertaken by two army headquarters.[63] The following day, Kemal's Seventh and Cemal's Fourth Armies absorbed the surviving remnants of the Eighth Army. Accordingly, the Eighth Army commander and his headquarters staff were ordered by the general staff to return to Constantinople. Also on this day, Liman von Sanders withdrew his headquarters, the Fourth Army headquarters and the German logistical elements by train from Dera to Damascus. Mustafa Kemal and his Seventh Army headquarters remained behind in Dera to manage the tactical withdrawal to Damascus. He made plans to abandon Dera on 27 September and pull the VII Corps north along the railway to Ezraa and the III and XX Corps north along the roads to Nava and Seyh. In order to screen this withdrawal, Kemal sent the 3rd Cavalry Division to his right flank to block Chaytor's cavalry at Tafas. A sharp battle ensued, but Esat's cavalrymen bought enough time for Kemal to pull his units out of the city.[64]

In the meantime, Indian and Australian cavalry were racing up the coast to the west of Lake Tiberius toward the bridge north of the lake at Benatı Yakup, which they took on 27 September. From there, Chauvel launched the Australian and New Zealand Mounted Division and the 5th Cavalry Division toward Damascus, while Chaytor's 4th Cavalry Division took Dera on the same day. To the west the Arabs launched minor attacks on the Hejaz railway. Alert to the fact that the Allenby's flanking operation on Damascus would trap almost the entire army group, Liman von Sanders ordered Kemal to move formations to blocking positions south west of the city. However, the geography of the operational situation was now working against the Ottomans. The distance from the British positions at the Benatı Yakup bridge to Damascus was 90km, while the distance from Dera to Damascus was 100km, placing Chauvel's cavalry closer to the city than Kemal's Seventh Army. Moreover, Liman von Sanders also had to contend with other enemy cavalry units which were pushing north from Haifa toward Beirut as well.

On 28 September, Chauvel's cavalry defeated a scratch defensive detachment Liman von Sanders had sent to Kuneytara and continued north east toward Damascus. To the east, Kemal withdrew the III Corps successfully to Sanamin and the XX and VIII Corps to Muhacce. The following day, Chauvel's cavalry pushed aside a blocking force at Sa Saassu, placing them about 20km south west of Damascus. Reacting to the dismal operational situation, Liman von Sanders intended that Cemal's Fourth Army would defend Damascus, while Kemal's Seventh Army withdrew through the city to Rayak, where it could reconstitute as well as threaten Allenby's drive on Beirut. However, Chauvel's rapid advance on Damascus demanded immediate action and Liman von Sanders was forced to order Kemal to block Chauvel's advance while Cemal attempted to fortify the city.

Marching rapidly north for two days, İsmet's III Corps reached Kisve station on the outskirts of Damascus on 30 September pivoting west just in time to establish a thin defensive line. This halted Chauvel's advancing cavalry while Kemal then positioned the 3rd Cavalry Division on İsmet's left flank. Simultaneously, Kemal employed Ali Fuat's XX Corps to block the Arabs, who were threatening to cut the route of retreat for the remainder of his army. In this way, Kemal hoped to hold the escape route open long enough to withdraw his forces. However, these units were badly worn down by combat and by retreat, and could not hold off the highly mobile enemy cavalry forces. The 3rd Cavalry Division fought a heroic rear guard action, which allowed the remainder of the Ottoman forces to escape northwards. The remnants of the Fourth and Seventh Armies followed and most of the units successfully moved though Damascus to safety beyond. However, the British pushed Kemal's battered forces back and entered Damascus on 1 October. Kemal's shattered 26th and 53rd Infantry Divisions as well as the 3rd Cavalry Division were trapped and forced to surrender. Although the Seventh Army lost some of its fighting formations, this difficult defensive manoeuvre arguably saved the surviving bulk of the Yildirim Army Group from certain extinction. The army group headquarters retired to Baalbek.

The British handed control of the city of Damascus over to the Arabs, who had earlier seized Dera where they had looted and killed many of its inhabitants. Chaos immediately descended on the city and Arab administration proved both indifferent and incapable of restoring the rule of law. As many as 20,000 starving Ottoman POWs and 800 hospitalized Ottoman soldiers fell into Arab custody.[65] In turn, hundreds of these Ottoman soldiers died of starvation and inadequate medical care.

Kemal now fell back on the railway to Baalbek with the XX Corps, which he reconstituted using the 24th and 43rd Infantry Divisions, while the III Corps blocked the roads north east of Damascus at Eski Han. To their rear the Fourth Army organized the defence of Homs. This was an important geographic location because it was the convergence point for the avenues of advance north into Syria as the coast lacked good roads. Although the British took Homs on 3 October their progress north now slowed to a crawl. Kemal now pulled his battered army north to Aleppo while the Fourth Army delayed the enemy at Homs, which fell six days later. Kemal's shrinking army still composed the III Corps and the XX Corps and he set to work in an attempt to defend Aleppo and established a defensive line south west of the city. The Ottomans lost the services of III Corps commander, Brigadier İsmet, on 5 October, when he fell sick and evacuated to Constantinople. He was replaced officially by Colonel Selahattin ten days later.[66]

The operational situation confronting Liman von Sanders on 6 October 1918 was grim to say the least. The Eighth Army had been destroyed and its headquarters dissolved. The Fourth and Seventh Armies were still intact and conducting a fighting retreat, however these organizations, as well as their subordinate infantry divisions, were armies, corps and divisions in name only. In addition to the crushed divisions of infantry, the Yildirim Army Group had lost most of its artillery and transport. In early October the 43rd Infantry Division arrived as a reinforcement from Rayak and was immediately committed to the defence of Beirut. Although the tactical situation appeared hopeless, the Ottomans and Germans kept fighting.

Allenby's pressure never stopped, and the British took Beirut on 8 October and kept driving northwards. On 13 October Liman von Sanders ordered the inactivation of the Fourth Army headquarters and three days later its last surviving elements were encircled and destroyed in the city of Humus.[67] The 48th Infantry Division attempted to set up blocking positions at Hama, south of Aleppo, but was thrown out of them on 19 October. The next day Kemal reorganized his command structure again by assigning the 1st and 11th Infantry Divisions to Ali Fuat's XX Corps. He tasked Selahattin to reconstitute the III Corps and assigned the 24th and 43rd Infantry Divisions to him. Kemal assigned the defence of Aleppo to the XX Corps which contained veteran and trusted infantry divisions. Although the city's defences were weak, the British chose not to assault Kemal's lines frontally and British cavalry swept to the north west of Aleppo in an attempt to envelop the city on 26 October. (See map 8.2.) According to the British official history, Kemal came up in person and directed a vigorous blocking operation with great boldness. However, his forces were too small and enemy cavalry seized Aleppo at 10.00 am that day. Fortunately for the Ottomans, Mustafa Kemal was able to withdraw his army from the city. Kemal's Seventh Army after conducting a brilliant and prolonged fighting retreat emerged as the sole survivor of the three Ottoman armies, which were stationed in Palestine on 19 September. On 25 October, Allenby's Army entered Aleppo. The campaign for Syria was over.

Supporting Operations by the Arab Armies

Arab attacks on the Medina railway drew to an end in August 1918 as Feisal's Northern Army positioned itself to assist Allenby's EEF in the final breaking of the Ottoman Army in Palestine. In the Turkish official history of the Palestine campaigns, the authors open the story after the Battle of Megiddo noting that, on 25 September 1918, Arab forces were conducting raiding, acts of revenge and sabotage.[68] Arab irregulars were again in action on 27 September near Dera and on 29 September south of Damascus. The Turkish official history does not give many details about specific actions by Feisal's men but noted that they were helpful to the British in the capture of Damascus on 30 September 1918. On the same day near Rayak, the Ottoman 43rd Infantry Division encountered difficulty in keeping its Arab soldiers from deserting their posts and joining the Arab army.[69] This forced the Mustafa Kemal's Seventh Army to send reinforcements there to hold the position. The next day, Feisal's men took the bridge near Tell es Şerif, cutting off temporarily the Ottoman force in Rayak.

As the retreating Ottomans withdrew to Aleppo, two groups of irregular cavalry harassed their flanks. On 10 October 1918, Feisal declared his authority over the city, although it had not yet been taken. On 17 October, the 'always industrious Feisal' approached Hama with 1,200 infantry and 300 cavalry.[70] This action again forced Mustafa Kemal to reinforce his flanks to avoid encirclement. By 23 October, Feisal delayed his attack on Aleppo until the British 5th Cavalry Division pushed to a position north of the city. Feisal's Arabs took Aleppo on 25 October as the Ottoman Seventh Army withdrew its forces. The campaign came to an end on 27 October when the British and Feisal's Arab Northern Army closed the pincers and encircled the few remaining Ottoman forces withdrawing from Aleppo.[71]

These operations had long since cut off Fahrettin's Hejaz Expeditionary Force in Medina as well as the independent Ottoman VII Corps in Yemen. At the time of the armistice, Fahrettin still

Map 8.2: The withdrawal from Aleppo, 25 October 1918

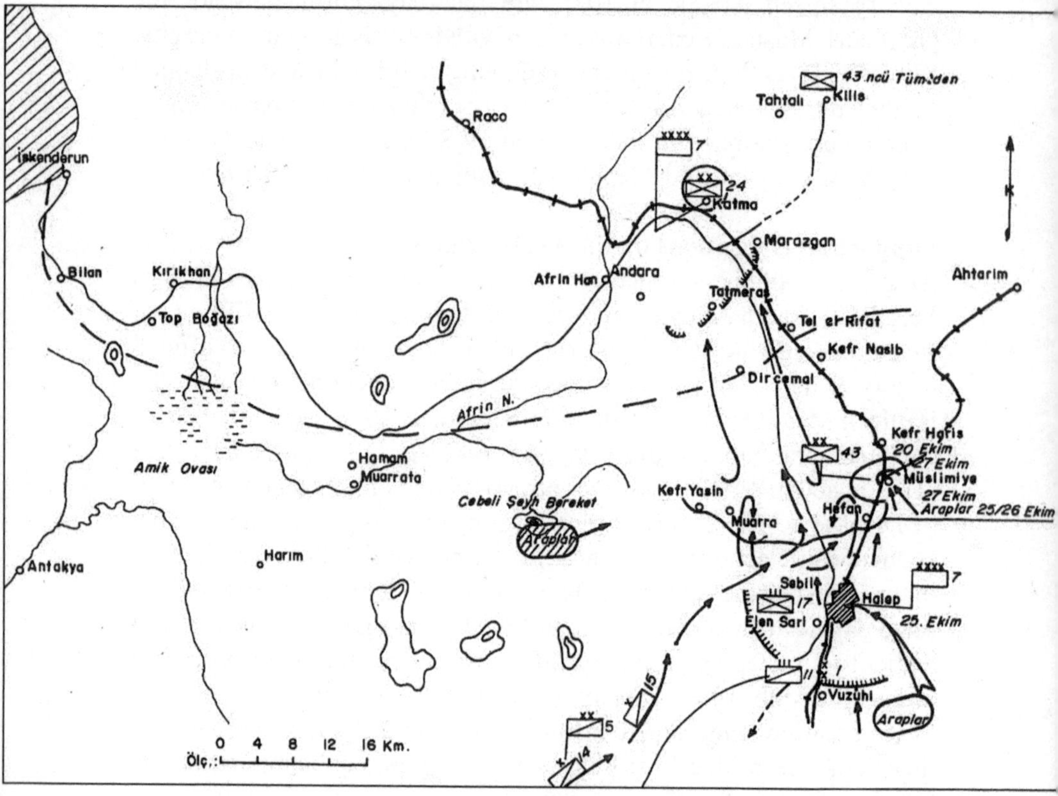

commanded over 10,500 men and maintained control of Medina and its hinterlands.[72] His force was largely self-sufficient in foodstuffs and water and, because the Arabs refused to attack him, his forces were able to conserve their munitions and medical supplies. British officers attached to Emir Ali's headquarters notified Fahrettin of the signing of the Mudros Armistice (which ended the war in the Middle East), especially of paragraph 16, which specified that the Ottoman Army would withdraw from Yemen, the Asir and the Hejaz. However, Fahrettin was unsure about the veracity of the information as well as to how to proceed should it be true. Thereupon he wrote to the new minister of war, Ahmet İzzet Pasha, for instructions while holding his position. In the meantime, he worked with the commander of the 58th Infantry Division on a plan to withdraw his forces to the north. Some of the men would go to Maan via the railway but many would also have to travel in an accompanying wagon train of supplies and equipment.[73] This was because, at this point in the war, fuel for the locomotives was almost non-existent in the Hejaz.

Fahrettin ordered the 2nd Railway Company to start moving some of his men north as early as 8 January and he ordered his staff to arrange transport for the remainder. Moreover, he ensured that the undefeated men of his Hejaz Expeditionary Force travelled in organized units of battalion strength under proper military command and control. It was not until 20 January 1919, that Fahrettin received instructions from Constantinople ordering him to stand down and surrender his men. As his story become known in the post-war Ottoman Empire, he became known to the public as the 'Lion of the Desert' and the 'Defender of Medina'.[74]

Retreat into the Heartland
Driven out of Aleppo on 25 October 1918, Mustafa Kemal re-established his headquarters at Katma and withdrew using the XX Corps' divisions to maintain contact with the enemy. The indefatigable Mustafa Kemal moved his headquarters to Raco and began to prepare yet another defensive line along what is now the southern border of modern Turkey. Behind him lay the Ottoman Second Army guarding the coast and the city of Adana and forces from it were assigned to reinforce him.

On 26 October 1918, the headquarters of the Yildirim Army Group had fallen back to the Anatolian city of Adana, where it was co-located with the headquarters of the Second Army and the XII Corps, as well as the headquarters of the 23rd Infantry Division (which had its main body at Tarsus). The headquarters of the Second Army's XV Corps, composed of the 41st and 44th Infantry Divisions, was located in Osmaniye. Mustafa Kemal's re-established Seventh Army headquarters was located in Raco and he deployed Selahattin's III Corps at Alexandretta (now composed of the 11th and 24th Infantry Divisions) and Ali Fuat's XX Corps near Katma (composed of the 1st and 43rd Infantry Divisions).

One of the last pitched battles of the First World War was also fought on 26 October 1918 at the small village of Haritan, which sits astride the Aleppo–Alexandretta road, 15km north west of Aleppo.[75] At the village 2,500 Ottoman soldiers, from the 24th Infantry Division, armed with 8 artillery pieces and some machine guns dug in and prepared to defend themselves.[76] Indian lancers from the 15th Cavalry Brigade charged the position at 10.45 am only to be driven off. A supporting attack by armoured cars was also beaten off with heavy machine-gun fire.[77] A subsequent charge by the Indians of the 14th Cavalry Brigade was also repulsed and the Ottomans captured eighty Indian soldiers.[78] That evening the division, threatened with a flanking encirclement, withdrew successfully 5km north west to a ridge overlooking the village of Bianum.

In the last days of October Mustafa Kemal's Seventh Army prepared to defend the core provinces of the Ottoman Empire. Under Kemal's confident and inspirational leadership, these small, badly equipped and exhausted forces began to dig in once again. However, morale was high and the soldiers were determined to halt the enemy.[79] Even on this late date, the Seventh Army still had assault troops listed on its order of battle. In the III Corps, the 24th and 43rd Infantry Divisions both had their own intact assault battalions, albeit greatly reduced in strength.[80] The divisional assault units in Ali Fuat's XX Corps divisions were dissolved but he retained an assault company at corps level.

However, before Allenby could marshal an attack on the Anatolian heartland the Ottoman Empire negotiated the Mudros Armistice on 30 October which brought the war to a close. On the same day, the newly installed Ottoman minister of war, Ahmet İzzet Pasha, recalled Liman von Sanders to Constantinople. Simultaneously, the minister of war appointed Mustafa Kemal to command the Yildirim Army Group and ordered him to report to the army group headquarters at Adana the next day. Liman von Sanders's farewell message to his armies praised their performance at Gallipoli, in Palestine and in Syria. He expressed how proud he was to command Ottoman forces from the first time he set foot in the empire and he thanked the Ottomans for their hospitality.[81] The tireless Mustafa Kemal went immediately to work planning for the defence of the Anatolian homeland. After the armistice on 7 November 1918, the Ottoman general staff inactivated the Yildirim Army Group and Seventh Army. Mustafa Kemal remained and was placed in command of the Second Army, which assumed control over the corps and divisions of the inactivated army group and army.

Conclusion

After the breakthrough on 19 September 1918, the final campaigns in the Palestine theatre are best characterized as campaigns and battles of manoeuvre. Allenby's EEF was a well-trained, well-led and highly mobile fighting force and, a cavalryman himself, Allenby relentlessly pushed his subordinate commanders north in pursuit of the Yildirim Army Group. The retreating Ottomans, on the other hand, had lost most of the transport and were penalized by the defeat and the disintegration of their armies. They were not penalized by inept commanders and, remarkably at that stage of the war, were capable of conducting a fighting retreat under intense pressure. A retreat under these conditions is thought to be one of the most difficult military operations to execute successfully. Of note were brilliant tactical performances by Mustafa Kemal and his Seventh Army, İsmet and his III Corps, Ali Fuat and his XX Corps, and Colonel Esat and his 3rd Cavalry Division.

The modern Turkish official history of the Sinai-Palestine campaign does not list the cost or the casualties that the Ottoman Empire sustained in these campaigns. In fact, the Turks today use the generalized British figures of 75,000 prisoners and 360 guns captured in the 6-week campaign from 18 September to 31 October 1918, which are taken from the British official history.[82] Additionally, Feisal's Arab armies claimed to have captured 8,000 Ottoman soldiers and 25–30 guns, as well as killing another 5,000 Ottoman soldiers.[83] The cost to the British was about 6,000 men killed, wounded and missing. Official tabulations of Ottoman casualties are unrecorded, possibly as a result of the loss of army records in the retreat from Palestine. Allenby's lopsided victory seemed near complete; however, it must be remembered that the Ottoman Army was still in the field and actively preparing its defence of the Anatolian heartland when the armistice was signed.

Notes

1. Falls and Becke, *Military Operations Egypt and Palestine, From June 1917 to the End of the War*, Part II, p. 467. Falls based this statement on an Ottoman intelligence map dated 17 September 1918, which was captured at Nazareth.
2. See Bruce, *The Last Crusade*, p. 220, Field Marshal Lord Carver, *The Turkish Front 1914–1918* (London: Sidgwick & Jackson, 2003), pp. 231–3, Falls, *Armageddon: 1918*, p. 46, Michael Hickey, *The First World War, The Mediterranean Front 1914–1923* (Oxford: Osprey Press, 2002), p. 60 and Perrett, *Megiddo 1918*, p. 36.
3. Onalp et al., *Sina-Filistin Cephesi, İkinci Gazze Muharebesi Sonundan Mütarekesi'ne Kadar Yapılan Harekât*, p. 620.
4. ATASE, Letter to Yildirim Army Group from Eighth Army, 17 September 1918, Archive 3787, Record H-37, File 11, reprinted in Onalp et al., *Sina-Filistin Cephesi, İkinci Gazze Muharebesi Sonundan Mütarekesi'ne Kadar Yapılan Harekât*, p. 621.
5. Falls and Becke, *Military Operations Egypt and Palestine, From June 1917 to the End of the War*, Part II, p. 468.
6. Liman von Sanders, *Five Years in Turkey*, pp. 272–80.
7. Belen, *Birinci Cihan Harbinde, Türk Harbi, 1918 Yılı Hareketler,* Kroki (Overlay) 15.
8. Onalp et al., *Sina-Filistin Cephesi, İkinci Gazze Muharebesi Sonundan Mütarekesi'ne Kadar Yapılan Harekât*, p. 625 and Belen, *Birinci Cihan Harbinde, Türk Harbi, 1918 Yılı Hareketleri*, Kroki (Overlay) 15.

9. For example, see ATASE, *20nci Piyade Alay Tarihçesi*, Record 26-327, p. 72 and ATASE, *21nci Piyade Alay Tarihçesi*, Record 26-327, p. 32.

10. In the German Army, for example, Georg Bruchmüller's famous 'flying circus' of artillery moved from battle to battle to support the army's main efforts. Bruce Gudmundsson, *On Artillery* (Westbrook, CT: Praeger, 1993), pp. 87–91.

11. Onalp et al., *Sina-Filistin Cephesi, İkinci Gazze Muharebesi Sonundan Mütarekesi'ne Kadar Yapılan Harekât*, p. 625.

12. Belen, *Birinci Cihan Harbinde, Türk Harbi, 1918 Yılı Hareketleri*, Kuruluş (Organizational Chart) 5.

13. See Erickson, *Ordered To Die*, pp. 137–42 for an examination of the Ottoman Army's campaigns in Galicia, which also included the 19th Infantry Division.

14. General Sir Archibald Wavell, *Allenby, A Study in Greatness* (New York: Oxford University Press, 1941), pp. 249–50.

15. Onalp et al., *Sina-Filistin Cephesi, İkinci Gazze Muharebesi Sonundan Mütarekesi'ne Kadar Yapılan Harekât*, p. 615.

16. Ibid., p. 617.

17. Wavell, *Allenby, A Study in Greatness*, p. 269.

18. See for example, Perrett, *Megiddo 1918*, p. 36 and Falls and Becke, *Military Operations Egypt and Palestine, From June 1917 to the End of the War*, Part II, pp. 452–3. Falls noted that British intelligence listed the total rifle strength of the 7th and 20th Divisions as 1,970 men.

19. Belen, *Birinci Cihan Harbinde, Türk Harbi, 1918 Yılı Hareketleri*, p. 73.

20. ATASE, *7nci Piyade Tümeni Tarihçesi*, unpublished staff study, ATASE Library, Record 26-518, p. 29.

21. ATASE, *20nci Piyade Alay Tarihçesi*, Record 26-327, p. 72.

22. Ibid., p. 64.

23. Ibid.

24. ATASE, *21nci Piyade Alay Tarihçesi*, Record 26-327, p. 32.

25. Ibid.

26. ATASE, *20nci Piyade Alay Tarihçesi*, Record 26-327, p. 73.

27. ATASE, *21nci Piyade Alay Tarihçesi*, Record 26-327, p. 32.

28. Onalp et al., *Sina-Filistin Cephesi, İkinci Gazze Muharebesi Sonundan Mütarekesi'ne Kadar Yapılan Harekât*, p. 626.

29. Ibid.

30. ATASE, Report to Yildirim Army Group from Eighth Army, 8.50 am, 19 September 1918, Archive 3787, Record H-37, File 1-14, reprinted in Onalp et al., *Sina-Filistin Cephesi, İkinci Gazze Muharebesi Sonundan Mütarekesi'ne Kadar Yapılan Harekât*, pp. 626–7.

31. Liman von Sanders, *Five Years in Turkey*, p. 275.

32. Onalp et al., *Sina-Filistin Cephesi, İkinci Gazze Muharebesi Sonundan Mütarekesi'ne Kadar Yapılan Harekât*, p. 627.

33. Falls and Becke, *Military Operations Egypt and Palestine, From June 1917 to the End of the War*, Part II, p. 476.

34. ATASE, *19ncu Piyade Tümeni Tarihçesi*, Record 26-349, p. 33.

35. ATASE, *16nci Piyade Tümeni Tarihçesi*, Record 26-441, p. 58. This division survived for a longer period in September 1918 and its war diaries are more complete than those of the 7th and 20th Infantry Divisions, which were destroyed as fighting organizations by 21 September.

36. Ibid.

37. Ibid.

38. Onalp et al., *Sina-Filistin Cephesi, İkinci Gazze Muharebesi Sonundan Mütarekesi'ne Kadar Yapılan Harekât*, p. 627.

39. Ibid.

40. Liman von Sanders, *Five Years in Turkey*, p. 277.

41. ATASE, *7nci Piyade Tümeni Tarihçesi*, Record 26-518, p. 30.

42. ATASE, *21nci Piyade Alay Tarihçesi*, Record 26-327, p. 32.

43. ATASE, *16nci Piyade Tümeni Tarihçesi*, Record 26-441, p. 61.

44. ATASE, Strength Report, 16th Infantry Division, 22 September 1918, Archive 3730, Record, H-4, File G-12. On this date, the division consisted of 200 men in the 2nd and 3rd Battalions, 125th Infantry Regiment, 100 men in the 47th Infantry Regiment and 80 men in the combined assault/engineer company.

45. ATASE, *16nci Piyade Tümeni Tarihçesi*, 61, Record 26-441.

46. Ibid., 62.

47. Onalp et al., *Sina-Filistin Cephesi, İkinci Gazze Muharebesi Sonundan Mütarekesi'ne Kadar Yapılan Harekât*, p. 629.

48. Ibid., p. 630.

49. Ibid., pp. 632–3.

50. Falls and Becke, *Military Operations Egypt and Palestine, From June 1917 to the End of the War*, Part II, p. 488.

51. Author's estimate. The Turks reported 19,157 soldiers in the Eighth Army, of whom 10,393 were infantrymen. Onalp et al., *Sina-Filistin Cephesi, İkinci Gazze Muharebesi Sonundan Mütarekesi'ne Kadar Yapılan Harekât*, p. 617.

52. Ibid., p. 640.

53. ATASE, Seventh Army orders, 1.30 pm, 20 September 1918, Archive 3705, Record F-7, File 1-2, reprinted in Onalp et al., *Sina-Filistin Cephesi, İkinci Gazze Muharebesi Sonundan Mütarekesi'ne Kadar Yapılan Harekât*, pp. 641–2.

54. Onalp et al., *Sina-Filistin Cephesi, İkinci Gazze Muharebesi Sonundan Mütarekesi'ne Kadar Yapılan Harekât*, pp. 642, 654.

55. Belen, *Birinci Cihan Harbinde, Türk Harbi, 1918 Yılı Hareketleri*, p. 81.

56. Ibid.

57. Onalp et al., *Sina-Filistin Cephesi, İkinci Gazze Muharebesi Sonundan Mütarekesi'ne Kadar Yapılan Harekât*, pp. 654–5.

58. Liman von Sanders, *Five Years in Turkey*, p. 269.

59. Onalp et al., *Sina-Filistin Cephesi, İkinci Gazze Muharebesi Sonundan Mütarekesi'ne Kadar Yapılan Harekât*, pp. 752–3. See *Sağlık, Veteriner Hizmetleri (Health, Veterinarian Services)*, p. 752 and *Hayvan Sağlıgı (Animal Health)*, p. 753.

60. Şerif Güralp, *1918 Yılında Türk Ordusunun Filistin ve Suriye'den Çekilişinde 3ncü Süvari Tümeninin Harekâtı (3rd Cavalry Division Operations in the Palestine Campaign and Retreat from Syria)* (Ankara: ATASE Yayınları, 2006), p. 13.

61. ATASE, Seventh Army orders, 25 September 1918, Archive 3705, Record 28, File 18-4, reprinted in Onalp et al., *Sina-Filistin Cephesi, İkinci Gazze Muharebesi Sonundan Mütarekesi'ne Kadar Yapılan Harekât*, p. 679.

62. Belen, *Birinci Cihan Harbinde, Türk Harbi, 1918 Yılı Hareketleri*, p. 94. Belen claims that 1¹/₂ million kilos of grains were lost but this seems unbelievably excessive.

63. Onalp et al., *Sina-Filistin Cephesi, İkinci Gazze Muharebesi Sonundan Mütarekesi'ne Kadar Yapılan Harekât*, p. 681.

64. Güralp, *3ncü Süvari Tümeninin Harekâtı*, pp. 15–19.

65. Yücel Güçlü, 'The Wounded Turks and the Fall of Damascus, 1 October 1918', *Belleten, Dört Ayda Bir Çıkar* (Ankara: Türk Tarih Kurumu Basımevi, 2003), 933–5.

66. Onalp et al., *Sina-Filistin Cephesi, İkinci Gazze Muharebesi Sonundan Mütarekesi'ne Kadar Yapılan Harekât*, p. 716.

67. Ibid., p. 822.

68. Ibid., p. 685.

69. Ibid., p. 705.

70. Ibid., p. 715.

71. Ibid., p. 726.

72. Erkal, *Hicaz, Asir, Yemen Cepheleri ve Libya Harekâtı*, p. 375.

73. Ibid., p. 385.

74. İsmail Bilgin, *Medine Müdafaası, Çöl Kaplanı Fahrettin Paşa* (Istanbul: Timaş Yayınları, 2009), *passim*.

75. Onalp et al., *Sina-Filistin Cephesi, İkinci Gazze Muharebesi Sonundan Mütarekesi'ne Kadar Yapılan Harekât*, pp. 726–8 and Falls and Becke, *Military Operations Egypt and Palestine, From June 1917 to the End of the War*, Part II, pp. 613–16.

76. Onalp et al., *Sina-Filistin Cephesi, İkinci Gazze Muharebesi Sonundan Mütarekesi'ne Kadar Yapılan Harekât*, Kroki (Sketch) 62.

77. Yücel Güçlü, 'The Last Pitched Battle of the First World War and the Determination of the Turkish-Syrian Boundary Line', *International Conference Atatürk and Modern Turkey (Yayın No: 582)* (Ankara: Ankara Üniversitesi Siyasal Bilgiler Fakültesi Yayını, 1998), 626–7.

78. Onalp et al., *Sina-Filistin Cephesi, İkinci Gazze Muharebesi Sonundan Mütarekesi'ne Kadar Yapılan Harekât*, pp. 726–7.

79. Güçlü, 'The Last Pitched Battle of the First World War and the Determination of the Turkish-Syrian Boundary Line', 630–1.

80. Belen, *Birinci Cihan Harbinde, Türk Harbi, 1918 Yılı Hareketleri*, Kuruluş 8 (Organizational Chart 8) following p. 110.

81. Ibid., p. 731.

82. Falls and Becke, *Military Operations Egypt and Palestine, From June 1917 to the End of the War*, Part II, p. 618.

83. Suleiman Mousa, *T.E. Lawrence An Arab View*, trans. Albert Butros (London and New York: Oxford University Press, 1966), p. 203.

Chapter 9

Combat Support: Logistics, Men and Airpower

Introduction

There is consensus among military historians that logistics and combat support are the *sine qua non* of all military operations. At the operational level 'logistics' (the 'wholesale' transportation of, stocking and storage of, and the distribution of bulk supplies) and at the tactical level 'combat service support' (the 'retail' end of logistics at the battlefield level but also the actual physical care and maintenance of men, animals and machines in the field) enables and limits what can or cannot be done on the battlefield. The combat effectiveness of an army in the field is not simply a function of its strength in the numbers of men and equipment it has on hand. At the operational level, logistics require the establishment and maintenance of a specialized transportation system which links the army in the field with the homeland. And in addition to the daily need for such items as artillery shells, ammunition, water, food, fodder, equipment and medical supplies a First World War army required continuous replenishment of new men and fresh animals. Moreover, men and animals on the front lines who are weakened by bad water and poor rations and lack of adequate medical and veterinary care are limited in their capability to execute the full range of their military potential. Shortfalls in operational and tactical logistics systems degrade firepower, mobility, health and morale – all of which affect the scope of what an army can and cannot do.

Murray and Allenby's armies were exceptionally well supported in comparison with their Ottoman opponents. In contrast, throughout the Palestine campaigns, the Ottoman Army in the field was penalized by a weak logistical infrastructure. The impact of this weakness was that the Ottoman armies in the Palestine theatre could never be maintained at full personnel and animal strength, were never maintained at full authorization of weapons and equipment, and were never provided with adequate amounts of munitions, food, fodder, equipment and medical supplies. Because of this, the Ottoman armies in Palestine were never able to exercise the full combat potential of their 'paper-strength' capability and capacity.

Ottoman Logistics in Palestine
Logistically, the Ottoman Army of 1914 patterned itself, its doctrines, its operational thought and its approach to war on the German Army. Logistically, the Ottomans separated their operational field armies from supporting logistics infrastructure by creating lines of communications inspectorates (LoCIs) in the rear areas upon mobilization (and mirroring the German system). These 'formed the conveyor of the army' and were 'the middleman between home and army'. In military doctrinal terms, the LoCIs were a service support organization (as opposed to a combat or combat support formation) and had no intrinsic combat capabilities. This system enabled combat commanders at the front to focus their energy on operational and tactical matters while logisticians handled supply matters.

As its capstone logistics command element the Ottoman general staff activated the General Lines of Communications Inspectorate (*Menzil Genel Müfettişliği*) on 5 August 1914 in Constantinople. This organization exercised command authority over the logistical lifelines of the empire at the strategic level. High-level logistical planning and co-ordination remained a function of the general staff's Fourth Division, while the GLC Inspectorate coordinated daily movements and logistical functions through lower level subordinate numbered army inspectorate commands.

In Syria and Palestine, the general staff activated the Fourth Army on 6 September 1914 and, in support, Cemal activated the Fourth Army Lines of Communications Inspectorate (*4ncü Ordu Menzil Müfettişliği*, hereafter referred to as 4 LoCI) on 12 November 1914 with its headquarters in Damascus.[1] The activation of 4 LoCI, which was commanded by Major Kazım, occurred after the declaration of war, and there were few opportunities to stockpile munitions or supplies. However, Kazım was assigned a variety of army support units, including ammunition depots and trains, transportation units, field hospitals, remount and veterinary stations, basic training depot battalions, bakeries and repair shops, supply depots and labour battalions.

In addition to Cemal's operational responsibility for logistics in his own army, the Fourth Army was responsible for the security and maintenance of the railway line that led from the Pozantı Gap to the Euphrates River and south through Palestine to Medina. The railway posed particular problems because it was constructed by European entrepreneurs rather than by military planners. There were two uncompleted gaps in the rugged Taurus mountains at Pozantı (54km) and through the Amanus mountains at Osmaniye (36km), there were different gauge tracks (for example: 1m wide from Remleh to Jerusalem but 105cm wide from there to Damascus) and the entire line was in an extremely poor state of repair. (See map 9.1.) Additionally, almost all of the supplies for the Mesopotamian theatre were shipped through the 4 LoCI area and competed for the inadequate transportation resources.

Bringing food, ammunition and supplies forward challenged Major Kâzım's organization to its fullest because of the weak infrastructure in the Palestine theatre. Unlike the great powers of Europe, which built railway nets to accommodate mobilization and supply armies, the Ottoman Empire's railways were built by foreigners for economic profits. Consequently, the railways in Syria and Palestine ran south to Medina on the east side of the Jordan River and the Dead Sea. This situation made supplying Ottoman forces in the Sinai very difficult. Moreover, in peacetime, much of trade in the Syrian and Palestinian provinces was carried by ship through coastal ports, but the tight Allied naval blockade made this impossible after early November 1914.

Cemal organized the 4 LoCI into a centralized command structure of zones with Damascus as its hub. To the north were the Adana and Aleppo Zones (*Mıntıkası*) and to the south were the Jerusalem Zone and the Desert Zones (with its headquarters at Beersheba). Each zone had a large number of subordinate depots where supplies were staged, maintained and stored. Because adequate supplies of water were so important in the dry and hot climate, the 4 LoCI established twelve 'water stations' which had the capacity to produce and store large quantities of water.[2] Additionally, along the critical road system itself, the 4 LoCI established ten Lines of Communications Command Posts, each with an authorization of eleven officers, five doctors and eighty-five soldiers.[3] The 4 LoCI also created seven Railroad Station Command Posts as well.

Going into January 1915, Cemal became extremely concerned about the inadequate logistics posture of his army along the Sinai frontier when he began to increase the numbers of men and animals stationed there in preparation for his invasion of Egypt. As mentioned previously, he assigned Lieutenant Colonel Behçet of the general staff as the commander of a specialized and autonomous Desert Lines of Communications Inspectorate.[4] Behçet was responsible for developing and pushing the logistics infrastructure forward which would support the offensive with water, food, munitions and other supplies. He initially set up two main supply bases at El Arish and Kalatünnahil. From the main bases von Kress and the VIII Corps staff also established a network of six smaller supply points to distribute supplies forward. The logistics goal for the campaign was to establish a fourteen-day supply of the vast array of consumables and commodities required by an army at war. At tactical level, Chapter 2 described the thought put into the Desert Ration and the daily water allotments for men and animals.[5]

The acquisition of large numbers of animals and transport placed a severe strain on the army. For example, by 23 February 1915, the 4 LoCI had 8,193 camels, 1,838 pack horses, 271 draught horses, 388 mules, 95 wagons and 150 artillery caissons travelling between Jerusalem and Maan alone.[6] Veterinary services for the army's vast array of animals became a critical component of support. The Fourth Army established forward veterinary hospitals in several of the towns in Palestine (for example, Beersheba, Kalatünnahil, Bisan, Nablus and five others) and five animal clinics in towns like Gaza and El Arish.[7] Two depot level camel hospitals were also established in Aleppo and Hama. These were critically important, for example, during the First Canal Expedition 8,098 of 12,120 camels deployed became sick and required treatment at some level. On average monthly, after that, 772 camels required medical attention in the expeditionary forces. The extremely hot climate took a significant toll on horses and mules in the Palestine theatre and they could not be used as frequently and as efficiently as they could in the cooler months. For its human capital, by April 1915, the 4 LoCI had established fifteen lines of communications hospitals in the major cities, three medical supply depots and five medical training companies. By that date the 4 LOCI established an additional nine animal hospitals and three veterinary medical supply depots as well.

By October 1915, the number of Lines of Communications Command Posts had risen to thirty-two, while the number of Railroad Station Command Posts had fallen to five. This indicates the increasing reliance on men and animals that the 4 LoCI encountered as the war progressed. By early 1917, the transportation system was faltering and the rations for men and animals in the Palestine theatre fell by one-third.[8]

The Fourth Army's stocks of ammunition and artillery shells were

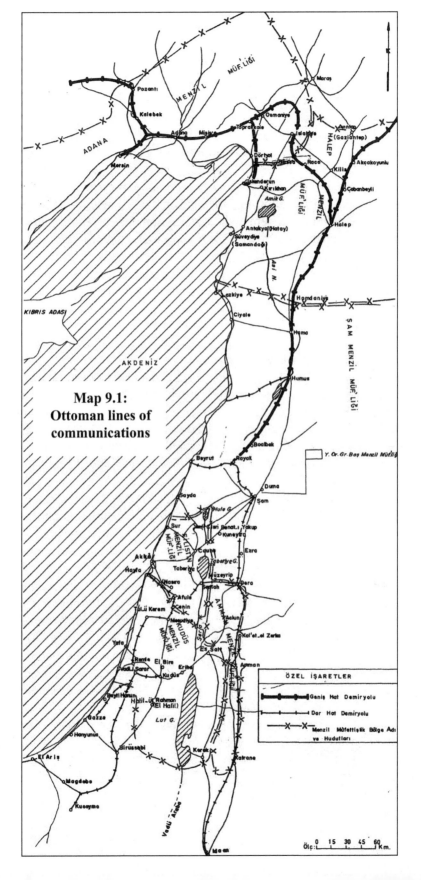

Map 9.1:
Ottoman lines of
communication

KIBRIS ADASI

AKDENIZ

ÖZEL İŞARETLER

Geniş Hat Demiryolu

Dar Hat Demiryolu

Menzil Müfettişlik Bölge Adı
ve Hudutları

Ölç.: 0 15 30 45 60
                              Km.

chronically short throughout the war. In 1916, the Fourth Army reported to the general staff that it only had enough rifle ammunition and artillery shells for fifteen days of combat.[9] Similar shortages existed in its supplies of communications equipment such as cable and field telephones. Most of this kind of material support came by rail from Germany to Constantinople where it was ferried across the Bosporus to the Haydarpaşa train station and reloaded on trains bound for Palestine. The unfinished tunnel system in the Pozantı Gap interrupted the journey by creating a choke point where everything was unloaded, transported and reloaded on different trains. By 1917, a large number of trucks and motor vehicles (as many as 600 at its highest) sent from Germany and operated by German soldiers were critically important in maintaining the flow of supplies through the Pozantı Gap to Palestine and Mesopotamia.

Ottoman Manpower in Palestine

Upon mobilization in the summer of 1914, including depot and jandarma (gendarmerie) units, the Fourth Army called 85,295 reservists to the colours.[10] Altogether, after its re-activation in September 1914, the Fourth Army comprised 1,563 officers, 52,858 soldiers and 22,031 animals, armed with 42,618 rifles, 112 cannons and 12 machine guns.[11] By 14 November, the Fourth Army had 67,963 rifles and carbines, 122 cannons and 10 machine guns on strength.

As the active Ottoman Army corps deployed to their war stations in 1914, their fixed-site pre-war administrative architecture remained in place for conscription, home defence and logistical duties. Thus, the Ottoman Army's conscription system that was used throughout the war maintained the pre-war army's thirteen numbered army corps areas (I–XIII) as administrative areas. Within these administrative areas, conscription offices were established to insure that eligible able-bodied men were identified and inducted into the army. Army Corps Area VIII (southern Syria, Lebanon and Palestine) and XII Army Corps Area (northern Syria) directly serviced the Palestine Front and together took in about 22,000 conscripted men per year. Increasingly as the war went on, conscripted men from Army Corps Area VI (south-east Anatolia) were sent to the Palestine theatre as well.

The bitter campaigns in Caucasia and Gallipoli made 1915 the worst year for casualties suffered by the Ottoman Army in the First World War.[12] This caused severe shortages of trained men and drained the Ottoman Army's manpower pool. In February 1916, the Fourth Army had 184,561 men assigned to its rolls and, after the Allied withdrawal from Gallipoli, the general staff determined to replenish the Palestine theatre with men for the second invasion of Egypt. The conscription offices began to organize the remaining men of the classes of 1896 and 1897 for induction and in army basic training that month the Fourth Army had 500 men at the Gaziantepe Depot Regiment, 3,544 men at the Bağlık Depot Regiment and 400 men at the Jerusalem Depot Regiment.[13] The Junior Officer Training Depot Regiment (*Astsubay*) had 1,500 men assigned, who were being taught to read and write. Because of the lower population densities (relative to Thrace, the straits and the Aegean provinces) in Ottoman Syria and Palestine the induction and training pipeline was never sufficient to maintain the strength of the operational forces in theatre. The Fourth Army estimated that the induction and depot system could only supply, at best without diversions to other theatres, about a third of its manpower requirements in combat.[14]

Unfortunately for the Fourth Army, the ongoing campaigns in Mesopotamia and Caucasia forced the general staff to send a large portion of its newly trained conscripts to the Second and Sixth Armies, respectively. This caused the Fourth Army's strength to drop to 172,065 men in August 1916. However, in November 1916, the general staff sent 10,000 replacements from the straits region to Palestine via the Haydarpaşa train station. Combined with returning men from hospital and an increased effort by the conscription offices, the Fourth Army gradually raised its strength to 191,270 men in February 1917. By 1 May the Fourth Army reported 224,355 men, 27,585 animals, 2,974 camels, 50,155 front-line rifles, 159 machine guns and 264 artillery pieces on hand. However, the end-strength of the Fourth Army would drop significantly by the time of Third Gaza, when many of its subordinate units were distributed to the newly activated Seventh and Eighth Armies.

In the first two years of war, the Ottoman Empire lost over 500,000 men (dead, missing and prisoners) and as many as 750,000 wounded.[15] This came from a total mobilized strength of about 2,900,000 men (jandarma included) and there was an annual input of newly conscripted men estimated at about 100,000 men.[16] The year group of 1900 was conscripted in 1917 and there were 90,767 of these young men available in training depots empire wide by mid-year.[17] Available in the Palestine theatre were the conscripted men of the VI Corps Area (9,601), the VIII Corps Area (12,197) and the XII Corps Area (2,318). The Yildirim Army Group, on 3 August 1917, reported that it required 70,000 soldiers to fill its depleted ranks. Even if every eligible man from the three corps areas was sent to Palestine, the remaining personnel shortfalls were significant. By mid-1917, the Eighth Army's infantry divisions on the Gaza–Beersheba line averaged 5,896 available soldiers, of whom an average of 4,580 were 'available for combat'.[18] The Fourth Army's divisions in Syria were maintained at a much lower troop strength and averaged 1,492 available soldiers, of whom 622 were 'available for combat'. The term 'available for combat' is not defined in the Turkish official histories and the author interprets the term to mean men who were medically fit, healthy and equipped and trained for combat.

In May of 1918, the general staff inactivated a number of training depots across the empire because the numbers of newly inducted men was decreasing. In the Yildirim Army Group, the following units were inactivated: the 13th Depot Regiment in Bağlik, the 17th Depot Regiment in Nasıra, the No. 1 Cavalry Depot in Damascus and its higher headquarters the Cavalry Depot Company as well as the No. 1 Artillery Depot Company in Nasıra. It is probable that the theatre-wide shortage of cavalry and artillery horses in combat units was also part of the decision to close these training facilities.

Desertion became such a problem in the Palestine theatre that the Yildirim Army Group established a Central Desertion Bureau, which reported directly to the 3rd Staff Directorate of the army group general staff.[19] The Desertion Bureau coordinated directly with the jandarma and conscription offices in identifying and apprehending deserters. Rather than being severely punished, deserters were incarcerated briefly and then returned to army units.

Spying was a persistent problem in Palestine, where many of the local inhabitants sympathized with the invaders. To prevent this, the Ottoman military authorities often used the mobile jandarma units to keep civilians away from the transportation hubs and railway lines.[20] Local tribal irregular cavalrymen, mounted on mules and paid at the rate of 2 gold lira per month, were also used to guard and secure the lines of communications as well.

Theatre Logistics in the Yildirim Army Group
On the establishment of the Yildirim Army Group, the Ottoman general staff determined that the logistical support of such a large force in a distant theatre demanded a reconsideration of how it would be supported with personnel and equipment. The general staff created the Yildirim Constantinople Dispatch of Troops Establishment (*Yıldırım İstanbul Sevk Kurulu*) and placed Lieutenant Colonel Esat in command.[21] Prior

to this, the epicentre of the support effort and staging point for Palestine and points east had been the city of Konya in central Anatolia. Under the reorganization, the general staff empowered Esat to provision and equip forces destined for Palestine and to use the Haydarpaşa train station (in Asia) as the main staging point. Esat was provided with a budget to purchase and provision the departing soldiers. Every week, on Friday, Esat dispatched a train loaded with officers, men, animals, wagons and military supplies from Haydarpaşa to the Pozantı tunnel portage in the Taurus Mountains. These trains were serial numbered and organized into a monitored programme, which tracked their progress, and Esat sent a written daily report via the empire's telegraph system to the Yildirim Army Group's 3rd Staff Directorate. In this way, the Ottoman general staff streamlined and built control measures into what had previously been a rather unstructured and problematic system.

An additional attempt to streamline the logistical system in Palestine involved the consolidation of the parallel lines of the German and Fourth Army Lines of Communications Inspectorates, which had evolved as increasing numbers of German units flowed into Palestine. By late 1917, the German lines of communications architecture included logistics command centres at Nasıra, Amman, Damascus and Aleppo.[22] A fifth German logistics command centre was being planned for establishment in Adana. This system grew in size and importance over time and also supported, in part, the elements of the Ottoman Army in Palestine, which used German equipment and munitions. In order to command all of these components, the Germans had established a German Principal Lines of Communications Inspectorate in Aleppo.

After the departure of Ahmet Cemal Pasha in late January and von Falkenhayn in March, the Yildirim Army Group headquarters inactivated both the 4 LoCI and the German Principal Lines of Communications Inspectorate on 15 April 1918. Consolidation in command by the army group to create unity of effort in tactical matters made the consolidation of logistics practicable as well. In their place the group headquarters activated a single Yildirim Head (or Principal) Lines of Communications Inspectorate (*Yıldırım Baş Menzil Müfettişliği*) in Aleppo to coordinate and control the logistics architecture of the Fourth, Seventh and Eighth Armies.[23] This overarching logistical command had powers over both Ottoman and German transportation and supply systems. Liman von Sanders appointed German Lieutenant Colonel Teerle von Kisling as the chief of the new combined inspectorate as well as forging a combined logistical staff composed of both German and Ottoman logistical specialists.[24] According to the Turkish official history, the inclusion of Germans within the army group logistical support staffs added discipline and organization to the logistical system. Of importance was the reconciliation of standardized practices, which further streamlined the system. Additionally, the presence of Germans embedded in the logistical system served to reduce the incidence of false reporting and corruption that accompanied the Ottoman service support administration.

Considerable effort was involved unloading every train at the uncompleted Pozantı tunnel complex, where the loads were hauled through the narrow mountain pass by animal power and by German motorized trucks, and then reloaded on new trains. Allied prisoners of war, especially British and Australians, were also used as construction crews and labour parties working on the tunnels and railway line. The tunnel complex was finally completed on 9 October 1918, which was too late to have any effect of supplying the Ottoman theatres in Palestine and Mesopotamia.

Air Operations in the Syria-Palestine-Hejaz Theatre

Air power was never a significant asset for the Ottoman forces in the Palestine theatre to the extent that, after 1917, it was for Allenby. Although the Ottomans had pioneered in the military use of aircraft in Libya in 1911, the empire could not compete with the advanced societies of the Allies in a global war. This was principally a function of a pauperized government and an unindustrialized society rather than a conscious decision not to build a viable military air arm. However, beginning in 1914 and continuing throughout the war, Germany provided military assistance to the Ottomans including aircraft, pilots and, eventually, entire air squadrons. The air squadrons that Germany sent to Palestine proved exceptionally valuable in keeping a small air presence to oppose the British to the end of the war.

In 1914, the Ottoman air arm was centred at Yeşilköy (near modern Atatürk Airport in Istanbul), where the army maintained a flying school. Very few aircraft were available and the empire had few trained pilots. To assist the Ottomans in developing an air arm, Germany sent a qualified pilot named Lieutenant Erich Serno and two aircraft to Yeşilköy, where he took command of the newly established Air Flying School Inspectorate in the rank of captain.[25] The Ottoman general staff established the 13th Staff Division to supervise air operations. The handful of miscellaneous aircraft that the armed forces possessed were organized into seven tiny squadrons of two or three aircraft and deployed to wartime stations in the fall of 1914. The 1st and 6th Air Squadrons went to Çanakkale (in Asia opposite Gallipoli), the 2nd Air Squadron to Mesopotamia, the 3rd Air Squadron to Uzunköprü (a town between Gallipoli and Constantinople), the 4th Squadron to Adana, the 5th Air Squadron to Second Army and the 7th Air Squadron to the Third Army. The navy also had a handful of aircraft but these remained in the Turkish straits region. There were two additional non-tactical air squadrons at Damascus and Keşan as well. These squadrons were active throughout 1915 and participated in combat operations at Gallipoli, in Caucasia and in Mesopotamia. In Cemal's area no complete air squadrons were initially sent to Palestine although the Fourth Army staff made plans to establish a fully capable military airfield at Beersheba.

In 1916, the Ottoman air service grew to twelve air squadrons and by the end of the year comprised sixty-seven airfields, eighty-one pilots, fifty-seven observers and ninety aircraft. Additionally, there were several naval air squadrons as well. The German general staff decided to reinforce the weak Ottoman air arm and sent Fliegerabteilung 300 to Constantinople. The squadron continued on to Palestine and reached Beersheba on 1 April. Fourth Army's air assets then included the 4th Air Squadron at Adana and the German 300th 'Pasha I' Air Squadron in Palestine.[26] Half of the German squadron deployed to Beersheba on 16 May 1916, where it began combat and night-flying training. On the night of 21/22 May, two aircraft dropped bombs on the Port Said harbour. The squadron carried out bombing training over the next few months and carried out several missions against British positions. On 18 June, eleven aircraft bombed and machine-gunned British positions near El Arish. Two aircraft were hit by anti-aircraft fire, wounding a pilot and two men. The squadron delivered miscellaneous bombing and strafing attacks over the summer months as well as conducting numerous observation and aerial photographic missions. On 19 July, part of the squadron moved forward to an airfield near El Arish, in order to better support the Ottoman forces operating in the Sinai. The squadron bombed the enemy during the Battle of Romani (4–6 August 1916) and attacked the British headquarters on 6 August.[27] Several missions were also launched against Port Said harbour and adjacent military depots.

A report from Cemal Pasha on 17 September 1916 detailed the previous three weeks of air operations. His report described bombing enemy regiments while the British bombed Ottoman headquarters at Romani and Muhammediye in return. He also reported that his aircraft had bombed the British railway that was being extended east from the canal. Finally, he noted that El Arish had been bombed twice and Beersheba three times.[28] German Captain Felmy arrived in mid-September with six Rumpler C-Is and two Fokker E-III fighters.[29] On 30 September, supplies of aviation fuel at El Arish were exhausted and the aircraft returned to Beersheba. The withdrawal of the Ottoman ground forces to the Gaza–Beersheba line forced the withdrawal of the air service ground elements and the aircraft to a more secure air station at Ramle at the end of the year.

The declining operational situation in the Hejaz demanded that the Fourth Army consider the deployment of aircraft to maintain observation on the Medina railway. The general staff alerted the 3rd Air Squadron for deployment to the Hejaz. The first elements of the squadron departed Constantinople on 23 June 1916, with orders to join the provisional force then assembling at Maan. The squadron consisted of four officers, one armourer, one mechanic and 103 soldiers. The squadron had the advantage of several months of training under German instructors and was considered combat ready. Temperatures were so hot that there were severe problems keeping the aircraft in flyable condition and the hot weather limited the aircraft to carrying bombs of 12–13 kg. Replacement aircraft had to be sent to Maan from the 300th Pasha Squadron on a frequent basis. The 3rd Air Squadron flew missions from Maan throughout the autumn of 1916, ranging along the railway as far as Medina to the south and Es Salt to the north. Two 12kg bombs were the standard bomb load. In early December 1916, the 3rd Air Squadron had four pilots, two observers and ten aircraft on its rolls.[30]

The 4th Air Squadron was based in Adana and had defensive responsibility over the Gulf of Alexandretta and the pass and tunnel complexes in the Taurus Mountains. The operational tempo of the 4th Air Squadron picked up in the fall of 1916 when the British stationed aircraft on the island of Cyprus, threatening the bay and the littoral coastlines. In turn, this drove the squadron to work closely with the 23rd Infantry Division in its coastal defence role. In early December 1916, the 4th Air Squadron had three pilots, two observers and two aircraft on its rolls.

In January 1917, eight Rumpler C-Is arrived to reinforce the German squadron and seven of its worn-out Rumplers were transferred to the air depot at Damascus. Over the next few months these aircraft were reconditioned and issued to the 3rd Air Squadron. As has been previously described, the 300th Pasha Squadron kept von Kress well appraised of British movements during the First and Second Battles of Gaza. Occasionally the squadron flew bombing missions against the British ground forces and the railways they were pushing east through the Sinai. In return, the squadron's base at Remle was frequently bombed in May 1917. In June and July, the tempo of British air operations accelerated as the Remle base continued to be bombed as well as army installations in Beersheba and Jerusalem. French aircraft also joined the fight to reinforce the British air effort. Photographic reconnaissance by enemy aircraft also picked up over the Gaza–Beersheba lines. The few fighter aircraft of the Pasha squadron were unable to prevent these raids and the only effective defence against enemy aircraft was a handful of anti-aircraft guns.

The air situation in Palestine was so dismal that the German general staff determined to send additional reinforcements to the theatre in July 1917. These reinforcements materialized as four flying units, the 301st–304th 'Pasha II' Air Squadrons. Each of these squadrons was equipped with four two-seat reconnaissance AEG C-IV aircraft and two modern Albatross D-III single-seat fighter aircraft. The new squadrons were sent to Palestine on trains from Germany via the Haydarpaşa station to Pozantı. The 301st remained at Remle, while the 302nd deployed to Elsafir, the 303rd went to Ettine and the 304th to Irakülmünşiye. The Yildirim Army Group established a small air reserve at Elhuç with a few aircraft from the 300th and 301st Pasha Air Squadrons. The retreat from the Gaza line and then from Jerusalem in the autumn of 1917 forced the air squadrons to withdraw to the north, and new bases were established at Nablus, Eriha and Avce.

In the Hejaz, the 3rd Air Squadron, under the command of Captain Fazıl, launched bombing missions from Maan against Arab headquarters and cantonments in January 1917. Aerial reconnaissance continued over the railway and what might be considered 'air presence' missions along the railway resulted in strafing Arabs who appeared to be up to no good near the tracks. Throughout the year, the German squadron in Palestine continued to replenish the Maan airfield with aircraft, spare parts and an occasional machinist repair party. In August, the 3rd Air Squadron conducted reconnaissance as far south as Aqaba and Medina. British air raids against the Maan airfield on 28 August and 10 November 1917 destroyed two aircraft and killed two men and wounded four.[31]

Up-to-date fighter aircraft appeared in January 1918, when Captain Felmy brought Lieutenant Maierdirch's Jasta 1 into Cenin with Albatross D-V fighters. These were similar in capability to the British SE-5a fighters used by the Royal Flying Corps but they were too few in number to wrest command of the air from Allenby. On 10 February 1918, the 3rd Air Squadron departed Maan and re-established its base to the north in Katrana. Other movements were in the planning stages as well and the army group activated a joint squadron composed of both German and Ottoman pilots known as the German 305th Air Squadron – Ottoman 14th Air Squadron.

The relief of von Falkenhayn by Liman von Sanders enabled the army group staff to redesign the architecture of air support in Palestine because the Second and Sixth Armies were detached simultaneously from Liman von Sanders's command. At the end of February 1918, the new air structure emerged, with its directing command in the Yildirim headquarters in Nasıra. The revised command arrangements decentralized tactical air support to the three Ottoman armies in theatre.[32] From Samah, the 300th Air Squadron, and the 302nd Air Squadron from air stations south of Haifa, supported the Eighth Army. The 301st and 303rd Air Squadrons from Cenin and the 304th Air Squadron from Afule supported the Seventh Army. From Dera, the 4th Air Squadron and the 305th Air Squadron supported the Fourth Army. The 3rd Air Squadron continued to move north to a new base in Amman, where it still provided air cover for the railway. The number of squadrons belied the actual size of the force, and altogether in the spring of 1918, the Ottomans and Germans had thirty-six aircraft of all types in Palestine.

Continued Arab attacks on the railway and on the town of Maan itself forced the Ottomans to re-deploy aircraft to that town in order to provide air support to the provisional division guarding the railway. Most of the Ottoman and German air activity in the spring of 1918 centred over the bridges supporting the British in the Jordan River Valley. Strafing and reconnaissance missions over the river in April were particularly costly and forced the general staff to dispatch Rumpler aircraft from Germany as reinforcements to replace the losses. On 1 May, the Yildirim Army Group consolidated the 3rd, 4th and 14th Air Squadrons into the Fourth Army Air Detachment under the command of German Major Zelich.[33] However, the centralization of air assets could not stop the overwhelmingly superior Royal Air Force (RAF – the RFC became the world's first separate air force on 1 April 1918) from bombing Amman on 31 May with 11 aircraft that dropped 100 bombs. Throughout the summer Zelich's air detachment was kept very busy with reconnaissance and bombing missions against the Arab armies which were steadily advancing from the south.

Diversionary RAF air attacks in support of Allenby's Megiddo offensive began on 18 September 1918 with large raids on the Seventh Army and III Corps headquarters. On the next day, the RAF unleashed a devastating series of air raids designed to knock out the Ottoman army, corps and division headquarters as well as disable all communications between these elements. The Ottoman and German air squadrons were completely unable to prevent this nor were they able to intervene effectively to alter the course of the battles. The ground elements of the 301st and 304th Air Squadrons as well as some aircraft and pilots were captured when Cenin and Afule fell. The 302nd Air Squadron's ground elements withdrew by motorized trucks to Haifa and then to Beirut. As the Fourth Army's position collapsed, the aircraft of the 302nd, 303rd and 305th Air squadrons, under Captain Elias, flew from Dera to Rayak. These squadrons continued to conduct strafing and bombing against the Arab armies as the Yildirim Army Group retreated north. The Ottoman 3rd and 4th Air Squadron personnel and equipment were lost on 21 September when their evacuation train from Amman was attacked at Mafraq.[34] The personnel of the 14th Air Squadron were captured on an evacuation train at Damascus on 30 September. On the same day, fifteen of the surviving aircraft flew from Rayak to Homs while a dozen un-flyable aircraft were abandoned on the airfield. Air operations continued sporadically throughout this period, including aerial reconnaissance missions over Cyprus. In October 1918, the surviving airmen and a few aircraft withdrew to Aleppo. Later that month five surviving aircraft were withdrawn to Konya (deep within the Anatolian Peninsula) ending Ottoman and German air operations in the Palestine theatre.[35]

Conclusion
Ottoman and German commanders in the Syrian and Palestine theatres were continuously plagued by logistics shortfalls of all kinds, which negatively affected the combat effectiveness of the Ottoman armies stationed there. For the Ottoman Army the campaigns it fought in Palestine were campaigns of operational poverty and were always managed on a 'shoe-string' logistical basis. The most remarkable aspect of this situation was that the Ottoman armies in Palestine managed to hold off their overwhelming British adversaries for so long. That they did so is a tribute to the Ottoman Army's overall combat effectiveness and to its effective interoperability with its German and Austro-Hungarian allies.

Notes

1. Fourth Army Orders, 12 November 1914 (Ek-6 (Appendix 6), reproduced in Okçu and Üstünsoy, *Sina-Filistin Cephesi, Harbin Başlangıcından İkinci Gazze Muharebeleri Sonuna Kadar*, pp. 765–7.
2. Ibid., p. 665.
3. Koral et al., *Idari Faaliyetler ve Lojistik*, p. 132.
4. Djemal Pasha, *Memories of a Turkish Statesman 1913–1919*, p. 148.
5. Ibid., p. 149.
6. Okçu and Üstünsoy, *Sina-Filistin Cephesi, Harbin Başlangıcından İkinci Gazze Muharebeleri Sonuna Kadar*, p. 677.
7. Ibid., p. 681.
8. Koral et al., *Idari Faaliyetler ve Lojistik*, p. 363.
9. Ibid., p. 381.
10. Ibid., p. 164.
11. Ibid. See field army and fortress infantry weapon and magazine situation (Ek 18), p. 639.
12. Erickson, *Ordered To Die*, Table F.4 'Consolidated Ottoman Losses by Year of the War', p. 241.
13. Koral et al., *Idari Faaliyetler ve Lojistik*, p. 327.
14. Ibid.
15. Erickson, *Ordered To Die*, Table F.4 'Consolidated Ottoman Losses by Year of the War', p. 241.
16. Erik J. Zurcher, 'Between Death and Desertion', *Turcica*, 28 (1996), 235–58, 241.
17. ATASE, Report, Midyear 1917, Soldiers taken from Year Group 1315 (1900), Archive 2024, Record 549A, File 1-157, reprinted in Koral et al., *Idari Faaliyetler ve Lojistik*, p. 413.
18. Koral et al., *Idari Faaliyetler ve Lojistik*, p. 414.
19. Onalp et al., *Sina-Filistin Cephesi, İkinci Gazze Muharebesi Sonundan Mütarekesi'ne Kadar Yapılan Harekât*, p. 762.
20. Ibid.
21. Ibid., p. 746. This was a different Esat, the officer commanding the cavalry.
22. Ibid., p. 747.
23. Ibid.
24. Ibid.
25. İhsan Göymen, *Birinci Dünya Harbi, IXncu Cilt, Türk Hava Harekâtı (First World War, Turkish War, Turkish Air Operations)* (Ankara: Genelkurmay Basımevi, 1969), pp. 32–3.
26. Ibid., p. 69.
27. Ibid., p. 115.
28. Commander, Fourth Army to General Staff Headquarters, 17 September 1916, summarized in Göymen, *Türk Hava Harekâtı*, p. 117.
29. Ole Nikolajsen, *Ottoman Aviation 1911–1919* (privately printed, n.d.), Chapter 8.
30. Göymen, *Türk Hava Harekâtı*, p. 70.
31. Ibid., pp. 206–7.
32. Ibid., pp. 238–9.
33. Ibid., p. 246.
34. Nikolajsen, *Ottoman Aviation*, Chapter 8.
35. Göymen, *Türk Hava Harekâtı*, pp. 249–51.

Appendix A

Ottoman Orders of Battle, Palestine Campaigns, 1914–18

1. Order of Battle, Sinai-Palestine, Beginning of the War
Fourth Army

	commander	BG Zeki Pasha (Halepli) (6 Sep–6 Dec 1914)
	commander	BG Ahmet Cemal Pasha (18 Nov, arrived 6 Dec 1914)
	chief of staff	Col Frankenberg
	chief of operations	Lt Col Ali Fuat (Gen Erden)
VIII Corps	commander	Col Cemal (Mersinli)
	chief of staff	Lt Col Ali Fuat (LTG Cebesoy)
	staff officer	Capt Halit (Akmanşu)
23 Div	commander	Lt Col Behçet
	chief of staff	Maj Mustafa İzzet
67 Regt	commander	Maj Rıza
68 Regt	commander	Maj Kemal
23 Art Regt	commander	Maj Ahmet Selahattin
25 Div	commander	Col Hilmi
	chief of staff	Maj Servetı
73 Regt	commander	Maj Mehmet Reşit
74 Regt	commander	Maj Fahrettin
75 Regt	commander	Maj Omer Fevzi
25 Art Regt	commander	Maj Mehmet Ali
27 Div	commander	Col Zeki
	chief of staff	Maj Etem
79 Regt	commander	Lt Col Etem
80 Regt	commander	Maj Rıfat
81 Regt	commander	Lt Col Hamdi
27 Art Regt	commander	Maj Mazhar

XII Corps	commander	BG Fahrettin Pasha (LTG Türkkan)
35 Div	commander	Lt Col Ahmet (division sent to Mesopotamia 14 Dec 1914)
36 Div	commander	Col Şamlı Yusuf Ziya (division sent to Caucasia June 1915)
22 Hejaz Div	commander	Col Vehip (Pasha – Kaçı)
Spec Vol Gp	commander	Maj Mümtaz
Spec Vol Gp	commander	Lt Col Eşref (Kuşçubaşı)
4 LoCI	commander	Maj Kâzım (MG Dirik)
Jerusalem Log	commander	Lt Col Ali Ruşen (Alb)
Border Cmd	commander	Lt Col Behçet – Beersheba Border Command
Jerusalem Zo	commander	Gen Back Pasha

2. Order of Battle, First Canal Expedition, 14 January–5 February 1915

Fourth Army	commander	BG Ahmet Cemal Pasha
	aide-de-camp	Cpt Selahattin
	chief of staff	Col Frankenberg
	chief of operations	Lt Col Ali Fuat (Erden)
	chief of engineers	Major Refet (Bele) until 27 Jan 1915
	asst ch of engineers	Cpt Çobanoğlü Zeki
	chief of medicine	Col Galip
Canal Exped	commander	BG Cemal (Mersinli) also **VIII Corps** commander
	aide-de-camp	Cpt Ekrem (LTG Baydar)
	chief of staff	Lt Col von Kress
	asst chief of staff	Maj Halit (Akmanşu)
	staff officer	Maj Sadullah (Col Güney)
Centre Column	commander	Lt Col Ali Fuat (Cebesoy)
25 Div	commander	Lt Col Ali Fuat (Cebesoy)
	chief of staff	Maj Mustafa İzzet
68 Regt	commander	Maj Kemal
73 Regt	commander	Maj Servet
1/73	commander	Maj Hüsnü
2/73	commander	Maj Ali Vehbi
74 Regt	commander	Maj Fahrettin

75 Regt	commander	Maj Omer Fevzi
Camel Cav	commander	Lt Col Sadık
25 Art Regt	commander	Maj Mehmet Ali
Right Wing	commander	Maj Refet (Bele) 27 January 1915
80 Regt	commander	Maj Refet (Bele)
Vol cavalry	commander	Maj Mümtaz
Left Wing	commander	Lt Col Musa Kâzım
69 Regt	commander	Lt Col Musa Kâzım
Vol cavalry	commander	Lt Col Eşref (Kuşçubaşı)
10 Div	commander	Col von Trommer
	chief of staff	Cpt Rüştü (LTG Akın)
22 Div	commander	Col Vehip (Kaçi) also Hejaz Expeditionary Force commander
Advance Log	commander	Cpt Ali Rıza (LTG Artunkal) Advanced Log Base at İbin

3. Order of Battle, Reorganization for the Second Canal Expedition, June 1915

Fourth Army	commander	MG Ahmet Cemal Pasha
	chief of staff	Lt Col Ali Fuat (Erden)
VIII Corps	commander	BG Cemal (Mersinli)
	chief of staff	Maj Anders (from 19 Feb 1915)
	staff officer	Maj Sadullah (Güney)
23 Div	commander	Lt Col Refet (Bele)
27 Div	commander	Col İbrahim
	commander	Col Mühittin (MG Kurtis)
XII Corps	commander	BG Fahrettin Pasha (Türkkan)
41 Div	commander	Lt Col Mehmet Emin
	chief of staff	Maj Mümtaz
131 Regt	commander	Maj Emin Lüftı
133 Regt	commander	Maj Rıfat
41 Art Regt	commander	Lt Col Asım
43 Div	commander	Lt Col Omer Nuri (MG Koptagel)
44 Div	commander	Lt Col Adıl
Desert Cmd	commander	Col von Kress
	chief of staff	Cpt Ali Rıza (Artunkal)
	staff officer	Cpt Ekrem (Baydar)

Left Det	commander	Lt Col Musa Kâzım – Left Wing Detachment
Centre Det	commander	
Right Det	ommander	Lt Col Laufer – Right Wing Detachment
Camel Regt	commander	Lt Col Sadık
Desert LoC	commander	Col Behçet (Desert Lines of Communications)
	chief of staff	Maj Şakır (MG Güleş)
25 Div	commander	Lt Col Ali Fuat (Cebesoy) 25 Div to Gallipoli 2 Jun 15

4. Order of Battle, Second Canal Expedition, July–14 August 1915

Canal Exped	commander	Col von Kress
	chief of staff	Maj Kadri (MG Demirkaya)
	staff officer	Maj Pohlman
3 Div	commander	Col Refet (Bele)
31 Regt	commander	Lt Col İsmail Hakkı
32 Regt	commander	Lt Col Hasan Basrı
39 Regt	commander	Maj Kamıl – taken POW 4 Aug 1915
1st Pasha	commander	Col Frankenberg – First Pasha Column
Camel Regt	commander	Lt Col Sadık
Irr Cav Regt	commander	Maj Mühlmann – Irregular Cavalry Regt
El Arish Log	commander	Col İbrahim – El Arish Logistics Command

5. Order of Battle, Fourth Army, end of 1916–19 April 1917

Fourth Army	commander	BG Ahmet Cemal Pasha
	chief of staff	Lt Col Ali Fuat (Erden)
	chief of artillery	BG Nicolai
III Corps	commander	Col İsmet (GEN İnönü)
41 Div	commander	Lt Col Cemil (MG Conk)
	chief of staff	Cpt Hasan
131 Regt	commander	Lt Col Nusret
132 Regt	commander	Lt Col Galip
133 Regt	commander	Maj Şerif
41 Art Regt	commander	Lt Col Asım

VIII Corps	commander	BG Cemal (Mersinli)
	chief of staff	Lt Col Sadullah (Güney)
	chief of artillery	BG Cemal (GEN Gürsel)
27 Div	commander	Col İbraham
43 Div	commander	Col Kâzım (Dirik)
XII Corps	commander	BG Remzi Pasha
23 Div	commander	Col Bahattin
44 Div	commander	Lt Col Şükrü
		Lt Col Mehmet Hayri (9 June–22 Aug 1917)
1st Exped Fr	commander	Col von Kress – First Expeditionary Force
	chief of staff	Maj Mühlmann
	staff officer	Cpt Ekrem (Baydar)
3 Div	commander	Lt Col Edip (Col Tör)
		Lt Col N. Nurettin (MG Özsü) after First Gaza
3 Cav Div	commander	Col Esat
16 Div	commander	Col Rüştü (MG Sakarya)
Gaza Group	commander	Maj Tiller
1st Prov Fr	commander	BG Cemal Pasha (3rd Cemal) – First Provisional Force
53 Div	commander	Lt Col Şerif – taken POW 26 March 1917
	commander	Col Refet (Bele)
XX Corps	commander	BG Abdülkerim (Öpelimi)
54 Div	commander	Lt Col von Kisling
Hejaz Exp Fr	commander	BG Fahrettin (Türkkan) – Hejaz Expeditionary Force
58 Div	commander	Col Ali Necip
	chief of staff	Cpt Yusuf Ziya
Medina Gar	commander	BG Basri Pasha (Noyan) – Medina Garrison Command

6. Order of Battle, Yildirim Army Group, July–September 1917

| **Yildirim AG** | commander | Marshal von Falkenhayn |

	chief of staff	Col von Dommes
	asst CoS	Lt Col Hüseyin Hüsnü Emir (MG Erkilet)
Sixth Army	commander	BG Halil Pasha (LTG Kut)
Seventh Army	commander	BG Mustafa Kemal Pasha (Atatürk)
	chief of staff	Maj Ömer Lütfü (12–18 July 1917)
	chief of operations	Maj Rüştü (LTG Akın)
III Corps	commander	Col İsmet (İnönü)
	chief of staff	Maj Şefik Avnı (Lt Col Özüdoğru)
	chief of operations	Maj Naci (LTG Tınaz)
24 Div	commander	Lt Col Willmer (division from Gallipoli)
50 Div	commander	Lt Col S. Naili (LTG Gökberk) (division sent to Mesopotamia)
59 Div	commander	Col Şefik (Col Aker) (division from Aydin)
XV Corps	commander	BG Ali Rıza Pasha (Sedes)
19 Div	commander	Lt Col Sedet (LTG Doğruer) (divison from Galicia)
	chief of staff	Maj Ömer Lütfü (to Yildirim AG staff 12–18 July 1917)
20 Div	commander	Lt Col Yasin Hilmi (division from Galicia)
Asia Corps	commander	Col Frankenberg – German Asia Corps
	chief of staff	Cpt Kurtcebe (GEN Noyan)

7. Order of Battle, Yildirim Army Group, October–December 1917

Yildirim AG	commander	FM von Falkenhayn
	aide-de-camp	Maj von Falkenhayn
	aide-de-camp	Cpt Ali Haydar (Germeyanoğlu)
	aide-de-camp	Cpt von Ernstein
	chief of staff	Col von Dommes
	assist CoS	Maj Ludlof

	chief of operations	Lt Col Hüseyin Hüsnü Emir (Erkilet)
	staff officer	Maj von Papen
	staff officer	Cpt Tevfik (Bıyıklıoğlu)
	staff officer	Cpt Mecit
	intelligence officer	Cpt Lübke
	intelligence officer	Cpt von Kamps Höffner
	railway officer	Cpt Gronevalt
	railway officer	Cpt Fots
	artillery officer	Maj Ostrovski
	personnel officer	Cpt Celâa
	personnel officer	Cpt von Groben
	engineer officer	Cpt Schmitt
	aviation officer	Cpt von Homskerk
	topographic officer	Cpt Andre
	medical director	MG Dr Steuber
	commissariat officer	Dr Yakobs
	HQ guard command	Cpt Hayrettin Fuat
	translator	Maj Kenan
	translator	Lt Ritter
Sixth Army	commander	BG Halil Pasha (Kut)
Seventh Army	commander	BG Fevzi Pasha (Marshal Çakmak)
	chief of staff	Maj Falkenhausen
	chief of operations	Maj Rüştü (Akın)
XV Corps	commander	BG Ali Rıza Pasha (Sedes)
19 Div	commander	Lt Col Sedet (Doğruer)
	chief of staff	Maj Ömer Lütfü
57 Regt	commander	Maj Hayri
72 Regt	commander	Maj Rıfat
77 Regt	commander	Lt Col Saip
20 Div	commander	Lt Col Yasin Hilmi
24 Div	commander	Lt Col Willmer
159 Regt	commander	
179 Regt	commander	Lt Col Osman Ata
Eighth Army	commander	Col von Kress

	commander	MG Cevat Pasha (Çobanlı) after 1 December 1917
	chief of staff	Lt Col Asım (GEN Gündüz)
	staff officer	Lt Col Hergote
	chief of operations	Maj Wolf
	asst chief of ops	Cpt İsmail Hakkı (Okday)
	artillery advisor	Lt Col Moderow
XX Corps	commander	Col Ali Fuat (Cebesoy)
	chief of staff	Maj Arıf (Ayıcı)
	staff officer	Cpt Ekrem (Baydar)
16 Div	commander	Col Rüştü (Sakarya)
	chief of staff	Cpt Lütfü
26 Div	commander	Col Fahrettin (GEN Altay)
	chief of staff	Maj Tevfik
54 Div	commander	Col von Kiesling
	chief of staff	Maj Hakkı Muhlis
XXII Corps	commander	Col Refet (Bele)
	chief of staff	Maj Rıfat (Lt Col Sözüer)
	staff officer	Cpt M. Mazlum (GEN İskora)
	staff officer	Cpt İzzet (GEN Aksalur)
	chief of artillery	Lt Col Ahmet Sabri (MG Erçetin)
3 Div	commander	Col H. Nurettin (Özsü)
	chief of staff	Cpt İskender
7 Div	commander	Col Kâzım (Dirik)
	chief of staff	Maj Fikri
53 Div	commander	Col Selahattin (Kiper)
	chief of staff	Cpt Ahmet Nüzhet
III Corps	commander	Col İsmet (İnönü)
	chief of staff	Maj Şefik Avnı (Özüdoğru)
	chief of operations	Maj Naci (Tınaz)
27 Div	commander	Lt Col O. Nuri (Koptagel)
	chief of staff	Cpt Tahsin
3 Cav Div	commander	Col Col Esat Pasha
	chief of staff	Maj Mahmut
Asia Corps	commander	Col Frankenberg – German Asia Corps
	chief of staff	Maj Solger
	asst CoS	Cpt Kurtcebe (Noyan)

701 Inf Bn	commander	Maj Staubwasser
702 Inf Bn	commander	Maj Merts
703 Inf Bn	commander	Lt Col Grasmann
701 Arty Bn	commander	Maj Hechtern
Yildirim LoC	commander	MG Ali Rıza (Sedes) – Lines of Communications Inspectorate
	chief of staff	Maj Kadri

8. Order of Battle, General Command of Syria and Western Arabia, 1 October 1917–18 January 1918

GC Syria	commander	MG Ahmet Cemal Pasha – Gen Cmd Syria and Western Arabia
Fourth Army	commander	BG Cemal Pasha (Mersinli)
	chief of staff	Maj von Papen
	staff officer	Cpt Keramettin (Kocaman)
VIII Corps	commander	Col Ali Fuat (Erden)
	chief of staff	Maj Şefik Avnı (Özüdoğru)
27 Div	commander	Col O. Nuri (Koptagel) (div reassigned to III Corps Oct 17)
4 Div	commander	Col Ali Rıza
48 Div	commander	Lt Col Hamdi Fahri — KIA 26 Oct 1918
	commander	Lt Col Asım (Gündüz)
	chief of staff	Maj Mehmet Nuri
43 Div	commander	inactivated 6 October 1917
XII Corps	commander	BG Abdülkerim Pasha
23 Div	commander	Col Bahattin
41 Div	commander	Col Cemil (Conk)
44 Div	commander	Col Hasan Askeri – div inactivated 25 Nov 1917
Hejaz Exp Fr	commander	BG Fahrettin (Türkkan) – Hejaz Expeditionary Force
	chief of staff	Lt Col Kemalettin Sami (LTG Gökçe)
58 Div	commander	Col Ali Necip
	chief of staff	Cpt Yusuf Ziya
Medina Gar	commander	BG Basri Pasha (Noyan) – Medina Garrison Command

1 Prov Force	commander	BG Cemal Psha (3rd Cemal)
2 Prov Force	commander	Lt Col Atıf (Ateşdağlı)
4 Army LoCI	commander	Sadullah (Güney) – 4th Army Line of Comms Inspectorate

9. Order of Battle, Yildirim Army Group, Jordan River Ops, 1 March–September 1918

Yildirim AG	commander	Gen Liman von Sanders
	aide-de-camp	Maj Ekrem Rüştü (Akömer)
	chief of staff	Col Kâzım (LTG İnanç)
	chief of operations	Maj von Papen
	staff officer	Lt Col Hüseyin Hüsnü Emir (Erkilet)
	staff officer	Cpt Tevfik (Bıyıklıoğlu)
	staff officer	Cpt Ali Haydar (Germeyanoğlu)
	staff officer	Cpt Mecit
Fourth Army	commander	BG Cemal Pasha (Mersinli)
	chief of staff	Maj von Papen
	staff officer	Cpt Keramettin (Kocaman)
VIII Corps	commander	Col Ali Fuat (Erden)
	chief of staff	Maj Şefik Avnı (Özüdoğru)
Prov Div	commander	Maj Ömer Lütfü
48 Div	commander	Lt Col Asım (Gündüz)
	chief of staff	Maj Mehmet Nuri
XII Corps	commander	BG Abdülkerim Pasha
23 Div	commander	Col Bahattin
41 Div	commander	Col Cemil (Conk)
44 Div	commander	Col Hasan Askeri – div inactivated 25 Nov 1917
XV Corps	commander	BG Ali Rıza Pasha (Sedes)
Hejaz Exp Fr	commander	BG Fahrettin (Türkkan) – Hejaz Expeditionary Force
	chief of staff	Lt Col Kemalettin Sami (Gökçe)
58 Div	commander	Col Ali Necip
Medina Gar	commander	BG Basri Pasha (Noyan) – Medina Garrison Command

1 Prov Force	commander	BG Cemal Psha (3rd Cemal)
2 Prov Force	commander	rLt Col Atıf (Ateşdağlı)

Seventh Army	commander	BG Fevzi Pasha (Çakmak) relieved for exhaustion Aug 1918
	commander	BG Nihat Pasha (LTG Anılmış)
	aide-de-camp	Lt İ. Hakkı (GEN Tunaboylu)
	chief of staff	Maj Falkenhausen
	chief of operations	Maj Ö. Halis (LTG Bıyıktay)

III Corps	commander	Col İsmet (İnönü)
	chief of staff	Maj Naci (Tınaz)
1 Div	commander	Lt Col Guhr
	chief of staff	Maj İbrahim
19 Div	commander	Lt Col Sedet (Doğruer)
	commander	Col Sami Sabit after May 1918
24 Div	commander	Lt Col Böhme
3 Cav Div	commander	Col Esat Pasha – WIA 2 May 1918
	commander	Lt Col Mahmut (Hendik)
	chief of staff	Lt Col Mahmut (Hendik)

XX Corps	commander	Col Ali Fuat (Cebesoy)
	chief of staff	Maj Arıf (Ayıcı)
53 Div	commander	Col Selahattin (Kiper)
	commander	Lt Col Mehmet Hayri (Tarhan) – in cmd 5 Aug–18 Nov 1918
	staff officer	Cpt Ekrem (Baydar)
26 Div	commander	Col Fahrettin (Altay)
	commander	Lt Col Mehmet Hayri (Tarhan)
	chief of staff	Cpt Fevzi (Akarçay)
78 Regt	commander	Maj Ömer Lütfü
163 Regt	commander	Cpt Aziz
27 Div	commander	Lt Col O. Nuri (Koptagel)

Eighth Army	commander	MG Cevat Pasha (Çobanlı)
	chief of staff	Lt Col Asım (Gündüz)
	chief of operations	Col Hergote
	asst chief of ops	Cpt İsmail Hakkı (Okday)

XXII Corps	commander	Col Refet (Bele)
	chief of staff	Maj Galip

	staff officer	Cpt M. Mazlum (İskora)
	chief of artillery	Lt Col Ahmet Sabri (Erçetin)
3 Div	commander	Col H. Nurettin (Özsü)
7 Div	commander	Col Kâzım (Dirik)
	commander	Lt Col Nasuhi
16 Div	commander	Col Rüştü (Sakarya)
20 Div	commander	Lt Col Yasin Hilmi
	chief of staff	Lt Col Veysel (Col Özgür)
54 Div	commander	Col von Kiesling
	chief of staff	
2 Cav Bde	commander	Lt Col Mehmet Ali – 2nd Caucasian Cavalry Brigade
Asia Corps	commander	Col Frankenberg – German Asia Corps
Yildirim LoC	commander	MG Ali Rıza (Sedes) – Lines of Communications Inspectorate
	chief of staff	Maj Kadri

10. Order of Battle, Yildirim Army Group, Megiddo–Aleppo, 19 September–25 October 1918

Yildirim AG	commander	Gen Liman von Sanders
	aide-de-camp	Maj Ekrem Rüştü (Akömer)
Fourth Army	commander	BG Cemal Pasha (Mersinli) – inactivated 12 Oct 18
	chief of staff	Lt Col Hüsnü Emir (Erkilet)
	chief of ops	Maj Rüştü
VIII Corps	commander	Col Ali Fuat (Erden)
	commander	Col Yasin Hilmi – after the fall of Damascus
	commander	Col Selahattin (Kiper)
48 Div	commander	Lt Col Asım (Gündüz) – captured 2 Oct 1918
	commander	Lt Col Nuri
	advisor	Lt Col Hunger
	cavalry cmdr	Lt Col Schierstüdt
Prov Div	commander	Lt Col Lütfi
Şeria Gp	commander	Col Esat
24 Div	commander	Lt Col Böhme
	commander	Lt Col Lütfü

3 Cav Div	commander	Lt Col Mahmut Nedim (Hendik)
	asst cmdr	Maj Vecihi – after 21 Sep 1918
II Corps	commander	Col Şevket
62 Div	commander	Unknown to the author
Havran Gp	commander	BG Hüsnü Pasha
Damascus Gp	commander	Unknown to the author
Maan G	commander	Unknown to the author
XII Corps	commander	BG Abdülkerim Pasha
23 Div	commander	Col Bahattin
41 Div	commander	Col Cemil (Conk)
44 Div	commander	Col Hasan Askeri – div inactivated 25 Nov 1917
Hejaz Exp Fr	commander	BG Fahrettin (Türkkan) – Hejaz Expeditionary Force
	chief of staff	Lt Col Kemalettin Sami (Gökçe)
58 Div	commander	Col Ali Necip
Medina Gar	commander	BG Basri Pasha (Noyan) – Medina Garrison Command
1 Prov Force	commander	BG Cemal Pasha (3rd Cemal)
2 Prov Force	commander	Lt Col Atıf (Ateşdağlı)
Seventh Army	commander	BG Mustafa Kemal (Atatürk)
	aide-de-camp	Lt İ. Hakkı (GEN Tunaboylu)
	chief of staff	Col Sedat (Doğreur)
	chief of operations	Maj Rüştü (Akin)
III Corps	commander	Col İsmet (İnönü)
	chief of staff	Maj Naci (Tınaz)
1 Div	commander	Lt Col Guhr
	chief of staff	Cpt Fikrit
11 Div	commander	Lt Col Mümtaz (Alb)
	chief of staff	Maj Mehmet Arif (Ayıcı)
XX Corps	commander	Col Ali Fuat (Cebesoy)
	chief of staff	Maj A. Galip (LTG Türker)
53 Div	commander	Lt Col Reşat
26 Div	commander	Lt Col Mehmet Hayri (Tarhan)

Eighth Army commander   MG Cevat Pasha (Çobanlı)
               chief of staff   Lt Col Sadullah (Güney)

XXII Corps commander   Col Refet (Bele)
               chief of staff   Cpt M. Mazlum (İskora)
7 Div   commander   Lt Col Nasuhi
20 Div   commander   Lt Col Veysel (Özgür)

Left Wing Gp commander   Col von Oppen – also German Asia Corps cmdr
16 Div   commander   Col Rüştü (Sakarya)
19 Div   commander   Lt Col Sami Sabit (MG Karaman)
46 Div   commander   Lt Col H. Hüsnü Emir (Erkilet)
               commander   Lt Col Tiller – after 24 Aug 1918
2 Cav Bde   commander   Lt Col Mehmet Ali – 2nd Caucasian Cavalry Brigade
Asia Corps   commander   Col von Oppen

11. Order of Battle, Yildirim Army Group, at the Mudros Armistice, 29 October–15 November 1918

Yildirim AG commander   Marshal Liman von Sanders
               commander   BG Mustafa Kemal (Atatürk) – after 30 Oct 1918

Seventh Army commander   BG Mustafa Kemal (Atatürk)
               aide-de-camp   Lt İ. Hakkı (GEN Tunaboylu)
               chief of staff   Lt Col Mehmet Hayri (Tarhan)
               chief of operations Maj Ömer Halis (Bıyıktay)

III Corps   commander   Col İsmet (İnönü)
               chief of staff   Maj Naci (Tınaz)
24 Div   commander
43 Div   commander   Lt Col Osman Nuri (Koptagel)

XX Corps   commander   Col Ali Fuat (Cebesoy)
1 Div   commander   Lt Col Veysel (Özgür)
11 Div   commander   Lt Col Mümtaz (Alb)
               chief of staff   Maj Maj Mehmet Arif (Ayıcı)

Second Army commander   BG Nihat Pasha (Anılmış)

XV Corps	commander	BG Ali Rıza Pasha (Sedes)
41 Div	commander	Lt Col Hüseyin Hüsnü (LTG Alptogan)
44 Div	commander	Lt Col Mustafa (GEN Muğlali)
XII Corps	commander	Col Fahrettin (LTG Altay)
	chief of staff	Cpt Fahri (LTG Belen)
23 Div	commander	Col Bahaettin
Asia Corps	commander	Col von Oppen

Sources:

İsmet Görgülü, *On Yillik Harbin Kadrosu 1912–1913, Balkan – Birinci Dünya ve Istiklal Harbi* (Ankara: Türk Tarih Kurum Basimevi, 1993)

Necati Ökse, Nusret Baycan and Salih Sakaryalı, *Türk Istiklal Harbi'ne Kalilan Tümen ve Daha Ust Kademelerdeki Komutanların Biyografileri* (Ankara: Genelkurmay Basımevi, 1989)

Appendix B

Palestine Campaigns Commanders in the War of Independence

Like the Gallipoli campaign the campaigns in Palestine proved to be the crucible of the school of command for the Ottoman Army and many of the commanders went on to important posts in the remaining years of the war. Later, during what the Turks call the War of Independence (1919–22), these commanders emerged as the seasoned and capable cadre around which Mustafa Kemal built his nationalist army. The table below shows the assignments of the Palestine commanders and their assignments in the War of Independence.

Name	Palestine Assignment	War of Independence Assignment (Ret. Rank)
	Army Level Commanders	
M. Kemal Atatürk	Seventh Army cmdr	National army cmdr in chief (Marshal)
M. Fevzi Çakmak	Seventh Army cmdr	Chief of general staff (Marshal)
İsmet İnönü	III Corps cmdr	Western Front cmdr (Gen)
	Corps Level Commanders	
Şükrü Naili Gökberk	50 Div cmdr	III Corps cmdr (LTG)
Mehmet Arif	III and XX Corps ch of staff	III Corps cmdr (Col)
Kemalettin S. Gökçe	VIII Corps ch of staff	Fourth Gp and IV Corps cmdr (LTG)
Fahrettin Altay	XII Corps ch of staff	V Cavalry Corps cmdr (Gen)

Kazıim İnançYildirim	AG ch of staff	VI Corps cmdr (LTG)
Çevat Cobanlı	Eighth Army cmdr	Elcezire Front cmdr (LTG)
Nihat Anılmış	Seventh Army ch of staff	Elcezire Front cmdr (LTG)

Division Level Commanders

Ömer Halis Bıyıktay	7 Army ch of op	23 Div cmdr (LTG)
Asım Gündüz	48 Div cmdr and 8 Army CoS	Western Front chief of staff (GEN)
Cemil Conk	41 Div cmdr	11 Div and 18 Div cmdr (MG)
Ö. Nuri Koptagel	43 Div cmdr	12 Div cmdr (MG)
Kazım Sevüktekin	7 and 11 Div cmdr	8 Div and 5 Caucasian Div cmdr (MG)
M. Munip Uzsoy	36 and 140 Regt cmdr	24 Div and 61 Div cmdr (Col)
Reşat Çiğiltepe	53 Div cmdr	11 Cauc Div and 21 Div cmdr (Col)
M. Şefik Aker	XXI Corps ch of staff	6 Div and 7 Div cmdr (Col)
Ali Sami Sabit	19 Div cmdr	13 Div and Urfa Prov Cav Div cmdr (MG)
H. Nurettin Özsu	43 and 48 Div cmdr	17 Div cmdr (MG)
Mehmet Hayri Tarhan	26 Div cmdr	9 Div and Gaziantepe area cmdr (MG)
Ahmet Fuat Bulca	23 Regt cmdr	1 Div, 29 Div and 11 Div cmdr (Col)
H. Hüsnü Emir Erkilet	46 Div cmdr	Second Army c/s and 1 Div cmdr (MG)
Ahmet Naci Tinaz	III Corps ch of staff	West Front c/s and 15 Div cmdr (LTG)
Ahmet Zeki Soydemir	48 Div ch of staff	2 Cav Div cmdr and general staff (MG)
Mehmet Salih Noyan	22 Div ch of staff	First Army CoS and 57 Div cdr (Gen)

Miscellaneous Commanders

İbrahim Refet Bele	XXII Corps cmdr	Minister of National Defence (MG)

Ali Fuat Cebesoy	XX Corps cmdr	Second Army LoCI (LTG)
Cafer Tayyar Eğilmez	VIII Corps cmdr	Edirne fortress cmdr (MG)
M. Rüstü Sakarya	16 Div cmdr	Konya area cmdr and IV area cmdr (MG)
M. Muhittin Kurtiş	27 Div cmdr	Istanbul delegation (MG)
M. Kâzım Dirik	7, 49 and 56 Div cmdr	Anatolian LoC cmdr (LTG)
Sadullah Güney	4 LoCI cfmdr	Ministry of Defence Logistics cmdr (Col)
Veysel Özgür	48 Div cmdr, XX Corps CoS	Erzincan Military District cmdr (Col)
Süleyman Sabri	8 Cav Regt cmdr	7 Cav Regt Cmdr (MG)

Sources:

İsmet Görgülü, *On Yillik Harbin Kadrosu 1912–1913, Balkan – Birinci Dünya ve Istiklal Harbi* (Ankara: Türk Tarih Kurum Basimevi, 1993)

Necati Ökse, Nusret Baycan and Salih Sakaryalı, *Türk Istiklal Harbi'ne Kalilan Tümen ve Daha Ust Kademelerdeki Komutanların Biyografileri* (Ankara: Genelkurmay Basımevi, 1989)

Select Bibliography

Archival Sources
Ankara: Askeri Tarıhı ve Stratejik Etut Başkanlığı (Strategic Studies Institute, Turkish General Staff) (ATASE)
Ankara: Askeri Tarıhı ve Stratejik Etut Başkanlığı Kutuphane (ATASE Library)
Canberra: Australian War Memorial (AWM)
Kew: United Kingdom National Archives (TNA)
Leeds: Brotherton Library, Liddle Collection (LC)
Washington, DC: National Archives and Records Administration (NARA)

Printed Document Collections
Arş.Ş.Mud.lüğü (ATASE staff). *Askeri Tarih Belgeleri Dergisi*, Auğustos 1989, Yıl 38, Sayı 88. Ankara: Genelkurmay Basımevi, 1989
Arş.Ş.Mud.lüğü (ATASE staff). *Arşiv Belgeleriye Ermeni Faaliyetleri 1914–1918, Cilt I*. Ankara: Genelkurmay Basımevi, 2005
Arş.Ş.Mud.lüğü (T. C. Başbakanlık Devlet Archives staff). *Osmanli Belgelerinde Ermenile (1915–1920)*. Ankara: Osmanlı Arşivi Daıre, 1995
Atılgan, İnanç and Garabet Moumdjian, *Archival Documents of the Viennese Armenian-Turkish Platform*. Klagenfurt: Wieser Verlag, 2010
Ghazarian, Vatche. *Boghos Nubar's Papers and the Armenian Question 1915–1918*. Waltham, MA: Mayreni Publishing, 1997
Gooch, G. P. and Harold Temperley (eds). *British Documents on the Origins of the War 1898–1914, Vol. XI*. London: HMSO, 1926
Ozdemir, Hikmet and Yusuf Sarinay (eds). *Turk-Ermeni Ihtilafi Belegeler*. Ankara: Egemenlik, n.d.

Official Histories and Studies Based on Official Records
Akbay, Cemal. *Birinci Dünya Harbinde Türk Harbi, 1nci Cilt, Osmanli Imparatorlugu'nun Siyası ve Askeri Hazırlıkları ve Harbe Girisi* (*Ottoman Empire Military Mobilisation and Entry into the War*). Ankara: Genelkurmay Basımevi, 1991
Ari, Kemal. *Birinci Dünya Savası Kronolojisi* (*First World War Chronology*). Ankara: Genelkurmay Basımevi, 1997
Atamer, M. *41nci Piyade Tumen Tarıhcesi* (*41st Infantry Division History*), ATASE, Archive Folder 26–344 (unpublished staff study)
ATASE. *3ncü Süvari Tümeni Tarihçesi* (*3rd Cavalry Division History*), ATASE Library, Record 26–421 (unpublished staff study)
ATASE. *7nci Piyade Tümeni Tarihçesi* (*7th Infantry Division History*), ATASE Library, Record 26-518 (unpublished staff study)

ATASE. *16nci Piyade Tümeni Tarihçesi* (*16th Infantry Division History*), ATASE Library, Record 26-441 (unpublished staff study)

ATASE. *19ncü Piyade Tümeni Tarihçesi* (*19th Infantry Division History*), ATASE Library, Record 26-349 (unpublished staff study)

Belen, Fahri. *Birinci Cihan Harbinde Türk Harbi 1914–1918 Yili Hareketleri, I–V Cilt* (*The Turkish Front in the First World War, Years 1914–1915, Vols 1–5*). Ankara: Genelkurmay Basımevi, 1964–7

Doğancı, Lüfti. *20nci Piyade Alay Tarihçesi* (*20th Infantry Regiment History*), ATASE Library, Record 26-326 (unpublished staff study)

Ererthem, Meki. *21nci Piyade Alay Tarihçesi* (*21st Infantry Regiment History*). ATASE Library, Record 26-361 (unpublished staff study)

Erkal, Şükrü. *Birinci Dünya Harbinde Türk Harbi VIncı, Hicaz, Asir, Yemen Cepheleri ve Libya Harekâtı 1914–1918* (*First World War, Turkish War, Hicaz, Asir and Yemen Front and Libya Operations*). Ankara: Genelkurmay Basımevi, 1978

Falls, Cyril and A. F. Becke. *Military Operations Egypt and Palestine, From June 1917 to the End of the War, Parts I and II*. London: HMSO, 1930

Göyman, İhsan. *Birinci Dünya Harbi IXncü Cilt, Türk Hava Harekatı* (*First World War, Turkish Air Operations*). Ankara: Genelkurmay Basımevi, 1969

Güralp, Şerif. *1918 Yılında Türk Ordusunun Filistin ve Suriye'den Çekilişinde 3ncü Süvari Tümeninin Harekâtı* (*3rd Cavalry Division Operations in the Palestine Campaign and Retreat from Syria*). Ankara: ATASE Yayınları, 2006

Iskora, Muharrem Mazlum. *Harp Akademileri Tarihçesi, 1846–1965, Cilt I (2nci Baskı)* (*History of the Staff College, 1846–1965*). Ankara: Genelkurmay Basımevi, 1966

Karamatu, Selâhattin. *Türk Silahli Kuvvetleri Tarihi, IIIncu Cilt 6ncu Kisim (1908–1920) 1nci Kitap* (*Turkish Armed Forces History, 1908–1920*). Ankara: Genelkurmay Basımevi, 1971

Koral, Necmi, Remzi Önal, Rauf Atakan, Nusret Baycan and Selâhattin Kızılırmak. *Türk Silahli Kuvvetleri Tarihi Osmanli Devri Birinci Dünya Harbi Idari Faaliyetler ve Lojistik, Xncu Cilt* (*Turkish Armed Forces History, Ottoman State in the First World War, Administration and Logistics*). Ankara: Genelkurmay Basımevi, 1985

MacMunn, George and Cyril Falls. *History of the Great War, based on Official Documents: Military Operations Egypt and Palestine, From the Outbreak of War with Germany to June 1917*. London: HMSO, 1928

Moberly, Brigadier General F. J. *Military Operations: Mesopotamia, Vol. IV, The Campaign in Upper Mesopotamia to the Armistice*. London: HMSO, 1927

Okçu, Yahya and Hilmi Üstünsoy. *Birinci Dünya Harbinde Türk Harbi IVnü Cilt, 1nci Kısım, Sina-Filistin Cephesi, Harbin Başlangıcından İkinci Gazze Muharebeleri Sonuna Kadar* (*First World War, Turkish War, Sinai-Palestine Front, From the Beginning of the War to the Second Gaza Battles*). Ankara: Genelkurmay Basımevi, 1979

Ökse, Necati, Nusret Baycan and Salih Sakaryalı. *Türk Istiklal Harbi'ne Kalilan Tümen ve Daha Ust Kademelerdeki Komutanların Biyografileri (Turkish War of Independence, Biographies of Divisional-level Commanders and Above).* Ankara: Genelkurmay Basımevi, 1989

Onalp, Merhum Kâmil, Hilmi Üstünsoy, Kâmuran Dengiz and Şükrü Erkal. *Birinci Dünya Harbinde Türk Harbi IVnü Cilt, 2nci Kısım, Sina-Filistin Cephesi, İkinci Gazze Muharebesi Sonundan Mütarekesi'ne Kadar Yapılan Harekât (21 Nisan 1917–30 Ekim 1918) (First World War, Turkish War, Sinai-Palestine Front, Operations from the Second Gaza Battle to the Mondros Armistice, 21 April 1917– 30 October 1918).* Ankara: Genelkurmay Basımevi, 1986

Saral, Muhratem, Alpaslan Orhon and Şükrü Erkal. *Birinci Dünya Harbinde Türk Harbi Vncü Cilt, Çanakkale Cephesi Harekati Inci Kitap (Haziran 1914–Nisan 1915) (First World War, Turkish War, Gallipoli Front Operations, June 1914–April 1915).* Ankara: Genelkurmay Basımevi, 1993

Şefik, Mete. *23ncu Piyade Tumen Tarıhcesi (23rd Infantry Division History).* ATASE, Record 26–412. Ankara: Genelkurmay Basımevi, n.d.

Memoirs and Primary Sources

Ahmad Izzet Pascha. *Denkwurdigkeiten Des Marschalls Izzet Pascha.* Leipzig: Verlag von K. F. Koehler, 1927

Çakmak, Fevzi. *Birinci Dünya Savaşı'nda Doğu Cephesi.* Ankara: Genelkurmay Basımevi, 2005

Cebesoy, Ali Fuat. *Birussebi – Gazze Maydan Muharebei ve Yirmici Kolordu.* Istanbul: Askeri Matbaa, 1938

Conk, Cemil. *Çanakkale Hatıraları ve Conkbayırı Savaşları (1955),* in *Çanakkale Hatiraları, 2. Cilt.* Istanbul: Arma Yayınları, 2002

De Nogales, Rafael. *Four Years Beneath the Crescent.* New York: Charles Scribner's Sons, 1926

Djemal Pasha (Cemal Pasha). *Memories of a Turkish Statesman 1913–1919.* New York: George H. Doran Company, 1922

Emir (Erkilet), Hüseyin Hüsnü. *Yildirim.* Ankara: Genelkurmay Basımevi, 2002

Erden, Ali Fuat. *Birinci Dünya Harbinde Suriye Hatiraları.* Istanbul: Arma Yayınları, 2003

Güralp, Şerif. *Çanakkale Cephesinden Filistin'e.* Istanbul: Güncel Yayıncılık, 2003

Intelligence Section, Cairo, British Army. *Handbook of the Turkish Army,* 8th Provisional edn, February 1916. Nashville: Battery Press, repr. 1996

Kaiser, Hilmar (ed.). *Eberhard Count Wolffskeel von Reichenberg, Zeitoun, Mousa Dagh, Ourfa: Letters on the Armenian Genocide, Second Edition.* London: Gomidas Institute, 2004

Kress von Kressenstein, Friedrich. *Zwischen Kaukasus und Sinai: Jahrbuch des Bundes der Asienkämpfer.* Berlin-Templehof: Deutsche Orientbuch-handlung Mulzer & Cleeman, 1921

Liman von Sanders, Otto. *Five Years in Turkey*. London: Bailliere, Tindall & Cox, 1928

Münim, Mustafa. *Cepheden Cepheye, Çanakkale ve Kanal Seferi Hatıraları*. Istanbul: Arma Yayınları, 1998 (repr. of 1940 edn)

Murray, Archibald. *Sir Archibald Murray's Dispatches (June 1916–June 1917)*. London: J. N. Dent & Sons Ltd, 1920

Steuber, Obergeneralarzt Dr. *'Jildirim' Deutsche Streiter auf heiligem Boden*. Oldenburg/Berlin: Gerhard Sialling, 1926

Torossian, Sarkis. *From Dardanelles to Palestine*. Boston, MA: Meador Publishing Company, 1929

Yengin, Sami. *Drama'dan Sina-Filistin'e Savaş Günlüğü*. Ankara: Genelkurmay Basımevi, 1967

Secondary Sources

Aksakal, Mustafa. *The Ottoman Road to War in 1914: The Ottoman Empire and the First World War*. Cambridge: Cambridge University Press, 2008

Barr, James. *Setting the Desert on Fire, T.E. Lawrence and Britain's Secret War in Arabia 1916–1918*. New York: W. W. Norton and Company, 2009

Bilgin, İsmail. *Medine Müdafaası, Çöl Kaplanı Fahrettin Paşa*. Istanbul: Timaş Yayınları, 2009

Bond, Brian (ed.). *The First World War and British Military History*. Oxford: Clarendon Press, 1991

Bruce, Anthony. *The Last Crusade, The Palestine Campaign in the First World War*. London: John Murray Publishers Ltd, 2002

Carver, Field Marshal Lord. *The Turkish Front 1914–1918*. London: Sidgwick & Jackson, 2003

Cassar, George H. *Kitchener's War, British Strategy from 1914 to 1916*. Washington, DC: Brassey's Inc., 2004

Churchill, Winston S. *The World Crisis*. New York: Charles Scribner's Sons, 1931

Cron, Herman. *The Imperial German Army, 1914–1918: Organisation, Structure, Orders-of-Battle*. Solihull: Helion and Company, 2002

Erickson, Edward J. *Defeat in Detail, The Ottoman Army in the Balkans 1912–1913*. Westport, CT: Praeger, 2003

Erickson, Edward J. *Gallipoli, The Ottoman Campaign*. Barnsley: Pen and Sword, 2010

Erickson, Edward J. *Ordered To Die, A History of the Ottoman Army in the First World War*. Westport, CT: Greenwood Press, 2000

Erickson, Edward J. *Ottoman Army Effectiveness in World War 1: A Comparative Study*. Abingdon: Routledge, 2007

Erickson, Edward J. *Ottomans and Armenians, A Study in Counterinsurgency*. New York: Palgrave Macmillan, 2013

Falls, Cyril. *Armageddon: 1918*. Philadelphia, PA: J. B. Lippincott Company, 1964

Falls, Cyril. *The Great War*. New York: G. P. Putnam's Sons, 1959

Ferguson, Niall. *The Pity of War*. New York: Basic Books, 1999

Fosten, D. S. V. and R. J. Marrion. *The British Army 1914–18*. London: Osprey Publishing Ltd, 1978

Gooch, John. *The Plans of War, The General Staff and British Military Strategy c.1900–1916*. New York: John Wiley & Sons, 1974

Görgülü, İsmet. *On Yillik Harbin Kadrosu 1912–1913, Balkan–Birinci Dünya ve Istiklal Harbi*. Ankara: Türk Tarih Kurum Basimevi, 1993

Görgülü, İsmet, *Türk Harp Tarıhı Derslerinde Adı Geçen Komutanlar*. Istanbul: Harp Akademileri Yayını, 1983

Güçlü, Yücel. *Armenians and the Allies in Cilicia 1914–1923*. Salt Lake City, UT: University of Utah Press, 2012

Gudmundsson, Bruce. *On Artillery*. Westbrook, CT: Praeger, 1993

Hankey, Maurice. *The Supreme Command, 1914–1918, Volume One*. London: George Allen & Unwin Limited, 1961

Heller, Joseph. *British Policy Towards The Ottoman Empire*. London: Frank Cass and Company, 1983

Hickey, Michael. *The First World War, The Mediterranean Front 1914–1923*. Oxford: Osprey Publishing Ltd, 2002

Hughes, Matthew. *Allenby and British Strategy in the Middle East 1917–1919*. London: Frank Cass, 1999

Keegan, John. *The First World War*. New York: Alfred A. Knopf, 1999

Kent, Marian (ed.). *The Great Powers and the End of the Ottoman Empire*. London: George Allen & Unwin, 1984

Kévorkian, Raymond H. *The Armenian Genocide, A Complete History*. London: I. B. Tauris, 2011

Langensiepen, Bernd and Ahmet Güleryuz. *The Ottoman Steam Navy*. Annapolis, MD: Naval Institute Press, 1995

Larcher, Commandant M. *La Guerre Turque Dans La Guerre Mondiale*. Paris: Chiron & Berger-Levrault, 1926

Lewy, Guenter. *The Armenian Massacres in Ottoman Turkey, A Disputed Genocide*. Salt Lake City, UT: University of Utah Press, 2005

McMeekin, Sean. *The Ottoman Endgame; War, Revolution, and the Making of the Modern Middle East*. New York: Penguin Press, 2015

Mango, Andrew. *Atatürk, The Biography of the Founder of Modern Turkey*. Woodstock, NY: Overlook Press, 1999

Middlebrook, Martin. *Your Country Needs You, From Six to Sixty-five Divisions*. Barnsley: Leo Cooper, 2000

Mousa, Suleiman. *T.E. Lawrence An Arab View*, trans. Albert Butros. London and New York: Oxford University Pres, 1966

Mühlmann, Carl. *Das Deutsch-Türkische Waffenbundnis im Weltkriege*. Leipzig: Verlag Koehler & Amelang, 1940

Murphy, David. *The Arab Revolt, 1916–18*. Oxford: Osprey Publishing Ltd, 2008

Nedim, Şükrü Mahmut. *Filistin Savasi (1914–1918)*. Ankara: Genelkurmay Basımevi, 1995

Nicolle, David. *The Ottoman Army 1914–1918*. Oxford: Osprey Publishing Ltd, 1994

Nikolajsen, Ole. *Ottoman Aviation 1911–1919*. Privately printed, n.d.

Örses, Tunca and Necmettin Özçelik. *I. Dünya Savaşı'nda, Türk Askeri Kıyafetleri*. Istanbul: Denizler Kitabevi, n.d.

Özdemir, Hikmet. *The Ottoman Army 1914–1918, Disease and Death on the Battlefield*. Salt Lake City, UT: University of Utah Press, 2008

Perrett, Bryan. *Megiddo 1918, The Last Great Cavalry Victory*. Oxford: Osprey Press, 1999

Schulte, Bernd F. *Vor dem Kriegsausbruch 1914, Deutschland, die Türkei und der Balkan*. Düsseldorf: Drost Verlag, 1980

Sedad, Ahmed. *Hücum Kıtaatının Talim ve Terbiyesi*. Istanbul: Erkaa-ı Harbiye Matbaası, 1336 (1920)

Shaw, Stanford. *The Ottoman Empire in World War I, Volumes 1 and 2*. Ankara: Türk Tarih Kurumu, 2007

Shaw, Stanford J. and Ezel Kural Shaw. *History of the Ottoman Empire, Volume 2: Reform, Revolution, and Republic: The Rise of Modern Turkey, 1808–1975*. Cambridge: Cambridge University Press, 1977

Sheffy, Yigal. *British Military Intelligence in the Palestine Campaign 1914–1918*. London: Frank Cass, 1998

Sonyel, Salahi. *The Great War and the Tragedy of Anatolia*. Ankara: Turk Tarih Kurumu, 2001

Strachan, Hew. *The First World War, Volume 1, To Arms*. Oxford: Oxford University Press, 2001

Tauber, Elizer. *The Arab Movements in World War I*. London: Frank Cass, 1993

Tetik, Ahmet. *Teşkilat-ı Mahsusa (Umûr-ı Şarkıyye Dairesi), Cilt I: 1914–1916*. Istanbul: Türkiye İş Bankası Kültür Yayınları, 2014

Trumpener, Ulrich. *Germany and the Ottoman Empire*. Princeton, NJ: Princeton University Press, 1968

Wallach, Jehuda L. *Anatomie Einer Militärhilfe, Die preussisch-deutschen Militärmissionen in der Türkei 1835–1919*. Düsseldorf: Droste Verlag, 1976

Wavell, General Sir Archibald. *Allenby, A Study in Greatness*. New York: Oxford University Press, 1941

Weber, Frank G. *Eagles on the Crescent: Germany Austria, and the Diplomacy of the Turkish Alliance, 1914–1918*. Ithaca, NY: Cornell University Press, 1970

Werfel, Franz. *The Forty Days of Musa Dagh*, trans. Geoffrey Dunlop. New York: Viking Press, 1934

Yalman, Ahmed Emin. *Turkey in the World War*. New Haven, CT: Yale University Press, 1930

Yilmaz, Veli. *Birinci Dünya Harbinde Türk-Alman Ittifaki ve Askeri Yardımları*. Istanbul: Gem Offset, 1993

Articles, Chapters and Papers

Erickson, Edward J. 'Ottoman Encirclement Operations, 1912–1922', *Middle Eastern Studies*, 40 (1) (January 2004)

Erickson, Edward J. 'The Turkish Official Military Histories of the First World War, A Bibliographic Essay', *Middle Eastern Studies*, 39 (3) (July 2003)

Erickson, Edward J. '*Wasp or Mosquito? The Arab Revolt in Turkish Military History*', British Journal for Military History, Volume 4, Issue 3, July 2018.

Güçlü, Yücel. 'The Last Pitched Battle of the First World War and the Determination of the Turkish-Syrian Boundary Line', *International Conference Atatürk and Modern Turkey (Yayın No: 582)*. Ankara: Ankara Üniversitesi Siyasal Bilgiler Fakültesi Yayımı, 1998

Güçlü, Yücel. 'The Wounded Turks and the Fall of Damascus, 1 October 1918', *Belleten, Dört Ayda Bir Çıkar*. Ankara: Türk Tarih Kurumu Basımevi, 2003

Kaiser, Hilmar. 'Regional Resistance to Central Government Policies: Ahmed Djemal Pasha, the Governors of Aleppo, and Armenian Deportees in the Spring and Summer of 1915', *Journal of Genocide Research*, Vol. 12, No. 3 (2010)

Neş'et, M. 'Büyük Harpte "Suriye" Cephesinde 48. Piyade Fırkası', *Askeri Mecmua*, No. 18, 1 July 1930. Istanbul: Askeri Matbaa, 1930

Newell, Jonathan. 'Allenby and the Palestine Campaign', in Brian Bond (ed.). *The First World War and British Military History*. Oxford: Clarendon Press, 1991

Sheffy, Yigal. 'Chemical Warfare and the Palestine Campaign, 1916–1918', *The Journal of Military History*, Vol. 73, No. 3 (July 2009)

Trumpener, Ulrich. 'Suez, Baku, Gallipoli: The Military Dimensions of the German-Ottoman Coalition, 1914–1918', in Bela K. Kiraly and Nandor F. Dreisziger (eds). *East Central European Society in World War I*. New York: Columbia University Press, 1985

Yanıkdağ, Yücel. 'Educating the Peasants: The Ottoman Army and Enlisted Men in Uniform', *Middle Eastern Studies*, 40 (6) (November 2004)

Yasamee, F. A. K. 'Abdülhamid II and the Ottoman Defence Problem', *Diplomacy & Statecraft*, 4 (1) (March 1993)

Yasamee, F. A. K. 'Some Military Problems faced by the Ottoman Empire at the beginning of the 20th Century', *KÖK Sosyal ve Stratejik Araştırmalar, Osmanlı Özel Sayısı*, 2000

Zürcher, Erik-Jan. 'The Ottoman Conscription System in Theory And Practice, 1844–1918', *International Review of Social History*, 43 (3) (1988)

Index